THE DEFEAT OF SOLIDARITY

THE DEFEAT OF
Solidarity

Anger and Politics in Postcommunist Europe

DAVID OST

Cornell University Press

Ithaca and London

First published 2005 by Cornell University Press
First printing, Cornell paperbacks, 2006
Printed in the United States of America

Library of Congress Cataloging-in-Publication Data

Ost, David.
   The defeat of Solidarity : anger and politics in postcommunist Europe / David Ost.
      p. cm.
   Includes bibliographical references and index.
   ISBN-13: 978-0-8014-4318-3 (cloth : alk. paper)
   ISBN-10: 0-8014-4318-0 (cloth : alk. paper)
   ISBN-13: 978-0-8014-7343-2 (pbk. : alk. paper)
   ISBN-10: 0-8014-7343-8 (pbk. : alk. paper)
      1. Europe, Eastern—Politics and government—1989– 2. Post-communism—Europe,
Eastern.   3. Democratization—Europe, Eastern.   I. Title.
   JN96.A58O75 2005
   322′.2′09438—dc22

                                                                                              2004030950

Cloth printing   10 9 8   7   6   5   4   3   2   1
Paperback printing   10 9 8 7 6 5 4 3 2 1

Contents

v

Acknowledgments

A book like this, based on research conducted in many cities over many years, is possible only thanks to much help from a great many people. Some help came from people whose names I never got to know—mid-level unionists in local offices who directed me to others, secretaries who facilitated access quickly and effectively, security guards who helped me get passes to worksites, people on trains who shared their own stories and gave me leads about firms I might visit. Field work often depends on the help of many unnamed people, so I want to acknowledge them first.

I had enormous help as well from people whose names I do know. Having traveled to Poland frequently for over twenty-five years now, I am very fortunate to have groups of friends and contacts in several different places. Among those who graciously provided various and valuable forms of assistance are Gosia Bilska, Ryszard Bugaj, Jonathan Fells, Kostek Gebert, Beata Grabowska, Ewa Grala, Frank Hantke, Beata Kozek, Magda Pustola, and Stanislaw Rudolf. Particular thanks go to those who helped in many ways and have become good friends, too: Magda Bochenska, Michal and Irena Federowicz, Nina Gladziuk, Nina Hoffman (and Piotr and Marta), Slawa Kaminska-Berezowska, Sergiusz Kowalski, Anna Kubiak, Dorota Morawetz, and Peggy Simpson.

Social scientists who work in Poland are fortunate to have wonderful colleagues there. Among those, from whom I have learned so much, are Henryk Domanski, Barbara Gaciarz, Jerzy Hausner, Aldona Jawlowska, Kazik Kloc, Jacek Kochanowicz, Tadeusz Kowalik, Wieslawa Kozek, Irek Krzeminski, Mira Marody, the late Edmund Mokrzycki, Witold Morawski, Janusz

Mucha, Maria Nawojczyk, Andrzej Rychard, and Aleksander Surdej. Very special thanks go to Juliusz Gardawski and Wlodzimierz Pankow, who shared with me not only their broad knowledge on labor but their friendship too. I owe them much.

I am also indebted to my many informants: the unionists, rank-and-file workers, and local political and governmental officials who were always willing to talk with me, answer my questions, give me their time, and help me understand the particularities and idiosyncrasies of Polish labor politics. I am truly amazed at and grateful for the generosity of spirit that allowed so many people to talk so freely and honestly with someone they didn't know—someone who sometimes just showed up at their workplace and asked to have a word. No matter how busy, people always found time for a real conversation, and I am immensely grateful. I am unable to mention everyone here, but I would like to thank Edward Ciepiera, Jacek Danel, Edward Graniczka, Wojciech Grzeszek, Marian Kokoszka, Ryszard Lepik, Jozef Lewczak, Elzbieta Majchrowicz, Andrzej Obutelewicz, and Jan Platek. Special thanks go also to the veteran national-level former Solidarity activists who have shared their time and ideas with me, such as Zbigniew Bujak, Wladyslaw Frasyniuk, Bronislaw Geremek, Aleksander Hall, Zbigniew Janas, Lech Kaczynski, Barbara Labuda, Jan Litynski, Adam Michnik, and Grazyna Staniszewska.

Many friends and scholars outside Poland have also helped as I have worked on this project, including Stewart Auyash, Sabina Avdagic, Jon Bailiff, Michael Bernhard, Dorothee Bohle, Basia Bolibok, Yitshak Brudny, Valerie Bunce, Mary Caponegro, Jodi Dean, Georgi Derluguian, David Dornisch, Elizabeth Dunn, Erzsebet Fazekas, Mary Fessenden, Cedric Johnson, Ewa Hauser, Andrea Hess, Michelline Ishay, Michael Kennedy, Padraic Kenney, Anna Klobucka, Paul Kubicek, Guglielmo Meardi, Mieke Meurs, Ann Michel, Joanna Mishtal, Dunbar Moodie, Erik Olsen, Anna Pollert, Anna Popiel, Brian Porter, Al Rainnie, Craig Rimmerman, S. N. Sang-Mpam, Dietmar Schirmer, Andrew Schwartz, Steven Stoltenberg, Anne Susskind, Deborah Tall, Andrew Tatarsky, Virginia Tilley, Phil Wilde, Ruth Yanai, and Patty Zimmerman. Several were particularly helpful in offering comments on my ideas and my written work: Laszlo Bruszt, Carola Frege, Julie Hemment, Bela Greskovits, Aida Hozic, Jan Kubik, Mitchell Orenstein, Cathy Schneider, Jonathan Terra, Andrzej Tymowski, and John Vail. And now that he is gone, one must be singled out for special mention: Paul Piccone. East European studies and political theory both owe a deep debt to Paul and to the journal, *Telos*, which he founded in 1968 and edited ever since. But I remember him especially as a good friend with a great mind and a gigantic heart, even if he did think I was wrong about almost everything. He is already sorely missed.

As for publication, a special thanks to Roger Haydon of Cornell Press, who supported and encouraged the project from the beginning, and to Karen Laun, who helped with the editing. In this context a long overdue and heart-felt thanks goes to Carmen Sirianni, who helped me first get published many years ago. Scholarly encounters often lead to long-term associations, and I am very grateful to Marc Weinstein and Stephen Crowley, initially my co-investigators on two grant projects and then my co-authors, friends, and the source of many good ideas.

Institutional support has been vital in making my field work possible, and I thank, in chronological order of their support, IREX, the American Council of Learned Societies, the National Council for Eurasian and East European Research (for two different grant projects), the Fulbright senior lecturer program, and particularly the Faculty Research Fund at Hobart and William Smith Colleges for their consistent support of summer research visits. In Poland, the sociology department of the Central European University in Warsaw proved to be a very supportive place to teach and work, as was the economics department at Warsaw University.

Finally, personal support remains indispensable. I am deeply indebted to my partners during the book's creation, for their emotional and intellectual support. In addition, David Weiss and Harry Segal have been like brothers. Then there's my amazing mother Ruth and her partner and my comrade Bill Mardo, and Fred, Dan, Joan, Nora, Janis, and Jeremy. It is to the next generation of Colette, Malcolm, Conrad, Carrie, Mitch, Jessica, Gabe, Celina, Carina, Cody, and, surely not least, the newest addition Molly (the name-sake, fittingly, of my grandmother born in the old shtetl of Mielec) that I dedicate this book.

David Ost

Ithaca, New York

THE DEFEAT OF SOLIDARITY

Introduction

Anger, solidarity, and democracy have traditionally gone together. Democracy has usually been advanced when people angry about their exclusion from wealth and power join together in solidarity. This does not mean just mass demonstrations or disruptive action. From New Deal America to Keynesian Western Europe, liberal and socialist parties resuscitated democracy in the West by organizing the anger of those long deprived of social protection. In Eastern Europe, the path to democratization opened up when workers angry about their political exclusion in Poland joined together in 1980 to form the trade union "Solidarity."

These solidarities had democratic consequences because the angry understood the meaning of "us" in a very inclusive way. Those who were targeted as "them" were seen as a small "economic other" (capitalists in the west, the communist bureaucracy known as the *nomenklatura* in the east) whose downfall would finally make possible the real participation of all citizens.

Democratic solidarities are much less common today. Technological change in the work process leads fewer people to see themselves as part of a majority working class, and global capitalism makes it harder for citizens to identify a concrete enemy the state can act against in a way that could benefit all. As a result, the solidarities that appear in domestic politics today are often highly exclusionary ones that target the most vulnerable of society's residents. These include anti-immigration and "law-and-order" movements, or "anti-terrorist" solidarities aimed not just at ethnic minorities but at dissidents in general. Meanwhile, those who seek to mobilize anger for democratic outcomes—for greater political and economic inclusion of the poor and the marginalized—are far less in evidence in national politics. Proponents of an alternative globalization, universal human rights, or "fair" rather than "free" trade are all more likely today to organize on the global rather than the domestic level.

Why has the nature of political solidarity changed so much in recent years? Why is anger mobilized increasingly toward exclusionary solidarities rather than inclusive ones? How does this tendency affect domestic politics? How does it affect workers and labor relations? This book explores these problems in the context of postcommunist Eastern Europe. I focus on Poland and the breakdown of its once-great Solidarity movement, but I believe that the arguments are more widely relevant. My general argument, concerning the consequences of how political actors mobilize class-driven emotions, pertains to all capitalist societies. My particular argument, that by organizing the anger of the economic "losers" along non-economic lines, Polish political and trade union leaders impeded the development of the emerging democratic system, has wide relevance to the rest of the postcommunist world.

The political importance of the organization of anger can be seen from the following story. In 1996, the Solidarity trade union in Poland announced that it would form a coalition of "right-wing" parties and movements in order to win control of parliament in the elections to take place the following year. Solidarity's president, Marian Krzaklewski, began to travel around the country speaking not only to the right-wing groups he hoped to organize but to the population as a whole. The main issues he addressed were the fight to keep abortion illegal and the need to install in the preamble to the constitution (being written at the time) a clause explicitly honoring God and Catholicism. "Communists," he said, were ruining the country and harming the labor movement. (The ex-communist Democratic Left Alliance controlled both parliament and the presidency at the time.) The chief way to counteract the damage the "communists" were causing was to strengthen Catholic moral values. Krzaklewski did sometimes speak about the economic difficulties workers faced, and he acknowledged that workers had lost a great deal of influence in the workplace. Wherever he went, in fact, these were the issues brought up by workers. But Krzaklewski told his listeners that these economic problems were not the result of economic causes. They were due, instead, to the fact that "communists" and "atheists" were running the system, which was thus not a real market system but only a "market-communist" one.[1] A right-wing government, he said, would solve the problems facing workers because moral people would be in power.

A Solidarity aligned with a politically illiberal "right wing," eager to place the fight for a religious public life at the center of its program, and virtually silent about the large percentage of its constituency that had plummeted into poverty—how had it come to this? How did a movement that did so much to revitalize liberal democracy, that reintroduced the notion of "civil society" into contemporary political discourse, that challenged and ultimately toppled a communist regime by stressing inclusion rather than exclusion—how did it turn into a self-proclaimed Catholic right-wing movement with a union membership less than one-tenth its 1981 size? Moreover, Solidarity's own right-wing turn helped revitalize the Polish right in general. In the 2001 parliamentary elections, two extremist right-wing parties not connected to Solidarity entered parliament. By 2004, both of them were talked about as potential governing parties before the decade was through.

So what happened here? What does this mean for democracy? What does it mean for workers? Is there a connection between the decline of Solidarity's union base and the rise of an illiberal politics? This book is an attempt to make sense of postcommunist politics through an exploration of the interconnection of unions, politics, and anger.

I deal with various big topics—democracy, labor, class, emotion, political mobilization—and several subsets of these topics—liberalism, illiberalism, trade unions, workers, anger, parties. The central player is Solidarity, the trade union movement founded in Gdansk in 1980 that brought about the collapse of the Polish communist system nine years later and had the chief responsibility for shaping the new one. It was a vast movement. Most of the new system's political and economic elite came out of the movement, as did virtually its entire intellectual elite. To the extent that those with communist pedigree maintained their positions, they did so only by playing by rules that the dissident intellectuals in Solidarity had shaped.

Indeed, precisely because the movement was so vast, a study of it can be vastly illuminating. Multiple-country studies, increasingly promoted in social science, must conflate too many particular events and cultural distinctions, minimizing the significance of each in ways that are often fatal for a proper understanding. Here we can keep cultural factors constant while studying processes perennially at the center of social science concerns: the building of democracy and the rise of capitalism. A close study of Poland's postcommunist experience allows us to discover some underlying lessons that are relevant in other contexts. At a time when passions and emotions are widely recognized as crucial factors affecting world politics, a book that looks at how anger is politically mobilized in a specific context to produce liberal or illiberal outcomes should offer ideas useful for other contexts as well.

In many ways, this book can be read as a continuation of my first one. *Solidarity and the Politics of Anti-Politics*[2] was not only a history of the movement but an exploration of the universal implications of its democratic theory and practice. Could Solidarity's concept of "anti-politics" and its "third way" notion of civil society (separate from both state and market but flourishing in a permanently open democratic public sphere) serve as tools for others seeking to democratize (or further democratize) their own societies without falling into the standard authoritarian traps of radicals past? Some scholars took up the book's challenge and tried to show what, for example, American democrats (small 'd') might learn from Solidarity.[3] For myself, I ended on a somewhat pessimistic note. Solidarity's grand program, I wrote, had failed due to its "lack of an institutional model for political interaction [between state and society]."[4] At its beginning in 1980, Solidarity had embraced "anti-politics," with its scorn for parties and states, both because this embodied the ethos of the 1968 generation who had given the movement its intellectual foundation and because the then-ruling communist party made renunciation of political goals a condition for accepting the movement. Over time, however, this renunciation became Solidarity's Achilles' heel, as the movement had no credible way of guaranteeing that it could control the highly mobilized civil society should the Party want to strike a deal. When the Party imposed martial law in December 1981, underground Solidarity leaders spent the next several years consolidating their political leadership, which finally bore fruit with the Round Table negotiations of 1989, soon followed by elections and the installation of a Solidarity government.

When I got to Poland again in April 1990 for the beginning of a four-month visit, I was fully prepared for Solidarity's increasingly politicized face, manifest in both parliament and government. I was not at all ready, however, for the eagerness with which it seemed to be shedding and disregarding its trade union base. The new elite seemed to be irrationally jettisoning the support network it would need to make its political agenda succeed. How to make sense of this?

Social scientists should enter a rapidly changing transformative political moment not with a fixed set of research questions but ready to learn whatever new questions the new situation compels one to ask. This was particularly true of the postcommunist moment, which was not just the time after communism but the period of what Ken Jowitt has aptly called the "Leninist extinction."[5] As Jowitt explains, "extinction" meant that everything was up for grabs. The old order no longer obtained, but it remained far from clear which factors were going to shape the new one. My initial impressions in 1990 confirmed that something new was happening. Solidarity officials at all levels, as well as the intellectuals and professionals who had always been so closely aligned with it, seemed increasingly not just to disregard but also to disown real workers. Right-wing nationalists who had formerly been suspicious of Polish workers now stood up to defend them. (They chose May Day

1990 to hold the first "Congress of the Polish Right.") Most workers, however, still trusted their former liberal leaders, even as those leaders now disowned them. Clearly this could not last for long. Workers and unionists were
too large and important a constituency to be ignored. If their former leaders, mostly dissident liberal intellectuals, did not try to retain their support,
some other group would. This was, after all, the founding period of democratic party formation. Parties needed these voters. They couldn't be safely
ignored for long.

By the spring of 1990, a diffuse popular anger began to emerge. Workers
losing out from the economic shock therapy program introduced in January
1990 began to express their dissatisfaction with what Solidarity had wrought,
but without quite being sure whom or what to blame. Lech Walesa forced a
snap presidential election in which he attacked "liberals" and their market
reforms but promised to hasten the establishment of "capitalism." Suddenly
the themes relevant to an understanding of the postcommunist moment became clear: widespread support for the idea of market reform clashed with
disappointment and anger over its effects, while emerging political actors
competed for the loyalties of workers (voters) who had become politically
homeless as a result of Solidarity spurning its social base.

In this book I take seriously Jowitt's claim of Leninism as a "civilization"
whose toppling threw the world into great uncertainty. In 1991 Jowitt hypothesized that the world had entered a political "Genesis moment," in
which the old ways of doing things were over and the new ways were still unclear.[6] As in Genesis, "the earth was without form and void." Jowitt was not
referring simply to the renunciation of power by the East European communist parties. He calls Leninism a "civilization" because it entailed much
more than who was running the political system. It meant also an institutional arrangement of running the economy, a set of rules outlining who
could participate in politics and how, an overarching ideology that motivated
people and explained why they should take part in the community, and a
language whose key terms referred back to these political, economic, and ideological arrangements, thereby reinforcing them. Christianity had also been
a civilization (before it became a private religion), which was then displaced
by a liberal civilization, which in the twentieth century came to be challenged
by the alternative Leninist civilization, which had now collapsed.[7]

The point about civilizations, then, is that they are much more than political systems. Rather, they are entire *existential* systems. Their demise,
therefore, is a time not only of political upheaval but also of enormous *emotional* upheaval. The extinction of Leninism, Jowitt hypothesized, would
usher in a time of rampant emotionalism, and thus liberal democracy will not

be enough. People need not only to construct new institutions but to construct new meanings. After 1989 the new elites focused only on building markets and parliaments, as they sought to adopt the economic and political elements of liberal civilization. But people, Jowitt proposed, will need new emotional lives too. Particularly those who lose out economically will need other ways of making sense of their lives. Whom do I trust? Where do I go to seek help? Where does my emotional energy go when it turns out it cannot be satisfied by fantasies about the market? Christianity offered an afterlife and Leninism offered a vanguard party. In late communist society, emotional energy went into the struggle *against* communism, but now that was gone as well. Liberalism, meanwhile, is notoriously weak on these issues. Encapsulating what a long line of critics of liberalism have argued, Jowitt notes that "liberal capitalism fails adequately to provide for the essential group needs and dimensions of human existence. . . . Its materialist bias and emphasis on achievement, its tendency to ignore or marginalize the human need for security, and its repression of expressive human action"—in a word, its "rational impersonalism"—have always been both central to liberalism and its key weakness.[8]

Jowitt was thus skeptical of the widespread notion, popularized by Fukuyama, that the demise of Leninism would usher in the triumph of liberalism. Just as liberal capitalism's rationalism and individualism—its "rejection of the heroic ethic, awe, and mystery"[9]—had led to diverse countermovements in the past (romanticism, fascism, Stalinism, religious fundamentalism), so, he anticipated, it would do so now. Jowitt ended up anticipating the emergence of "movements of rage" as the possible future in the postcommunist world. "Movements of rage are nihilistic political responses to failure; the failure . . . to create productive economies, equitable societies, ethical elites, and sovereign nations."[10] And so Jowitt predicts a "surge of anger"[11] in postcommunist societies, as they show themselves unable to meet either the material or emotional and existential needs of their populations.

I have taken this time to outline Jowitt's argument because it seems to me fundamentally to be right, and because my book is exactly an attempt to show, bit by bit, year by year, how this existential void gets filled—how labor anger gets organized, and with what political consequences. Unlike other social scientists, who seem quite unsure how to handle Jowitt with his untestable hypotheses, I took his approach seriously because it seemed to accurately describe what I found as I spent time in Poland in the early 1990s traveling around the country, outside the major cities, and talking with workers and unionists whose lives were quite simply coming undone. Instead of an easy embrace of the new market economy, people were confused, frustrated, and angry. They were glad to have the old Party out of power, but not at all glad about the rapid decline of living conditions and the lack of any clear sense of the future. It's not that they expected instant success. What bothered them was how the new system set them up for failure, and seemed to treat their failure as a sign of the system's revitalization. The specifics of this will be discussed in the following chapters. The point, however, is that postcommunism did indeed generate an enormous amount of anger. "Movements of rage" may be too strong a term for Poland, where cultural homogeneity and the still-fresh legacy of Solidarity's inclusiveness vitiated any recourse to violence. Still, the subsequent emergence of strong right-wing movements, in and outside of Solidarity, that built themselves precisely by capturing the burgeoning social anger, suggests that the term is not inapt.

Elsewhere in the region, in countries without Poland's civic legacy or cultural homogeneity, "movements of rage" in fact seems a remarkably apt phrase. How else to describe the paroxysms of fury that engulfed the former Yugoslavia, meticulously egged on by nationalist politicians? In Czechoslovakia and the Soviet Union too, secessionist movements successfully aroused popular anger at the central authorities and thereby brought down these states as well. Violence there was minimal, since Czechs and Russians, unlike Serbs, were able to maintain a dominant position even in a truncated state.[12] Passions, however, were no less central to these developments. Indeed, everywhere one looked, anger, rage, disappointment, and bewilderment became aspects not just of individual psychology but of collective behavior. "Rage" would be too strong a term to capture all these phenomena, but the point was clear and on the mark. Just as Jowitt had predicted, emotion had become a crucial political variable.

Something else seemed to unite these different experiences. Not only were negative emotions politically salient throughout the region, but they seemed everywhere to be driven by economic developments. The nationalist tensions in Yugoslavia that would soon burst into war mushroomed precisely when the country underwent an extremely painful market reform program, creating large-scale unemployment and enormous fear of what was going to happen in the future.[13] In Czechoslovakia, it was Slovaks fearful of the costs of marketization who voted the secessionists into power. In Poland, the emerging anger was most visible among workers, particularly the less-skilled outside of the big cities, frightened by what hard budget constraints (the elimination of subsidies) would mean for their futures.

Economics was clearly not the only factor driving this chaotic, fragmenting, and mostly illiberal political expression of anger. But in the context of a traumatic "extinction" of the only political system most citizens had ever known, economic decline—and even more, the fear of decline—was the one factor they could feel most palpably. It was the one that made them politically available. Above all, it was the one that made anger *legitimate*.

In his book *The Passions and the Interests*, Albert Hirschman shows that its original eighteenth-century ideologues defended capitalism on the grounds that people engaged in the pursuit of wealth would be less inclined to wage war. Pursuing interests would cool passions. In his more recent account of the same topic, Christopher Lasch puts it somewhat differently. Capitalism, he says, is based on an ideology of progress. Unruly passions can be kept out of the public sphere only to the extent that people believe their interests will be met.[14] (The contrast between 1930s and 1950s Europe and America makes Lasch's point clear: labor passions were high in the earlier period when the pursuit of interests did not pan out, and low in the later one when they did.) Communism, of course, did not break from capitalism on this point but merely claimed it could do a better job of delivering progress. Both capitalism and communism thus defended their systems on the grounds that they would improve things for people economically. When they no longer do, people are allowed to get angry.

In Eastern Europe, people had joined in anticommunist opposition movements because they wanted a better life, and when that better life grew increasingly elusive, due to the costs of the post-1989 economic transformation, they were open to substitute satisfactions and solidarities instead. These substitutes depended on the particular national context, and also on the particular group of politicians savvy enough to recognize the opportunities that frustrated people offer. Where national distinctions existed, these became an easy target for political entrepreneurs to zero in on: they calculated, correctly, that despite decades of stability and majority populations that identified with the multinational state, old national cleavages could always be revived (even if it sometimes took an initial dose of violence to get it started).[15] In more homogeneous settings, lustration fever and religious fundamentalism became the substitute satisfactions of choice. We may not be able to fix the economic situation, this political appeal goes, but we can beat up on "communists" and "atheists" for supposedly getting us into this mess. When people cannot put their faith in progress, in other words, passions return.

This book deals with the substitute satisfactions offered to Polish workers, and the consequences this has had for the quality and inclusiveness of the political system that has emerged. The starting fact is that when Solidarity won, Polish workers lost. Given that Solidarity's triumph ushered in the onset of a capitalist economy, this was no surprise: any new government was going to make economic changes that would violate the social contract of the communist system. But the argument of this book is that this starting fact, occurring in the context of a society oriented around large factories and a recent political history dominated by a trade union, elicited an enormous level of anger, discontent, and confusions—passions, in a word, which no political organization had control over. With the one group that *could* control them, Solidarity, interested chiefly in promoting the marketization *causing* this emotional distress, a political crisis was inevitable. The passions would be up for grabs.

Who would politically capture the unruly passions necessarily emerging in the country, and along what lines would they do so? This was the question I learned to ask in my initial post-1989 visits to Poland. To answer it, I studied previous democratization processes in other capitalist countries and developed the following six claims that inform this book:

1. The emotions generated by capitalism, or what I call "economic anger," need to be organized along some lines or cleavages.
2. For liberal democratic outcomes, economic anger is best organized along class lines, meaning that economic conflicts get expressed as economic conflicts, rather than as ethnic, racial, national, or religious ones.
3. In postcommunist societies, class sensibilities are extremely low, due to the legacy both of communism and of the struggle against communism.
4. East European liberal parties are reluctant to promote class cleavages, because they see class only as an anticapitalist identity rather than a politically liberal one.
5. Liberals are reluctant to mobilize emotions, because they see them as a threat to their interests.
6. Illiberals, who are always anxious to mobilize around emotions, are able to score great successes as they organize economic anger along noneconomic cleavages.

While I discuss my understanding of democracy more fully in chapter 1, a few words are in order here. When I speak of dangers to "liberal democracy," I am not referring to the demise of parliamentary forms of government. I believe we need a "thicker" understanding of liberal democracy than most transition literature has embraced. For does it really get us anywhere to see democracy as merely "a political system in which the formal and actual leaders of the government are chosen within regular intervals through elections"?[16] Given that Eastern Europe's elite political actors agreed on this minimal definition in 1989, and that the international bodies they wanted to join insisted on it as a condition of entry, competitive elections were not at risk. Indeed, it does a condescending disservice to East Europeans to set the democratic threshold so low. I am more interested in the quality and openness of the democratic system: the degree to which it accepts all citizens as legitimate actors deserving of respect, while not singling out whole categories of people for exclusion. In chapter 1 I call this "inclusive democracy," but it is no more than the essence of "liberal democracy"—*if* we take that adjective seriously. Political liberalism, after all, means precisely this attitude of treating all people in a community as citizens equally deserving of rights, opportunity, respect, and dignity. When parliaments pass radical lustration or privilege one religion or nationality over another, they are being illiberal by creating whole groups of citizens subject to persecution by the state. They'll still have elections and parliaments and laws and privatization, but they'll be backsliding on the universalist promises of democracy that 1989 was all about. That is what this book deals with: the challenges to inclusive, liberal democracy after 1989, which, I argue, derive from the combination of neoliberal economics, new class formation, the anger that these economic policies produce, and the way politicians mobilize this anger.

This is probably the place to warn against a likely misreading of the book. For reasons that are quite misguided (as I discuss in chapter 1), any study today that takes class as seriously as this one runs the risk of being taken for a radical, left-wing book. Serious left-wing readers, however, will see that it is nothing of the kind. I am not boasting about this—if anything, the book may still stay too close to the narrow model of democracy that it criticizes. But the book has its origins in the discussion of capitalist democratization that followed 1989. My focus is on managing class conflicts in a capitalist society, not overcoming them in the name of achieving a classless future. I am saying to those who do want a politically liberal capitalist system to prevail that they ruin the chances of it when they allow labor to be organized by their opponents. Democratic capitalism works best with a strong class-conscious labor movement, not a weak one concerned with maintaining moral purity. One would have thought this lesson had been learned long ago. Actually it *was* learned long ago, and had become common wisdom in the West after World War II, until opportunities presented by globalization allowed capital to break free of its ties to labor, meaning apparently that "all the old crap" needs to be learned once again. Left-wing readers will see in this book a social democratic logic that many regard as having given exploitative capitalism its staying power. Of course, in this era of globalization and worldwide cutbacks on labor rights, most left-leaning readers now probably view social democracy as a time of great labor victory. And perhaps it was. The point, though, is that this book focuses only on the need for the inclusion of labor in any politically liberal capitalism. If such an outcome smacks of radical leftism these days, it certainly would not have seemed so a relatively short while ago.

As for methodology, the empirical part of this book is based on extensive field work, a national survey, and a thorough reading of the excellent sociological work coming out of Poland. Most of my on-site research was conducted in the southeastern area once known as the Central Industrial Region, Silesia, and the cities of Warsaw, Gdansk, and Krakow. I chose the first two because they are the most heavily industrialized regions in the country, the areas where I anticipated that the economic transformation would be particularly painful for labor and, because so many of the cities were so dependent on single factories, have a large political impact. In the former Central Industrial Region—so named by the interwar government, which began a massive industrialization program there in the 1930s—I visited industrial enterprises in Mielec, Stalowa Wola, Starachowice, and Rzeszow. In Silesia, I visited mines and other industrial sites in Bytom, Katowice, Chorzow, Gliwice, and Oswiecim. The three cities were chosen because of their obvious political importance: Gdansk is Solidarity's headquarters, Warsaw is the capital, and Krakow is Poland's second-largest city and the site of the important Nowa Huta steel mill. I tried to visit both factory union offices and regional headquarters in the various regions. I went always to the Solidarity unionists first, since it was by far the most important actor in shaping new industrial relations and labor politics, while in areas where I spent long periods of time, like Mielec, Krakow, and Warsaw, I met extensively with unionists from other unions as well. Altogether, I did my research during visits in 1989, 1990, 1992, 1993–94, 1995, 1996, 1998–99, 2001, 2002, and 2004, for a total stay of about two and a half years.

Because I wanted to know what the unionists I spoke with thought the relevant issues were, I did not come with a set list of questions. I usually began with very general questions, such as how they see their role as unionists, and then tried to get them to pursue the various trains of thought that such a broad question inevitably sparked. My very presence prevented me from being the fly on the wall that I wanted to be, listening and watching unobtrusively as the unions conducted their daily business, but by refraining from too many prepared questions I tried the best I could to get people to say what they wanted to say rather than what they thought I wanted to hear. While the disadvantage of this method is that one cannot get exactly comparable data, the advantage is that by not forcing one's own categories into the discussion, one learns the issues, questions, and categories that are central to one's interlocutors. The overwhelming majority of union officials I met with were men, which is what the overwhelming majority of union officials in Polish factories are.

Other empirical data came from a 1994 survey I organized with Marc Weinstein of unionists and managers in ninety-five manufacturing plants throughout the country. This is discussed in chapter 5. Other than my field work and the survey, the book is based on the solid work produced by Polish sociologists. Poland has a superb sociological tradition and a rich history in industrial sociology, practiced during the communist years by authors like Kazimierz Doktor, Leszek Gilejko, Maria Jarosz, Jolanta Kulpinska, Jan Malanowski, Witold Morawski, and Adam Sarapata and continued today (with some overlap) by scholars such as Michal Federowicz, Barbara Gaciarz, Juliusz Gardawski, Wieslawa Kozek, Maria Nowojczyk, and Wlodzimierz Pankow. These authors have produced extremely valuable case studies and have organized and analyzed numerous micro-level and nationwide labor surveys both broad in scope and rigorous in detail. Much of my analysis here is based on these studies, even though I only scratch the surface—a fact that future researchers should bear in mind. I was able to make extensive use of the press as well, particularly the weekly *Polityka* and the daily *Gazeta Wyborcza*, not only because of the generally high quality of Polish journalism but also because, unlike in the American press, newspapers regularly summarize recent sociological studies and print interviews with industrial sociologists.

It is my hope that this book will be read by more than those interested in East European politics. For the issues that postcommunist societies raise— the questions they help us answer—are the very stuff of a universal social science. A recent book argues that contemporary Eastern Europe offers sociologists an incomparable research site "for exploring the development of new capitalist possibilities all over the world and into the twenty-first century."[17] In the same way, the region offers political scientists an unparalleled venue for understanding how inclusive democracies can emerge, and the role played by labor, parties, and emotions in making this happen or not. The question of how economic anger, in the context of low class consciousness, can be mobilized to produce inclusive outcomes should be relevant both to underdeveloped states forced by globalization and Western pressure to open up their markets, a process causing a great deal of political instability, and to the western capitalist democracies, where old class cleavages are breaking down and conflicts based on ethnicity and religion are emerging as potentially dominant. Studying Poland during its fascinating fifteen years of complete systemic transformation can yield insights that are relevant far beyond its borders.

1

Democracy and the Organization of Anger

I t's not immediately obvious why a book dealing with postcommunist politics should take labor as its focus. Indeed, some would think the same about any book on politics. If Michael Burawoy could write, in 1985, that his book on politics in the labor process was an "unfashionable book . . . about an unfashionable class," how much more true is that two decades later?[1] For reasons having to do with globalization, the collapse of communism, and theoretical fashions that the first two helped create, the topic seems quite out of date. Yet for understanding this subject, that is simply not so. Labor remains as crucial as it was once seen to be. Thus, much of my book concerns the organization, ideas, and political impact of traditional blue-collar workers in manufacturing. It is this group, I argue, that is crucial for understanding political developments in postcommunist Eastern Europe.

Workers are important for one very important reason: communism produced an industrial society, not a postindustrial one. When the system collapsed in the late twentieth century, none of the characteristic features of *fin de millenium* postindustrialism—dying factories, a booming service sector, declining cities, burgeoning suburbs—was anywhere in evidence. Communism created a gritty industrial society and stopped there. The system was largely *about* the construction of heavy industry and of a proletariat—the development of both of which was central to these countries' very notion of national identity. When communism ended, the countries of Eastern Europe had a significantly higher percentage of workers working in blue-collar jobs in large factories than in the increasingly postindustrial West. As one author

Table 1. Percentage of labor force employed
in industry and construction in the 1980s

Poland	36.3
Hungary	38.3
Soviet Union	38.9
Romania	43.1
Bulgaria	46.6
East Germany	49.4
Czechoslovakia	49.8
Holland	23.9
Belgium	25.1
Canada	25.6
United States	26.7
Great Britain	26.7
France	27.2
Italy	28.2
Sweden	29.0
Spain	30.4
Japan	33.5
Switzerland	37.4
Austria	37.5
West Germany	39.1

Source: Rocznik Statystyczny 1991 (Warsaw: GUS,
1991), pp. 500, xxv. All figures from 1987 to 1989,
except for Czechoslovakia (1980), Bulgaria (1985),
and Belgium and Switzerland (1986).

put it, communist governments succeeded in building "the world's most advanced late nineteenth-century economy."[2] And what such economies do best is create large working classes.

In 1989, 36.3 percent of Poland's working population was employed in industry and construction, only one-tenth of a percent less than in 1970. As can be seen in table 1, figures elsewhere in the former Soviet bloc were normally even higher, ranging from 38.3 percent in Hungary to 49.8 percent in Czechoslovakia. Comparable western figures, however, were much lower: most employed about a quarter of their workforce in industry and construction, with only technologically sophisticated Switzerland, Austria, and West Germany approaching East European numbers. The percentage of the western workforce employed in services, meanwhile, typically hovered over 30, and in trade just under 20, while averages in Eastern Europe were about 10 percent lower in each category.[3]

Poland's industrial workforce in the late 1980s was even greater than table 1 indicates, however, because we must also add a large number of its agricultural laborers. Ever since it stopped its collectivization campaign in 1956, Poland had more people working in agriculture than anywhere else in Eastern Europe, not to mention the West. (In 1988, 27.1 percent of Poland's workforce worked in agriculture, compared to the well under 10 percent common in the West.)[4] Most of Poland's rural laborers, however, *also* worked part-time in industry, because although the state formally allowed the private ownership of farms, in practice it so restricted rural opportunities that farmers had to enter the urban labor market to survive. The state controlled the prices of inputs, virtually monopolized the market for agricultural outputs, and prevented the consolidation of large farms or the hiring of outside labor. In such conditions, farmers had no choice but to look for part-time industrial work. In the early 1970s, for example, 80 percent of Polish families living on small farms of under five acres supported themselves with outside employment.[5]

All this means that the percentage of blue-collar workers was in fact extraordinarily high in Poland. One survey showed the 1988 Polish workforce to be stratified as follows: 23 percent skilled manual laborers, 22 percent unskilled or semi-skilled laborers, 15 percent either farmers or farm workers.[6] In other words, 60 percent of the workforce without a desk job. Such figures only confirm what anyone who actually traveled around any of the former communist countries could see: these places were populated by people who looked like they had stepped from the pages of fading *Life* magazines from over half a century ago.

It is a commonplace of contemporary sociology to say that classes are no longer dominant collective actors. As one typical article puts it, the key groups today are not classes but "non-economic, non-class groups based on ethnicity, gender, lifestyle, values, and consumption."[7] But such a line-up makes little sense in Eastern Europe, particularly for the first postcommunist decade. You can look hard in the region and, with the notable exception of ethnicity, you still won't find such collective actors making much of a difference. What you do find, however, is that where there are protests there are likely to be workers, marching and striking—more so in Poland or Romania than in the Czech Republic or Hungary, though even there protests are far more likely to be organized by workers' groups than, say, women's groups.[8] Domestic conflicts in Eastern Europe still overwhelmingly take place along old industrial lines. Even the national conflicts that have racked the region can be seen as substitutes for industrial conflicts: Slovak workers hoping to save their industry coming to believe that Czech dominance held them back, or Yugoslav workers, reeling from market reforms by the late 1980s, having their class anger diverted into nationalist passions by elite politicians trying to save their skins. Politicians, meanwhile, have needed to appeal to workers since East European capitalism is developing out of a communist framework, not a feudal or premodern one. Since communist discourse privileged the working class, all calls for change had to be couched within pro–working class language, and the postcommunist system has had to reckon with the expectations thereby created.

To say labor discontent has been prominent does not mean that workers and their unions are strong. In fact, I argue the opposite. It means only that we're still dealing with an industrial society, not a postindustrial one. And this, in turn, means that the classic political issue facing industrial society— how to incorporate labor—has been the key political question since 1989.

Of course, workers are even more important to Poland than to the rest of the region. After workers on the Baltic coast went on strike in 1980, and stayed out until the ruling Communist Party accepted their demand for an independent trade union, the resulting union movement, Solidarity, became the key political force in the country for the next two decades. It was also, of course, the chief force shaping industrial relations. As one industrial sociologist has put it, "The field of industrial relations in the enterprise is completely dominated by Solidarity. This union is seen by employees, directors, and union activists [of all unions] as the main player in dealings with enterprise management."[9] As we shall see, Solidarity was not just a labor movement. It also served as the vehicle for the technical intelligentsia in its drive to become the new dominant class. But it very much was and is a labor movement too, totally separate from those emerging new elites. If for other countries in the region the question of how to incorporate labor was the key *underlying* political issue, for Poland it was always right there on the surface.

Most scholarship on democratization in postcommunist society has not dealt much with workers. Initial work on democratization focused on pactmaking between elites, and then turned to broad economic topics like marketization and privatization, or broad political issues like constitutions and political parties. The assumption, in other words, was that democratization follows from institutional changes made by governing elites, and these were said to be matters in which workers not only had little say but *ought* to have little say. Indeed, all of civil society was now pushed to the background. It had made political democracy possible, but now that that democracy existed, its role was to accept these changes peacefully. Most of the literature on democratization thus either ignored labor or insisted that it needed to accept what's coming—which, of course, was simply another way of ignoring labor. The real issues faced by real workers were essentially simply seen as unimportant to the democratic transformation at hand.

I still vividly recall a conference on democratic transitions held at Berkeley in 1993. I was presenting a paper on the decline of labor in postcommunist society and noticed a prominent social scientist in the audience looking quite annoyed. He raised his hand as soon as I finished and, still quite worked up, expressed his displeasure that I had chosen to talk about such a topic.

"Look," he said, "workers are going to suffer in this transition, and there's nothing anyone can do about it. Labor *must* lose. Do you really think it can be any other way?" His question, it turned out, was not just rhetorical. He wanted me to answer it. But I was simply bewildered. What did it matter, I thought, whether I agreed or disagreed with what "must" happen? The point is that people in Eastern Europe might not agree, and it is their anger about the hardships that await them that was going to be politically significant.

The social scientist had made clear his conviction that workers did not matter. They weren't players in this transformation, only the "played." Not subjects but objects. Their plight might be morally regrettable, but that did not matter as far as politics and democracy were concerned. Indeed, for most social scientists the only way workers seemed to "matter" was as a potential *obstacle* to democratization. Since they were going to pay a stiff price, they had to be disciplined to accept it. Democratic transformation, wrote Adam Przeworski, can succeed only with "an almost complete docility and patience on the part of organized workers."[10] Indeed, many post-1989 Polish reformers felt that successful democratization was possible precisely *because* Solidarity was in a good position to discipline workers.[11]

There are several problems with this. First, it runs counter to everything we know about the history of democratization, where labor has typically played a crucial role as the mobilizer of agitation on behalf of democracy. Second, it makes us blind to the problems posed by the *marginalization* of labor, by the dramatically reduced status of workers. One of these problems is indeed moral. Isn't it a blight on postcommunist democratization that the chief losers were those who made the transformation possible? That those whose solidarity strikes had helped make capitalist democracy possible would soon find themselves working in firms whose managers tolerated neither unions nor collective bargaining, or perhaps working as "independent contractors" without benefits or legal protection and subject to dismissal at any time? That by the late 1990s the typical Polish suicide victim was not a teenager in an existential crisis but a married man in his early forties living in one of the myriad small towns and villages where state firms and farm bankruptcies combined with the collapse of the old welfare state to produce a particularly searing kind of despair?[12] The dominant postcommunist "democratization" narrative defining labor as an obstacle has largely kept people from even commenting on such outcomes, much less recognizing them as indicators of a democratization gone awry.

But these are, of course, not just moral problems but political ones, as they leave open the question of how workers are going to react to their marginalization. For contrary to the assumption that entitled workers threaten democracy and therefore must be disciplined, it is certainly more historically accurate to see *excluded* workers as a danger. This is particularly true in the postcommunist case, as should be clear when we compare it to the Latin American experience upon which Przeworski, like others, based his recommendation of labor quiescence. Such a recommendation indeed made sense in Latin America, where labor militance had been a key factor leading to the imposition of dictatorship in the first place. Capital had been so threatened by labor mobilization in the 1960s and 1970s that it turned to the military to defend its interests, so it stood to reason that democratization efforts needed to be accompanied by labor moderation so as to keep business from turning to the military again. In postcommunist society, however, there was no capitalist class that needed to be "protected" from labor. Far from leading to the installation of dictatorship, labor militance instead helped unravel it. And so it should stand to the same reason that this makes *labor* important in Eastern Europe, both as a bastion of the new civil society underpinning democracy and as the key group that *could* reject liberal democracy (by supporting a demagogue at the ballot box) if its interests are grossly violated. In other words, just as capital's interests need to be looked after in a postcapitalist democracy, labor's interests need to be protected in a postcommunist one.

But mine is decidedly the minority view. All in all, working people have been rendered marginal to the postcommunist democratization discourse. This is surely one of the most remarkable developments in the history of political sociology. A century ago, democratization was synonymous with the entry of workers ("the masses") into politics, which is why conservatives so opposed democracy. Workers were the ones demanding inclusion, and their success in winning it meant the expansion of democracy. The recasting of labor as the obstacle to democracy is thus quite a novel one. Moreover, as noted, it is yet another way of saying that workers do not really matter for democracy: the way they are incorporated into the system does not matter, industrial relations do not matter, all that matters is their acceptance of the new elite. Their "importance" is framed as a negative one only.

Even works that do speak of labor tend to share this view. Bela Greskovits, for example, writes that workers have indeed lost out since the fall of communism but that this has not adversely affected democracy since they have not done much to protest their fall.[13] Ekiert and Kubik have a different take, but one that only reinforces the same theme: workers *do* protest, they say, particularly in Poland, but this doesn't threaten democracy both because the protesters are not trying to overthrow the system and because democracy is fully compatible with protest.[14] The fact that they have to assert these points—the central ones of their book—only underscores how pervasive the "labor = danger to democracy" theme really is. Why, after all, should anyone even think that labor protests would be a sign of antidemocratic activity, since historically they usually represent precisely the opposite, unless a general conviction had already pervaded the likely readership that workers constituted a threat? Both Greskovits and Ekiert and Kubik, in other words, agree that labor matters only "negatively": democracy does not require any positive measures to bring labor in, it only requires ensuring that labor does not challenge the new elites running the show.[15]

My argument here is quite different. The focus of the book is to show how workers are central to liberal democracy. Demonstrating this requires a discussion of other topics in this introductory chapter: class, anger, and democracy. We begin with class.

The Emergence of Class

Talking about class after 1989 seems to some like talking about flappers after the 1920s: it is a concept past its time, obsolete, over. If communism is dead, they say, then certainly its key conceptual unit—class—should be put to rest as well. But this is based on a fundamental misunderstanding: class has always been a concept for understanding capitalism, not socialism. Class language may have become *identified* with communism, but class analysis never had much success in dealing with communist society.[16] It has been in the dissection of market societies that class analysis has been most fruitful. Retiring "class" together with communism, therefore, just will not do. It is only now, *after* communism, that class becomes relevant, because it is only now, with the building of capitalism, that the class cleavages common to market societies are being created in Eastern Europe. Far from signifying the death of class, 1989 inaugurated a period in which economic class divisions finally became salient.

In subsequent chapters I talk about the post-1989 decline in workers' living standards and employment rights. Here I just want to stress the fact that economic class divisions do emerge after 1989, and that labor is suddenly relegated to the bottom.

Who ended up on top? The most serious account of class formation in postcommunist society is Eyal, Szelenyi, and Townsley's *Making Capitalism Without Capitalists*, coming on the heels of a long series of works by Szelenyi on class in Eastern Europe.[17] Using Bourdieu's notion of different types of capital, they argue that political capital (ties to the establishment) became greatly devalued after 1989, that the possession of economic capital helped only slightly in moving up the class hierarchy, and that those who possess cultural capital (education) had become the new dominant elite in Eastern Europe. In other words, those who owed their former status solely to affiliation with the ruling Communist Party lost out after 1989, while those who combined that affiliation with sound credentials as specialists, or who cultivated specialist skills without Party affiliation, emerged on top. "The coalition that governs postcommunist societies," they conclude, "is comprised of technocrats and managers—many of whom held senior positions in communist institutions—and former dissident intellectuals who contributed to the fall of communist regimes at the end of the 1980s."[18]

Eyal et al. write only about the emergence of the new elite, but their categories help us understand in theoretical terms what all the empirical accounts have shown: the relative, and often absolute, decline of labor since 1989.[19] Whatever clout workers had in the communist system derived from their political capital, which itself came from their symbolic capital. In other words, labor's power came from being in a system that symbolically privileged workers. In the absence of elections, that system could derive legitimacy only to the extent that it made good on its claims that workers lived well. I will explore this more in Chapter 5, but the point is that by breaking with communism's privileging of political capital and linking advancement to possession of both cultural and economic capital, which workers lacked, postcommunism inexorably brought about this dramatic decline in the standing of labor. As Eyal et al. put it, in one of their few comments on labor, postcommunism entailed the transformation of workers from "clients . . . into wage laborers."[20] This came about because the only capital workers possessed was the only one to be fully disavowed.

It should be clear, then, how this brings us to anger. Put simply, postcommunism is a period in which the new elites seek to bring labor down. One of their aims is to wipe out the ways in which being part of the working class brought economic dividends. In Poland, this meant that those who made possible the political transformation were the ones made to pay the price. Not their intellectual allies in the old dissident coalition, and not even all of the old Party elite either. The practical economic repercussions of this, as well as its clash with most people's notions of justice, brought a stream of negative emotions into the political world. How the new parties managed these emotions would become a key factor shaping the political future.

Anger and Politics

I do not have space here to develop a theory in full, but let me outline the key ways in which I understand political anger, and why it is one of the crucial concepts of politics, central to the process of democratization. What I am interested in here is anger brought into the public sphere, anger that becomes the basis of conflicts between social groups and the state, or of conflicts between particular social groups that can affect state policy. My starting point is the connection between anger and structure. All social systems generate popular anger, but they do so in different ways and with different results. Political and economic systems thus have different types of what might be called "anger regimes," or structured economic and political arrangements that cause anger to be expressed in different ways. What is crucial for political outcomes is how anger that is structurally created becomes politically organized: by whom and for what political ends. "Anger regimes" can be seen as the broad political equivalent of what Arlie Hochschild, in her work on the sociology of emotions, calls "feeling rules." That concept, which she refers to as "a private emotion use," is too disconnected to politics to be of use here—even with her later contention that the political "authorities . . . are the keepers of feeling rules."[21] But just as political authorities ultimately affect what feelings we are able to express and how ("feeling rules"), so the structural nature of the political and economic system shapes how and against whom we are able to express our anger ("anger regimes").

The central distinction between communist and postcommunist anger regimes—and, more generally, between state socialist and democratic capitalist anger regimes—derives from the fact that political power is transparent in the former and opaque in the latter. In communist society the ruling Party openly declares that it is in charge of everything, its claim backed up by its nationalization of the entire economy. In democratic capitalist society the government declares that the people are in charge, its claim backed up by elections and by ownership of productive property in diverse private hands. In the former system, all citizens know who's in control, or think they know, which, as far as anger is concerned, is the same thing. In the latter, no one can be sure: people "learn" who's in control only by accepting the line put forth by some political actor, such as a party or movement. Power transparency means that social anger is naturally directed at a common target; the anger requires no organization. Power opacity means parties and movements must tell people where to direct their anger; politics in capitalist society is all about the organization of anger.[22]

Communism loses out in this arrangement. By explicitly claiming to control all public matters, the Party only invites people to blame it for all public shortcomings. If prices go up, there are no economic others to blame, only political others. If work norms go up, it is not the managers but the Party that is responsible. If I'm not successful in life, it's not because of what I did but because of what the Party did: it didn't allow me my freedom, it kept me from advancing in my profession, it prevented me from publishing my poems. And since the Party is the sole voice of the entire system, it is the system as a whole that is the recipient of all these negative emotions. The same mechanisms that allowed communist systems to control their publics also made the systems extraordinarily vulnerable: all social grievances could only be directed at one target, the Party. As Valerie Bunce puts it, "what . . . socialist dictatorships lacked . . . was the capacity to obfuscate regime responsibility for unpopular outcomes."[23]

Political authorities have three ways to stave off anger: they can organize antipathy against external others, arouse hope of future salvation, or increase standards of living. All East European communist authorities tried all three. In the early years, the Party both blamed the West for present privations and promised that continuing hardships would be compensated for by a communist future. When these claims wore thin, about a decade after taking power, the authorities turned to the third strategy: buying consent by improving the standard of living, or what has been called the "new social contract."[24] It is when this failed, starting with the region's debt crisis in the late 1970s, that the system entered its terminal phase. If the Party could not lead them to a glorious future *or* provide goods in the here and now, people had no reason to offer consent. By claiming to be in charge of everything but being unable to deliver the goods, the authorities succeeded in what they had always wanted to do: uniting society. Unfortunately for them, however, they united society only against themselves. In the end, communist political structures allow no other way for social anger to be organized.

If communism attracts anger onto itself, democratic capitalist society deflects it onto unknown others.[25] Capitalist power opacity means it is unclear who exactly rules, and unclear who exactly should receive the blame for people's problems. If prices go up, I don't know who's responsible, since no one claims to be responsible. If the economy is bad, is that because the government did wrong, businesses did wrong, I did wrong, or because market forces are what they are? It's all quite unclear. This is what Marx long ago called "commodity fetishism": the way capitalism hides the human exploitation at its foundation by promoting the belief that impersonal economic forces structure economic relations.[26] The opacity of power is probably capitalism's leading political asset since it creates a fragmented opposition, with everyone proposing a different enemy said to be responsible for whatever mess people may find themselves in.

This leads to the next key point. None of this means that there is no anger in capitalist societies, only that anger must be politically organized.

That capitalism inexorably generates anger became clear to social scientists a long time ago. In fact, the effort to explain social anger lies at the very *foundation* of social science. What else, Albert Hirschman asks, are the concepts of "alienation, *anomie, ressentiment, Vermassung,* class struggle" but attempts to make sense of the "passionate anger, fear, and resentment" that capitalism and modernity were so obviously creating?[27] The link between capitalism and anger is particularly clear in early capitalist societies, such as nineteenth century Western Europe or postcommunist Eastern Europe, when poverty abounds and notions of radical individualism still ring unfair to those raised on communitarian sensibilities. In its early days capitalism not only produces deteriorating economic outcomes for a great many people, but seems to those people as contrary to prevailing notions of justice. This seems to be a universal truth. Studies of early capitalist societies, whether in Europe, North America, southeast Asia, or South Africa, always show strong social resistance to the onset of a market society.[28]

But capitalism in more advanced forms produces anger as well. Let us call this "economic anger": the anger that is systematically generated in and by the workplace, from production to compensation. People who complain about their working conditions, their pay, their benefits, or their poverty, are all expressing their economic anger. (I understand "anger" here as including disappointment and frustration, other negative emotions that systematically emerge from the working experience. I include them under "anger" because that is what political parties try to convert these other emotions into.) Since journalists and social scientists have written about workers' protests for as long as there have been workers, we can say that the experience of economic anger is also universal. This does not mean that all workers are always angry, but it does mean that there always exists a reservoir of anger that, in democratic society, is out there to be tapped politically.

So now we get to the critical importance of anger for democratic capitalist politics. Since anger is pervasive but power opaque, political actors are needed to capture that anger, to explain, channel, and make sense of it. Identifying enemies and mobilizing emotions against those enemies is the way that political leaders get citizens to do what these political leaders want them to do—whether that means voting for their party, participating in a protest, or supporting a certain policy in an opinion poll. As Debra Javeline demonstrates in her work on protests in post-Soviet Russia, "mobilizing resources to answer the question of whom to blame" is the key task for political activists, since citizens who do not "know" who to blame are unlikely to get politically involved.[29] Or as Della Porta and Diani put it more generally, "A crucial step in the social construction of a problem consists of the identification of those responsible for the situation in which the aggrieved population finds itself."[30] Political mobilization means getting citizens to respond to the narrative and target that you put forward. It means, to use Carl Schmitt's language, getting citizens to accept *your* friend-enemy dichotomy.

How different it all was before! The transparency of communist power established an anger regime that always struck at the Party itself; thus the grand collectivist flavor of East Europe's various rebellions from 1956 to 1989. In the anger regime of postcommunism, however, anger is up for grabs. Political activists will shape the future by what they do with the anger they capture. The task, then, is not to hope for labor "docility and patience," as Przeworski put it, but to pay attention to who captures the anger that emerges. The question is not whether anger will emerge—it will—but rather who will own it? Which party or trade union? Offering what kind of narrative? Promoting what kind of cleavages? Economic anger is the given that all politics must take into account. The question of politics is not how to eliminate that anger but how to manage it.

Politics as the Organization of Anger

Organizing anger is the task of the political actors who lead and set the discursive agenda (that is, develop the "frame" or ideology) for associations like parties, unions, movements, and states. Let's go through each of these in turn, moving from the least to the most obvious. The last-named might seem anomalous, since passions are typically associated with societal groups in opposition to states, but I follow Carl Schmitt in seeing states as the original and primal organizers of anger. Schmitt argues this in his famous definition of politics as founded on the dichotomy states make of friend versus enemy. States, he says, "group themselves according to the friend and enemy antithesis," and do not shed this central founding rationale even while living in peace.[31] The dichotomy, in other words, is for Schmitt the *beginning* of politics, not the end. The "enemy" is not someone to destroy but simply someone who, as another state with its own myths and ambitions, might someday seek to destroy you, and thus against whom you must define yourself. Politics is thus not primarily about moral suasion but about understanding that there are rival, competing sides who will never be won over. Schmitt stresses that the political other is only a "public enemy," not a private one, meaning that "the enemy in the political sense need not be hated personally."[32] But this public other must be recognized as an enemy and maintained as such in order for a political conflict to be waged.

Maintaining the political other as an "enemy" thus requires mobilizing anger against that other. This is most apparent in the case of political parties. Much has been written on how parties express domestic cleavages.[33] More important, I think, is how parties shape and promote cleavages, consciously choosing to emphasize some and deemphasize others. Parties, like movements, succeed to the extent that they can get people to accept their version of what's wrong with things rather then someone else's version. To say that parties aggregate interests, which is the standard definition of what parties do, is to put the cart before the horse. Before it can aggregate interests, parties must tell people what their interests should be, which they do by presenting a narrative explaining how the world ought to be interpreted. For interests refer not to each group's desire to live better—everyone wants that—but to the specific policies that are supposed to help me, in my group, live better.[34]

In other words, before parties aggregate interests, they must organize anger. My experiences may give me a feeling of anger and injustice, but they do not tell me who or what is responsible for that anger. Parties present a narrative that identifies the cause of people's dissatisfactions and promises to take action against that cause. As a worker, for example, I have an interest in higher taxes if the taxes are progressive and the proceeds are used for class-based collective goods such as health or unemployment insurance or safety inspections. But I come to *know* these are my interests only if I am first persuaded by a narrative that identifies the untaxed income of corporations and the wealthy as the problem. I know my interest only by knowing the designated other. Which is, of course, why many workers do *not* organize and historically have not organized around class issues such as these. If I am persuaded to believe, as were many Europeans a century ago, that Jews prevent me from living a good life, then persecuting or eliminating Jews comes to be in my interest. If I am persuaded, to use another real example, that my anger generated economically is "really" caused by the moral rot in society at large, then establishing a religious state becomes my interest. For what matters in politics is not my "real" interests but my perceived interests. People act on the basis of what they perceive their interests to be, not according to what those interests "actually" are. Of course, if their perceived interests are implemented but their frustration continues—in other words, if their perceived interests are not their real interests—this poses a serious political problem. But it is usually resolved not by protest and collective action, but by the dissatisfied being won over by another party with another narrative claiming to represent their interests, in a cycle that can go on for a very long time. (As Piven and Cloward note, the electoral system is usually the "principal structuring institution . . . in the early phases of protest," an argument Bela Greskovits echoes in his account of why labor opposition in post-1989 Eastern Europe has been less than might have been expected.)[35]

Of course, the proffered enemy must be minimally plausible. Brazilians will have a hard time believing that Norwegians are responsible for declining wages, and any political entrepreneur proposing such an enemy is not likely to be in politics for long. But if the problems of a market society can be blamed, to take a few historical examples, on Jews in Europe, Asians in

Uganda, Moslems in Bosnia, Chinese in Indonesia, blacks in South Africa, or blacks and "secular humanism" in the United States, there are, clearly, many potential enemies out there. The one citizens target is the one they have been persuaded to target by the political narratives of parties and movements.[36]

Parties are not the only important agents creating and promoting narratives of opposition. Trade unions do this too. Unions play a key role in producing political stability in that they channel the inchoate social anger that comes from being a subordinate in the workplace into a formal economic grievance capable of being redressed. At least ideally this is what they do—advanced capitalist societies have achieved social peace to the extent that unions do this in practice. They might, however, choose to organize workplace anger differently. Like parties, unions can channel anger at various possible targets. In nineteenth-century America, unions in California decided that Chinese workers were labor's chief enemy, while organized labor in much of the rest of the country was learning to blame blacks. Like parties, trade unions are powerful political mobilizers, and the way they mobilize anger powerfully affects political outcomes. Mobilizing economic anger at non-economic others can be done—we will see how Solidarity did this repeatedly over the course of the 1990s—but it is a sure way to produce an illiberal outcome.

Summing up, my approach differs from those presented in both "malintegration" and "resource mobilization" perspectives, both of which see anger as something that appears solely from the intervention of social actors. Rather than approaching anger as produced either by the ignorant and uneducated (whom Hofstadter called "paranoid," a concept appropriated by Lipset as the centerpiece of his "working class authoritarianism"—a perspective, as we shall see, close to the heart of Polish liberals)[37] or by ambitious politicians (the "political entrepreneurs" emphasized by McCarthy and Zald),[38] I see anger as *structurally intrinsic* to the capitalist system. It is something that the system inexorably produces, and must produce, and which is therefore always present, either as collective action or, more commonly, in a congealed political form that political scientists call "stability." Marx calls capital "congealed labor"; we can call political stability "congealed anger." The nature of a particular stable political system depends on the cleavages around which political actors have organized social anger.

Toward an Inclusive Model of Democracy

If labor has been largely left out of the literature on postcommunism because of the assumptions and lapses of the "transition to democracy" paradigm, then we have to revise that paradigm in order to bring labor back in. The first way to do so is to challenge the unfruitful distinction between "procedural-ist" and "substantive" democracy and substitute instead the concept of "in-clusive democracy." The reason transition theorists have given for offering their sometimes trivially minimal definitions of democracy is the fear that anything else leads to the shaky ground of "substantive" democracy, the def-inition of which notoriously eludes consensus. On the one hand, substantive democracy implies material benefits for citizens. But how much? And for which citizens? Transition theorists did not want to go there. Since we will not be able to agree on all the good things "real" democracy should have, they argued, and since existing democracies are already so different from each other, it is better not to try to come up with "substantive" features and to limit the definition to its bare minimum of free elections and rights to par-ticipate.³⁹ With this definition, workers with their "substantive" demands constitute a danger to democracy, diverting attention from the procedural consensus.⁴⁰ The "substantive" demands of capital, of course, are something else—they're built-in. Since private ownership is assumed as the basis of lib-eral democracy, capital's insistence on, say, privatization, is not considered a problem. Instead, it is smuggled in as part of the procedural consensus.

The problem with the procedural definition is that it ignores the extent to which non-elites, and particularly urban workers, have always been central to democracy. Indeed, societies adopted procedural democracy chiefly be-cause non-elites demanded it, seeing no other way to secure their inclusion in the modern world without it. Demands for democracy did not arise in pre-modern rural society since people there were embedded within a communi-tarian framework in which rules of reciprocity prevailed. One had one's place in a hierarchy presented by the dominant class as divine. Inequalities were rampant, but anger from below was normally contained by the communitar-ian consensus and by measures taken by the elite to sustain the poor in times of dire crisis.⁴¹

Modern market society changed all that.⁴² Its ideology stripped the elite of its moral obligation to keep communities intact. Community affairs were now to be satisfied by the *deus ex machina* of the "invisible hand" said to emerge out of everyone pursuing their own individual interests. The poor, in its new incarnation as an urban working class, lost its guaranteed, intrin-sic connection to the wider community. It lost its moral claim to a share of the economic product. It lost its guarantee of inclusion. And so it had to fight for that inclusion—which it did, starting in the nineteenth century, by pick-ing up the political language of the bourgeoisie and talking about "rights." They organized to get the right to vote. They turned to politics to provide the guarantees that the pre-market economy provided in the past, and that the market economy took away. Their anger was turned against the system that excluded them, becoming a force for inclusion, which, when realized, we called "democracy."

Procedural democracy is thus a partial answer to the problem of how to include people in decision making. The extent to which it is able plausibly to resolve social problems suggests that people are already demanding inclusion. Procedural democracy, in other words, is premised on the notion of inclusion.

Of course, democracy in the real world has never meant the franchise alone. The demand for inclusion has never stopped there. Historically, this has meant the evolution from electoral rights to social rights, from political citizenship to social citizenship, to use T. H. Marshall's well-known language. No democracies have been stabilized without entailing some degree of welfare state. Consolidating democracy in Western Europe was not possible until after World War II, precisely because the lack of social safety guarantees led to recurrent crises of legitimacy. Until such guarantees were in place, challenges from the left and right could not be defeated. There was no gainsaying the charge that democracy was only "bourgeois democracy" until democracy showed it could include the excluded in more than a formal way. Until it did, political liberalism came under effective attack from both left and right. Procedural democracy had—and has—no chance in the real world unless it provides some degree of inclusion. The entity providing the inclusion is usually the state, providing benefits to its citizens. And this points to yet another "inclusion" evident in any democracy: the symbolic inclusiveness of the nation-state.[43]

Political democracy thus becomes consolidated only when wedded to policies that guarantee economic inclusion for workers as a class. Transition studies have so far missed this point, leading most theorists to see democratization as a political process alone, without getting at the class arrangements that underpin them. Fortunately, recent years have seen the publication of a good deal of serious work on the connection between class and the consolidation of democracy. Some of this literature notes the large contribution of labor to bringing about stable democratic outcomes. In their large comparative study based on European and Latin American examples, Rueschemeyer, Stephens, and Stephens argue that labor has historically stood out as "the most consistently pro-democratic force." While the bourgeoisie fought for its own political rights, the working class consistently fought for the extension of such rights.[44] Working-class mobilization has also been the key factor in winning social welfare guarantees, the other crucial element necessary for embedding democracy in a given national society.[45]

Other studies focus precisely on the question of inclusion. Gregory Luebbert, for example, shows that political stability in interwar Europe depended on the incorporation of the working class. Elite theorists may have railed against "mass politics," but they couldn't do anything about it. Practical politicians had to act within this new context. The political outcome, Luebbert demonstrates, would be determined by which party would be able to win over this newly mobilized working class, which party would be able to capture its anger. A democratic system resulted either when workers were won over by liberals, or when they organized themselves and then won over the agrarian middle class. Where liberals failed to win over workers, or where workers failed to win over farmers, fascists were able to win the support of those who felt excluded and thereby come to power themselves.[46] Luebbert's account demonstrates how any kind of political democracy, whether of the liberal or social democratic kind, requires the inclusion of labor as a condition of its existence. While societies in which economic liberalism fails to take hold, he says, can still be "governed as representative democracies, . . . it [is] not possible for them to be governed as stable, effective representative democracies without the acquiescence of labor." The "stability, effectiveness, and even legitimacy" of a political system requires the "acquiescence or actual support of labor."[47] Luebbert speaks of the importance of labor inclusion for democracy in Europe. Other recent research shows how this shapes systemic outcomes elsewhere as well.[48] The result of all this work is that they get us to see labor inclusion not as a "substantive" issue but as an indispensable aspect of political democracy. The key question for politics in the modern era is not whether workers will be included, but how, and on what grounds.

Class as the Cleavage of Democracy

If capitalism creates anger but democracy is about inclusion, then democratic politics requires the organization of anger to secure the inclusion of labor. Of course, all stable political systems provide for labor inclusion in some way. (Franco, after all, in classic "state corporatist" fascist fashion, created the *sindicatos* to capture labor, and provided health insurance and authoritarian morality to keep workers content.) The question, then, is what kind of inclusion leads to what kind of outcomes. This, again, is Luebbert's main point: that how labor is included, by whom and along what lines, is what shapes political outcomes. The question for a *democratic* polity, then, is: how can labor anger be organized in order to facilitate democratic outcomes?

The answer, supported by the historical record, is that for liberal democracy to succeed, class anger is best organized along class lines. For a system in which rights for all citizens are guaranteed and secure, workers need to accept a narrative that explains their anger as a product of economic class divisions, rather than of national, religious, or racial divisions. Class, in other words, is the optimal cleavage of democracy.

I should note that I use class here not as a sociological concept but as a political one. I am interested not in identifying who is in what class but in showing how the term serves to organize conflicts. Class is one of a variety of concepts around which to organize political conflict (nation, religion, and race are obvious others). But it is the one, I argue, that pays the kind of political dividends that make it particularly well-fitted for inclusive liberal democratic societies.

The organization of labor's economic anger along class cleavages is democratic because the proffered enemy is an impersonal economic system and not an ethnic, political, or religious "other" slated for expulsion from the community. Class conflicts lead to liberal democratic outcomes because they seek to resolve conflicts through bargaining among different groups of people, all of whom are accepted as citizens of the same state. Unlike the enemy of racial, nationalist, or fundamentalist politics, the class other is a group with different interests, not with alien identities. Alien identities are to be eliminated from the polity. Different interests are to be negotiated with in order to come up with a fairer distribution of wealth.

It is the simultaneously abstract and concrete nature of class that make it the ideal democratic cleavage. It is abstract in that it does not define the other according to ascriptive criteria. It is concrete in that it points to the real underlying causes of economic anger. As a result, it impersonally structures antagonisms in a way that gets at the root cause of the anger, thus making inclusive, or positive-sum, compromise possible.

Class, of course, is not a natural category for the organization of social conflicts. Classes may exist objectively without becoming real subjectively.[49] People do not naturally or inevitably come to think in terms of class. This was particularly true when the concept first came into wide use, in the mid–nineteenth century, when the relationship between employer and employee was far more personal than it would soon become. It was much easier at that time for workers to think of their bosses as people much like them. Why, after all, is the owner not on your side? If he goes bankrupt, there goes your job. You may have known him before he was your employer, and you may like him. You may be grateful that he gave you a job. Moreover, why oppose the boss when he can so easily do you such harm? If you are upset about your economic situation, as you may well become, why not blame someone else—someone who does not pay your wages, someone who cannot cause you such harm?

And indeed, historically it has been much easier for workers to blame not owners or managers but some ascriptive other. In many European countries, for example, it was long easier to blame "Jews" for economic problems than to blame "capital." Kept off the land and out of the traditional feudal class structure, many Jews moved to then-small cities and gravitated to then-marginalized positions in trading, which eventually turned Jews into human signifiers of the new market economy when cities and capital replaced feudal estates and gentry. From Paris to Russia, villagers and workers were mobilized by domestic elites to direct their economic anger not at capital but at Jews. In North America and South Africa, meanwhile, workers traumatized by the emergence of large-scale capitalist factory production were mobilized to express their anger not by opposing the industrialists but by opposing blacks.[50] In both ways, class anger became organized along non-class lines, with tragic results for the quality of democracy.

It is precisely the ability to identify the enemy on the basis of his interests rather than his identity that is crucial to democratic politics. When the other is defined according to ascriptive features or according to cultural attributes the other can do nothing about, the only way to defeat that other is to eliminate from the community those with the "wrong" features or attributes. Class-based critiques lead to a more inclusive polity precisely because they target their enemies on an abstract rather than concrete basis. Unlike nationalist, communitarian, religious, racial, or ethnic antagonisms, which exclude whole categories of people from citizenship on the basis of attributes one can do nothing about, class-based antagonisms target only an abstract distributional arrangement as the problem. Thus, they can be resolved by adjusting the economic system, rather than, say, by killing Jews, subjugating blacks, or expelling Muslims.

Of course, the language of class can be organized towards murderous ends, too. In communist practice, if not in theory, "class" has frequently been interpreted in a tragically concrete way, with those designated as "class enemies" liquidated on a massive scale in Stalinist Russia, Maoist China, and the Khmer Rouge's Cambodia. In these cases, governing communist party-states used the language of class, their chief available discourse, in order to suppress opposition and build state power. In capitalist society, however, class has regularly been the language of democratic inclusion. It has been a concept promoted only by labor—capital always presents its interests as universal—and used by labor parties seeking to expand the democratic terrain. Parties offering class narratives to explain injustice have usually pushed for the political inclusion of minority groups, opposed distinctions based on race or ethnicity, and promoted a broad-based concept of community, just as liberal democracy commands. It is this that has led left-wing parties to consistently oppose racisms and other ascriptive hatreds. Long before Stalinism, early Russian Marxists fought workers' spontaneous tendencies to direct economic anger at ethnic others. When strikes turned to pogroms, Bolsheviks and Mensheviks alike admonished workers for attacking the wrong enemy.[51] In America, communists consistently opposed Jim Crow, precisely because they saw class as the only legitimate cleavage. In Western Europe, socialists and social democrats played the crucial role, appealing to the notion of class inclusion in order to introduce comprehensive and inclusive welfare states in the postwar era. Promoting the organization of anger along class lines means discouraging it along other lines, and that helps promote full democratic inclusivity.

Class is the democratic cleavage because it offers economic anger an economic narrative. No pretending here that the anger derived from the work experience is "really" caused by alien nations or peoples. Instead, class narratives claim that economic anger is caused by economic problems and that the complaints can only be redressed by changing economic rules. In this way, anger is confronted directly and compromise becomes possible. Of course, this does not mean that class cleavages are the only ones present in democratic systems, just as economic anger is not the only source of political unrest. It only means that social anger *ought* to be organized around class lines, if the aim is to build an inclusive democratic polity.

In a sense, what I'm advocating here can be called a realist approach to domestic politics and civic relations, similar to what is meant by a realist approach in international relations. The core of realism is a recognition that conflicts between states are inexorable, meaning that the focus becomes how to manage conflicts, not prevent them. Whereas some realists see conflict as something you can't do anything about, I agree with those, like Charles Kupchan, who see a need, and claim there's a way, to promote the organization of conflict in certain specific ways, since some ways are better than others. "By recognizing the system's tendency to gravitate to conflict and by identifying and seeking to repair fault lines before they erupt," writes Kupchan, "leadership and planning can mitigate . . . the logic of realism and the rivalry that derives from it."[52] I'm arguing, similarly, that liberal democratic political actors should recognize that anger is intrinsic to market economies and try to channel the ensuing social conflicts along class rather than ascriptive lines. In this way, they will be promoting an inclusive liberal democratic outcome.

Class conflict with a key role played by trade unions and social democratic parties has been the glue of liberal democracy for another reason. It provides one of the key existential needs that capitalism does not offer those at the bottom: passion. Elites can find their passions satisfied by avarice. As Hirschman has shown, capitalism's original theorists explicitly *promoted* avarice because they thought that it could placate the passions (that is, satisfy the emotional needs) of the elites, who in early capitalist times were the only ones even thought to have passions.[53] By the middle of the nineteenth century, however, it became clear that non-elites had passions too, expressed in the labor movements they began to form. The appearance of poor people with passions threw elite theorists into a real crisis. Would it be possible to discipline "the masses" so they would accept the established order? Elites had their doubts. Conservatives like Spencer or Ortega despaired of the decline of civilization, while capitalist liberals like Cecil Rhodes proposed colonization of faraway places to capture the passions—and sop up the superfluous labor—of the working poor. As it turned out, however, socialism solved the problem in a liberal manner. Class struggle not only succeeded in winning material benefits for workers, but it offered passion to them as well. And since this way of satisfying passion, like greed and avarice, did not require killing or excluding anyone from the community, it proved fundamentally compatible with liberal political notions of inclusivity. Indeed, class conflict was the stuff that consolidated political liberalism in the West, since it satisfied both the material and emotional needs of workers.

The democratic core of the concept of class is evident in its very genealogy. The word came to be used widely only in the modern capitalist era. Raymond Williams traces its initial usage to the period between 1770 and 1840, its appearance signifying "the increasing consciousness that social position is made rather than merely inherited."[54] The liberal emphasis on human agency is thus implicit in the term itself, which explains why conservatives long refused to accept it, preferring "rank" or "order" instead. The term became a concept around which to organize political anger only when used as "working class," for this invariably posits an other. That phrase emerged around the 1830s as a critique of the unequal distribution of wealth of early capitalist society. Contained within it was the implicit claim that wealth not only should, but could, be distributed more equally, with those who produce it getting their fair share. Radical thinkers offering "class" as the concept through which to understand injustice and inequality thus shared with liberals an anti-aristocratic belief in distribution according to work. They only asked that liberals live up to their ideology. The concept itself is steeped in rationality. It offers no scapegoats, appeals to no magical solutions, banks on no savior to provide redemption. Rather, it represents an economic response to economic inequalities, proposing a rational redistribution of material resources as a way of resolving burgeoning social conflicts. (The ability of class conflict to satisfy emotions, discussed in the preceding paragraph, is the extra ingredient that makes it actually work in the real world.) Politically, therefore, the idea of class—the sense that social divisions and political conflicts can be traced to a situation that humans created and can therefore redress—is inextricably linked to the liberal notion that conflicts should and can be resolved by reason exercised by the relevant parties. The concept of class thus constitutes not a rejection of liberalism but an immanent, internal critique of liberalism. Proponents of class narratives agree with the liberal agenda of citizenship for all. They demand only that that agenda be realized.

The key question for politics, then, is how the economic anger that capitalist systems produce, particularly in their early phase, is politically organized, and by whom. If anger is captured by parties and trade unions seeking to organize it along economic lines—by defining the enemy as an unjust economic system that needs to be redressed—then it can be channeled in a politically liberal way. If it is captured by nationalist parties blaming ascriptive characteristics of others about which nothing can be done, then the resulting anger congeals in politically dangerous ways leading to illiberal outcomes.

How Polish Liberals Promoted Anti-Liberalism

Unions and parties are the key subjects of the following chapters. In many ways, of course, the book tells a story of union *as* party, for in Poland it has been Solidarity, in its dual role of union and party, that has played the chief role in organizing labor's anger. Labor movements emerging from dictatorship in the capitalist world have typically had a socialist party to latch onto. In Poland, however, like elsewhere in Eastern Europe, the former communists claimed the mantle of socialism, and were for that reason largely dismissed as a legitimate partner. In 1989, however, no other party was available. Whereas opposition proto-parties had emerged in Hungary during the communist era, in Poland all opposition energies had gone into the putative labor movement. Any party seeking to grab labor's support in the new era would have to emerge from there.

And indeed it did. Initially, Solidarity was not completely party-free. In late 1988, union leader Lech Walesa created the "Civic Committee" as Solidarity's direct political arm. Composed chiefly and led almost exclusively by the union's leading liberal intellectuals, the Civic Committee was authorized to lead the 1989 Round Table negotiations on Solidarity's behalf and to organize the subsequent election campaign. It is commonly said that "Solidarity" won those elections, but in fact the union had barely revived when the elections were being held. Instead it was the Civic Committee, backed by reemerging union cells and particularly by nascent local Civic Committee party structures, that actually organized the campaign and triumphed. When its slate of candidates overwhelmingly won those elections, propelling its leaders first into parliament and then into power, the Civic Committee seemed poised to emerge as the hegemonic party of Polish labor.

It began with an apparently unbeatable set of resources, including domestic fame, international clout, huge popular support, local networks, political skills, money, name recognition, and the most popular national daily newspaper as its virtual house organ. As the following chapters show, however, the Committee's liberal leaders systematically—and very consciously—squandered its opportunities, going on to create political parties that proudly boasted a middle-class, pro-business orientation and that enjoyed telling workers honestly (for it was "honesty" that these liberals valued most) that labor should expect to find no succor under its wings. My argument, developed in chapter 4, is that it squandered these assets by repeatedly refusing to act—refusing even to *pretend* to act—as a defender of labor interests. By positioning themselves as the party of professionals, intellectuals, and young reformers, by appealing to voters as future bourgeois citizens rather than as present-day workers in a time of difficult transition, the liberals lost their popular base with astonishing speed. Five years into the postcommunist era, Solidarity's old liberals ended up with a wavering base of about 10 percent popular support, giving them an important say in elite circles and policymaking but stripping them of any chance of running a dominant party.

And this is how it happened that Solidarity the trade union had to pick up the pieces and enter the formal political fray on its own. Beginning in 1996, the union, now largely shorn of its political liberals, became the political mobilizer of labor, not just at the workplace but in the voting booths as well.

On what grounds? For most sociologists, the answer seemed obvious. As organizations representing labor's interests in the workplace—the most common definition of unions—unions would seek to direct labor anger against the new elite responsible for the dramatic post-1989 economic depression. This is why many transition theorists commonly identified labor as the main obstacle to successful transformation. Solidarity, however, has never acted as a trade union "should"—meaning, as unions have acted in most capitalist societies. Instead, as the next chapters show, Solidarity consistently sought to organize labor anger *away* from class cleavages and toward identity cleavages instead, with negative consequences both for the quality of Polish democracy and for the effectiveness of its trade unions. Parties and unions that mobilize labor by identifying "capitalism" and "owners" as the other contribute to an inclusive democratic system in a way that those targeting political, ethnic, or religious others do not. Yet despite its identity as a trade union, class was a language that Solidarity was both unwilling and unable to embrace. Far from trying to fight the new market economy, the union embraced it, channeling the anger it caused onto political or religious others, thus leaving a profoundly illiberal legacy in its wake. With party liberals abdicating the responsibility of organizing labor, and unions mobilizing workers along non-economic cleavages, the result has been a labor movement incorporated politically in an undemocratic way: Polish workers are accustomed to protesting but direct their anger at targets whose persecution contravenes basic principles of inclusion, and whose defeat does nothing to fix the problems they were angry about in the first place.

And so, by looking at how anger has been organized, we can understand why postcommunist politics has developed the way it has. For this book is also about the strength of the political right in postcommunist Eastern Europe. How did it happen that political liberals, everywhere so prominent after the fall of communism, lost their dominance and were replaced by nationalist or religious parties of the right or by the successor parties of the former regime? As will be argued in subsequent chapters, the turn of a large part of Polish labor to the political right results from their economic anger being captured by parties proposing non-economic solutions. And these parties and tendencies were able to do so because the political liberals who led the country after 1989 consistently refused to organize workers. On the contrary, they presented labor as the chief threat to democracy and set out to reduce its power radically. With the former communists still unpopular in most labor circles, labor anger then gravitated to political illiberals, who spoke constantly of the economic issues confronting workers as a class, even as they proposed non-class-based answers to these problems.[55]

Most accounts of the rise of the extreme right in postcommunist Eastern Europe explain people's susceptibility to authoritarian or fundamentalist populism as a product of irrationalism. Tismaneanu, for example, depicts postcommunist anti-liberalism as a "longing for political myth" in a context where "old ideological certainties are dead" and people need "quick and satisfactory answers to excruciating dilemmas."[56] I stress economic and organizational factors instead. My argument, laid out in a detailed account of Poland's postcommunist years, is that many turned to the right because the right offered them an outlet for their economic anger and a narrative to explain their economic problems that liberals, believing they held sway over workers, consistently failed to provide. In the end, workers drifted to the right because their erstwhile intellectual allies pushed them there. The implications, I argue in the conclusion, extend far beyond Eastern Europe: in order to stabilize an inclusive liberal democracy, liberals must seek to organize labor and channel their discontent along economic lines, encouraging class conflict. If their anger is not organized along class lines, chances are it will be organized along more intractable and politically exclusionary lines. That is precisely what happened in Poland in its first postcommunist decade.

2

Solidarity Against Itself

"We will not catch up to Europe if we build a strong trade union."   —Lech Walesa, September 1989.

Rarely has a social group fallen so fast from such dizzying heights. From their glory days as the heroes of 1980, the undisputed vanguard of a nonviolent revolution that meant all things to all people, Polish workers found their social prestige steadily devalued throughout the 1980s. When the decade was over, labor ended up being recast as the epitome of a social pathology: a deformed remnant of the old system fighting irrationally (a key term in the new narrative) to hold onto privileges it neither earned nor deserved and which, if maintained, would ruin the chances for the new system to succeed. From the harbinger of the new, they were reinterpreted as a specter from the past.

This was no mere intellectual fad, relevant only to the history of ideas. On the contrary, what makes this so important is the identity of those who did the "recasting" and "reinterpreting." For it was Solidarity's leaders themselves who promoted this new approach. Those who enjoyed such authority in 1980–81, the very people workers considered their legitimate leaders throughout the years when Solidarity was banned, were developing the new antilabor ideas that would prove so damaging to labor (and to democracy) once the ban was lifted. Lech Walesa was surely not the theorist of this new approach, but that it became his approach as well is clear from the epigraph that opens this chapter: like virtually all the other leaders of Solidarity, Walesa simply opposed building up unions once it was possible to do so. What happened theoretically in the 1980s, therefore, is crucial to understanding what happened practically after 1989.

The 1980s assault against labor was multi-leveled, occurring not just in politics and economics but in ideology and culture too. Even as Solidarity won a decisive electoral victory in 1989, even as Walesa was elected president in 1990, Poland saw a bizarre embrace of old Victorian sensibilities in which the working class became the "dangerous class" that must be restrained. Most surprising, this attitude affected workers, too. Having fought so hard for independent trade unions in 1980, ten years later even they were looking skeptically on trade unions and other institutions claiming to represent their interests, such as political parties and self-management bodies.

In the course of a decade, therefore, we see a sea change in the master frame of the political opposition, ending in the emergence of a new overarching narrative explaining Solidarity's mission. And just as the "anti-politics" paradigm of the 1970s opposition played such a key role in shaping the nature of the first Solidarity, this reconceptualization and downgrading of labor in the 1980s, part of a more general embrace of property and capital, powerfully influenced the Solidarity of the 1990s. For, as I will argue, it was this intellectual devaluation of labor in the 1980s that helped spark an illiberal backlash in the next decade. By defining workers as irrational, even dangerous, and doing their best to marginalize labor influence, liberals pushed away huge swaths of voters who should have been theirs, driving many of them into right-wing populism. The aim of this chapter is to explore this transformation in the views of elite opinion-makers. How and why did they turn labor from friend to foe, from exalted subject to marginalized object, in the course of a mere ten years?

In short, this chapter deals with the change, over the course of the 1980s, in Solidarity's ideas about the relationship of labor to democracy. Changes in public policy, if they are going to be durable, require changes in public consciousness. Just as the Keynesian turn in the postwar West, like the neoliberal turn more recently, was made possible by the arduous efforts of intellectuals and publicists who argued their case beforehand, so the post-1989 policies marginalizing labor in Poland were preceded by a newly dominant strand in intellectual discourse that defined workers as a potential danger to democracy. Ideas have "the power to change the perceptions a group [has] of its own interests," writes Peter Hall,[1] and subsequent chapters will show how trade union activists themselves embraced this new antilabor consensus and largely ceased to represent their members. This chapter focuses on the intellectual effort that made such a shift possible, the way these new ideas were institutionalized by Solidarity's political leadership in 1989, and the consequences this reorientation has had for Polish labor and politics.

From Fawning to Discarding

We must, of course, begin with 1980, for that was when intellectuals first proclaimed an inseparable *connection* of labor and democracy, thus establishing the claim they would spend most of the rest of the decade trying to dismantle. For in 1980 Polish workers suddenly found themselves overwhelmed by the affection of intellectuals. How it was overwhelming, and even destructive, will be discussed later on. But there is no gainsaying its powerful intensity. In August 1980, intellectuals in the political opposition greeted the general strike in Gdansk with nothing short of awe. After decades of discussing strategies of opposition chiefly among themselves, they now evinced a profound astonishment: perhaps we can learn from *them*. Gdansk seemed to lay to rest the pervasive image of worker as *robol* (the uncultured brute who cares only about his next drink), revealing instead a citizen who cared for dignity and autonomy—precisely the values that intellectuals saw as their own.[2] Even more, the strike showed that workers knew how to win, too. The Warsaw intellectuals advising the Gdansk strikers famously urged them *not* to press the demand for free trade unions, and Solidarity came about only because the strikers ignored this advice. Intellectuals came to see Gdansk as a rebellion against hopelessness, and they took it as a profound critique of themselves.[3] They now saw their own previous protests against the regime as somehow shallow and insignificant, as superficial resistance masking a deeper layer of complicity. Workers, it appeared, had the courage and tenacity to bring about the changes that intellectuals only talked about.

Gdansk set in motion a deferential exaltation that was positively Maoist in its self-flagellation. One can see it in the difference between Andrzej Wajda's two films, *Man of Marble* (1977) and *Man of Iron* (1981). The heroine of the first film is a young filmmaker who cuts through bureaucratic obstacles to learn the truth about the Stalinist past. In the second film, the same woman comes to realize that her struggles are nothing compared to those of the average worker. The intellectual gives up her craft to become a wife to the Gdansk shipworker valiantly fighting for social justice.[4] Changing one's career in response to Gdansk was what a real-life filmmaker told me he was going to do himself. Janusz Kijowski, from the same production company as Wajda, had directed the powerful 1979 film *Kung Fu*, which explored the way that student radicals from 1968 became complicit in the Polish reality of the 1970s. After Gdansk, however, Kijowski saw that film only as a sign of his *own* complicity. We thought we were so profound, he told me, but "the things happening on the streets, in the offices and factories, were a lot bolder and more interesting than any of our films and screenplays." He vowed to abandon his subtle films in favor of "anti-films" and documentaries.[5] The subtlety of the intellectuals needed to be replaced by the forthrightness of the workers.[6]

Musia Sierotwinska, a teacher from Krakow, was even more blunt in describing what Solidarity taught her. "I used to think that books and culture were the important things. But it turned out that these were completely marginal. It's the factories, economics, the workers who are important. Their issues are the crucial ones." Solidarity showed workers to be morally superior too, she added: "In intellectual circles, we all got along. The oppositionist and the party secretary meet and we're all polite with each other. But for the worker, everything's clear: that one's a red! And that's that! The nuts-and-bolts wisdom of the working man is the healthiest thing. They alone knew how to judge what's true and what's false."[7]

This adoration of the working class was different from the more famous and widespread wave of reverence of the 1930s and 1940s. That earlier moment was mostly a fascination with the *idea* of the working class—labor as "agent of History"—and manifested chiefly in support for the Communist Party. It was a worship of the "naïve," in the Schillerian sense, meaning fealty to the simple truths of premodern values brought to bear on the industrial world, excitement at the physical strength that could build a world of modern righteousness.[8] But 1980 elicited an admiration based on wonder, as if to say: We thought we knew who these people were, but look what they can teach us! They know how to topple the system while we pretend. They are morally righteous while we are complicit. They build structures and organizations while we talk about culture. This veneration of labor valued not just workers' brawn but their brains. Poet Stanislaw Baranczak beams as he recalls how workers in the giant Cegielski metal plant in Poznan wanted to hear *him* talk, not about politics but about censorship. "It was precisely censorship that they were interested in," he notes proudly, and two years later he was already having trouble believing it.[9] Of course, the love affair did not stop with admiration from afar. Intellectuals traveled to the workplaces to form Solidarity with workers and worked with them in strike committees and union offices. Polish academics even abandoned the union they had formed soon after the strike in Gdansk in order to join Solidarity, before the latter became the powerhouse it would become. Intellectuals established multiple venues of direct contact with workers and maintained them for the sixteen months of legal Solidarity.

The theoretical basis of this adoration for labor was the idea of civil society. The liberal intellectuals so closely affiliated with Solidarity saw labor activism as the embodiment of the free, autonomous public activity that they believed to be the grounding of a democratic system.[10] Their 1980 fascination with Solidarity was not just aesthetic but profoundly political: this trade union movement, they believed, had made a democratic transformation possible. By acting in a participatory, democratic way, even without legal sanction to do so, workers were living out the democratic ideals that these intellectuals had long been advocating.

We can get a sense of how quickly intellectuals changed their view of labor and democracy by looking at one of Adam Michnik's works of 1985. The most influential member of the liberal intellectual opposition, Michnik explodes here with one of the most stinging indictments of working-class activism ever written by an ostensible supporter. Far from being the guarantor of democracy, says Michnik, labor activism was one of the main dangers to democracy. The rational intellectual elite, he argues, would have to take the place of workers in the Solidarity leadership if the organization was truly to be the agent of democratic transformation.

Long live Solidarity, writes Michnik, but beware of its proletarian rank and file. In 1980 we may have thought of them as sensible and rational actors. In fact, says Michnik, they are really irrational hotheads, hostile to reason and common sense, contemptuous of the notion of compromise, and incapable of recognizing the "limits and realities" of the real world.[11] Michnik describes Polish unionists as antipluralist and "susceptible to a cult of the Leader," and characterizes Lech Walesa himself as a "sultanic" despot. Local Solidarity leaders, he says, have been blinded by the ambition to become petty despots themselves. With their limited knowledge of the world— Michnik is particularly harsh on their meager intellectual qualifications— they resorted to easy slogans in order to speak to the masses and win their support. The characteristics he ascribes to these workers—"new radicals," he calls them, in contrast to veterans like himself—are, for Michnik, the building blocks of a new totalitarianism. Michnik stands as a strong defender of Solidarity, but only if led by intellectuals. A Solidarity outside of their control, he suggests, is a dangerous one.

Michnik was writing here from the perspective that Solidarity might actually succeed. The view, popular in the West, that no one anticipated the upheavals of 1989 may make a good sound-bite, but it is not good history. For as gloomy as the situation appeared to be in Poland in the mid-1980s, it was even gloomier from the point of view of the ruling Polish United Workers Party. Despite the imposition of martial law in December 1981, the Party had proved unable to break social resistance. Even despite the numerous social concessions it was making—improving relations with the Church, promoting small business, introducing some real market reforms, and soon to make concessions to the political opposition as well—the Party was simply unable to attract support. In short, martial law proved unable to restore the public order and social acceptance the Party needed to accomplish its goals, suggesting that eventually the Party might have to turn to the opposition to broker a deal. In this context, Michnik's broadside signaled that the next round of conflict must be different from the past. If Solidarity was to succeed, Michnik was saying, it would have to do so on a different basis from 1981, when labor took itself so seriously.

This was no isolated voice. Few other interventions of the time criticized labor so directly, but the wave of pro-Solidarity writing embracing property rights and the move to a market economy constituted a clear, if indirect, attack on the prominence of labor in the opposition pantheon.[12] Opposition members formerly known for their praise of self-management, such as Jadwiga Staniszkis or Leszek Balcerowicz, now came out as eager free marketeers, organizing conferences devoted to Hayek and the theory of property rights. Prominent Solidarity intellectuals in Gdansk and Krakow put their efforts not into maintaining an underground union but into building liberal think tanks. Little by little, a new intellectual consensus began to emerge: that democracy was grounded not in an active citizenry, as had been argued from the mid-1970s through 1981, but in private property and a free market.

Efforts to promote this new consensus intensified as the opposition began to sense it might succeed. And contrary to the usual view of 1989 as a sudden collapse of communism, perceptive dissidents could smell victory much earlier than that. Bronislaw Geremek, Walesa's closest adviser during the underground period, maintained as early as 1984 that he did not consider the Solidarity period over.[13] The appearance of Gorbachev and glasnost in 1985, followed by a general amnesty in 1986, only reinforced that conviction. Indeed, the Party's inability to win public support, along with its genuine attempts at economic reform, made it clear that no "normalization" was happening this time, even if the exigencies of mobilization forced Solidarity supporters to say otherwise in public.

Liberal intellectual attacks on labor must be seen in this context of anticipated success. Intellectuals embraced labor when their aim was simply to challenge an apparently omnipotent Party-state. In that struggle all of society shared common aims, above all for an independent civil society and the right to self-representation. But when success seemed possible, the intellectuals who dominated the union's official politics came to see that interests now diverged. As democratic reform became a real possibility, intellectuals sought to legitimate their emerging class interests. Political liberalism they shared with labor, but not economic liberalism, which is what they emphasized now.[14] In doing so, they spoke the language that the Party was now speaking, which eventually made them attractive partners for the Party elite. That is, the rival elites were coming together on the question of economic reform, over the heads of labor, coming to see the emerging class interests they had in common. Ivan Szelenyi et al. argues this thesis at some length in their recent book:

> By the end of the communist period, dissidents had joined forces with the technocratic fraction of the communist ruling estate in a commitment to transform the socialist economy and build capitalism. . . . So although it appeared that the dissident emphasis on civil society and the technocrats' interest in free markets and monetarist discipline had little in common during the 1980s, as soon as they both reached the conclusion that socialism was dead, they also realized that what seemed so different were merely two sides of the same coin—that is, liberal capitalist society.[15]

Jan Kubik's notion of workers and intellectuals constituting a single "cultural-political class" may have been valid in 1980,[16] but the prospect, five years later, of an imminent capitalist system meant that market economic classes were finally beginning to form, and here interests began to diverge. Hence Solidarity intellectuals' attacks against labor. To be sure, they usually spoke of the Party as the enemy, not labor. But this new deemphasis on labor, manifested in practice by the Solidarity underground leadership's unwillingness in the late 1980s to give workers much to do other than pay dues and distribute the *samizdat* press, isolated workers both practically and theoretically. The struggle for democratization would be led by the union's elite, not by its rank and file. Labor would never again be the object of the ebullient adoration of 1980.

Elites Only: Solidarity's Path to the Round Table

In the late 1980s, the Solidarity leadership pushed hard to make a deal with the Party on a common platform featuring a market economy and a liberalized political system. To force the Party to the table, Solidarity still needed the specter of a militant rank and file fighting for its rights. But unlike in 1980–81, Solidarity no longer made labor issues a key part of its program, aside from the right of independent trade unions to exist. Even as it still needed labor, the leadership began systematically to underemphasize labor activism, setting in motion the kind of exclusionary practice that would become official policy after 1989.

From the moment Solidarity was outlawed in December 1981, all Solidarity representatives, whether operating under or above ground, put forth one central demand: that the Party open negotiations with the previously elected leaders of Solidarity. Because a few of those leaders could be bribed or blackmailed, the demand soon switched to opening negotiations with Lech Walesa and his own group of advisers. In this way, Solidarity turned the underground conflict into an exclusively political one led by a central leadership. Former Solidarity leaders who rejected this policy found themselves shut out of leadership positions in the underground, increasingly steered by Walesa.

Given the nature of the system, the political strategy certainly made sense. The effort to have independent trade unions without explicit political bargaining with the authorities (the strategy of "anti-politics") had been the hallmark of the 1980–81 period, and it had come up short. The striking thing about the new strategy, then, was not its political focus but its meticulously non-labor focus. For instead of a political strategy that sought to mobilize labor activism in order to push the authorities to the bargaining table, Solidarity pursued a political strategy that explicitly downplayed labor activism, that tried to keep workers from getting involved in independent activity. In sharp contrast to the opposition program of the late 1970s through 1981, which advocated uncentralized independent activity as the harbinger of a democratic society, Solidarity's post-1981 policy favored elite supervision over the activity of others.

This can be seen in Solidarity's policy regarding participation in union activities. All trade union activity had been "suspended" by the December 1981 imposition of martial law, until in 1984 the Party gave permission for its revival. There were restrictions in place that prevented the reemergence of Solidarity, most notably a ban on nationwide unions—unions could operate only in individual enterprises. Still, with an autonomous leadership, one no longer linked to management or the local party cell, and a legal right to strike, these new union rules were a big improvement over those before Solidarity and constituted a sign that the Party recognized its weakness. Some Solidarity worker activists were inclined to test the new bill, to form local unions and to see how far they could go in recreating a Solidarity-type organization. The union's underground leaders, however, rejected such entreaties. Solidarity activists were instructed to abstain from forming unions on the basis of the new law, and to keep away from those that were formed. (Another innovation of 1984 trade unionism was the de facto abandonment of universal membership.) Anyone that joined was branded a traitor. In this way, the Party succeeded in building a trade union movement, the National Association of Trade Unions (OPZZ), devoid of political opponents. OPZZ was, and is, not a single national union but an association of thousands of formally independent workplace unions.

Because political arrests and detention were still widespread in 1984, few committed Solidarity activists questioned the wisdom of this decision. Under these conditions, participation did seem like betrayal to most worker activists. Three years later, however, things were quite different. A general amnesty had been declared in 1986, leading to the reconstitution of aboveground Solidarity politics. Walesa created a Provisional Council and later a National Executive Commission, charged with bringing about negotiations leading to union relegalization. Why not, some worker activists thought, use the moment to revive *union* activity too—that is, to exploit the letter of the 1984 union law in order to form trade unions and push for change from within? Their idea was to go through the official procedures and formally submit an application for a new workplace union called Solidarity. When the courts refused, they would resubmit the application over and over again, hoping thereby to mobilize employee activism. So local activists began doing just this in 1986 and 1987. Instead of the national support they expected, however, they came up against the opposition of the Solidarity leadership, who first tried to ignore the local activists' efforts and then actively discouraged them. By 1988, the campaign ceased.

Why should national Solidarity have discouraged a grassroots campaign to revive trade unionism, which would have put additional pressure on the government to make democratic reforms? The policy makes sense only from the standpoint of Solidarity's new skeptical attitude towards labor. This new Solidarity did not approve of workers taking matters into their own hands. The union's leaders rejected such activity because they did not want to be bound to labor and because their current plans for opposition explicitly bypassed labor activism in favor of an elite-based strategy. They did not trust workers to be loyal to the political strategy adopted by the moderates within the organization. They did not want this second Solidarity to be as symbolically or ritually linked to labor as the first one. Michnik's fears of 1985 now seemed to be those of the leadership as a whole: they now saw labor not as the agent of democratic reform but as one of the great obstacles to reform.

What were workers to do? The answer was not much. Underground union cells, where they existed, focused mainly on collecting dues, paying benefits (particularly for families of the persecuted), and distributing *samizdat* publications. They usually did not get directly involved in workplace issues or enter into dialogue with local management. Solidarity thus gave workers very little to do *as workers*. In the eyes of the national leadership, the mission of local Solidarity unions was not to conduct negotiations in the workplace but to demonstrate, through their mere existence, society's continued rejection of Party rule. These underground unions were thus dramatically different from the underground unions that appear in capitalist dictatorships—such as in late Francoist Spain, where the *Comisiones Obreras* negotiated with management as avidly as it mobilized against the dictatorship, seeing both as central to the struggle for democracy. Members of underground Solidarity locals were treated by their late-1980s leadership more as symbols than as citizens.

One of the key reasons for the leadership's distrust of labor activism was its adoption of a radical pro-marketization program contrary to workers' immediate interests. According to the union's 1987 programmatic statement, workers would get independent trade unions and basic democratic rights, but also wage cuts and large cutbacks on social welfare guarantees. Knowing that such a program would not benefit its members, Solidarity did not wish to promote activism on the part of the soon-to-be disfranchised.

Not surprisingly, the policy was not a big success. That the leadership needed workers more than it wished became clear in May 1988, when workers went on strike in several key factories, including the famous Lenin Shipyard in Gdansk—and official Solidarity knew almost nothing about it. The strikers, mostly young workers with little experience from 1980–81, did make the relegalization of Solidarity one of its main demands. The name still enjoyed universal currency as a symbol of opposition. But the immediate cause of the strike was their rejection of the government's economic reform—a program that official Solidarity had denounced as too *timid*. Clearly, this was not a base with which Solidarity could feel comfortable. Yet it was the only real base the union had, so it had to reassert control.

Walesa went personally to the Lenin Shipyard, and he did reestablish his authority, although just barely. The real outcome of the strike was that Solidarity realized it needed to reestablish links with the rank and file. In the subsequent months, Solidarity reengaged with workplace politics in the hopes of reestablishing its base. Even then, however, its goal was not to promote workers' economic interests but to use this new labor activism as a club with which to force the Party to open elite-level negotiations over broad political issues.

Thus, Solidarity spent the period after the events of May 1988 trying to organize proper political strikes. By August, they had succeeded. "The August strikes were fully planned out," according to leading Solidarity official Lech Kaczynski. "They were supposed to take place in August, and they did."[17] Union leaders also sought to insert themselves into strikes that they did not play a role in planning in order to guide them in the "correct" direction—namely, to promote top-level negotiations. Jan Litynski, for example, another key Solidarity official at the time, had a friend smuggle him into the "July Manifesto" mine in Silesia, where workers had gone on strike without official imprimatur and with a series of economic demands. Litynski laid down the union's official line and eventually succeeded in getting the miners to turn their economic strike into a purely political one.[18] As it turned out, this strike was the proverbial straw that broke the camel's back, pushing the government toward resumption of formal negotiations with Solidarity. According to the prime minister at the time, Mieczyslaw Rakowski, only after Solidarity demonstrated its influence within the workplace by taking control in Silesia did the Party acknowledge that it was time "to go further" toward general negotiations with Solidarity.[19] The Round Table negotiations commenced in February 1989. A few months later, the communist political system was dismantled, and elected Solidarity officials took over the government.

Though it had used labor activism to force the Round Table talks, official Solidarity did not return the favor. In the talks themselves, workers all but disappeared. Having allowed Solidarity to reaffirm its role as the representative of civil society, labor was given very little role in the Round Table talks. Few workers made it onto the negotiating team,[20] workplace issues were scarcely considered, and communication between negotiators and the rank and file was conducted almost solely through state television. The "sub-table" on trade unions dealt with little more than how Solidarity would be relegalized.[21] It was the only sub-table not to issue a final report. As a result of their important strike, miners got their own "mini-table" (something less than a sub-table), but did not do much with it. Litynski, who led Solidarity's negotiating team in the "mini-table" on miners due to his role in the "July Manifesto" strike, did not want to propose anything concrete. Specific issues, he thought, should be left to the trade unions later on, thus illustrating the point that he, like the rest of official Solidarity, did not see the Round Table discussions as having anything to do with labor matters. The miners who participated in the talks spoke about occupational diseases and called for changes in the labor code, but Litynski, representing the national leadership, considered all this "utopian." For Litynski, the only thing that really needed to be said was "marketization." Other than that, "we didn't have anything to propose."[22]

As for communication, it might be argued that negotiations by definition are elite-centered affairs, but Solidarity had had a very different pedigree. In 1980, the strikers in Gdansk insisted that all negotiations be broadcast live. In 1989, only the formal opening and closing ceremonies were broadcast live. In between, "sub-tables" and "mini-tables" met in private, while the very top leaders of the two sides met occasionally in secret at a government villa outside Warsaw. By sitting in Warsaw for virtually the entire time of the Round Table talks, Solidarity leaders conveyed the impression that they were interested exclusively in "big picture" arrangements, with workers assigned the role of cheerleading. Unsurprisingly, such (in)action dampened the enthusiasm of their working-class base. But union officials were not dissatisfied with this outcome. Solidarity *wanted* to convey that it spoke for workers, that it knew best what was in labor's interests. It *preferred* to have quiet followers rather than active ones. In this way, it conveyed to supporters its new understanding of democracy as a system grounded not in a democratic citizenry but in private property and a market economy.

As it happened, though, it still needed the democratic citizenry in order to get the new system it wanted. For although Solidarity authorities had tried to channel class anger into support for their own political efforts ever since the government-opposition dialogue began in 1988, they would gain nothing by suppressing that anger altogether. For they still needed a potentially unruly social movement, with its accompanying threat of a social explosion that only they could control, as a means of forcing the Party to continue to make concessions. This ultimately led the union to countenance one, but only one, strike wave in 1989, a political strike beginning in August. The national leadership did not lead the strikes but did not want to stop them either, for it still needed bargaining chips to propel its political agenda.

The strikes—initiated independently by miners, transport workers, and metal workers, with textile and postal employees soon to follow—were prompted by both political and economic factors: the Party's reaction to its June electoral defeat, and the hyperinflation unleashed by its August 1 freeing of prices. Despite having lost 99.9 percent of all freely contested seats and suffering the ignominy of defeat even for candidates who ran without opposition (because a majority of voters crossed out their names), the Party refused even to act humbled. Instead of acknowledging the depth of their defeat and promising to draw the proper conclusions, the Party simply shuffled its leadership and proceeded to keep governing as if it had won a mandate. Solidarity's political leaders, who had agreed at the Round Table to allow the Party to maintain power regardless of the result of the elections, did not object. Lower-level activists, however, mobilized by the electoral victory and looking at least for signs of humility, were outraged. Rank-and-file workers, on the other hand, were more upset by the second development. The August 1 decision freeing prices led to inflation far more serious than anything in the past—and without wage hikes to compensate. Even worse, stores were still largely empty, due to supply breakdowns and the lack of competition.

That the strikes were driven by economic factors rather than political ones is clear by the fact that they commenced only after the price hikes, not after the Party congress, and that they ceased as soon as the workers won their wage demands. Although the union's national authorities had nothing to do with starting these strikes,[23] they quickly understood that it was not in their interest to stop them. The elections and the strikes had changed the political situation, rendering the Round Table deal obsolete much sooner than expected. Solidarity now demanded the right to appoint the next prime minister. In order to pursue this new political agenda, Solidarity needed to capture the anger of the strikers, not squander it.

For Lech Kaczynski, the de facto leader of the trade union part of Solidarity (with Walesa focusing on politics), the situation was clear: only a political deal could end the wave of strikes and restore some internal coherence to the union.[24] He entered into negotiations with the representatives of the two satellite parties whose parliamentary votes, combined with those controlled by Solidarity, would be enough to push through a Solidarity prime minister. And the union quickly sought to recast the economic strikes as political ones. In the rhetoric of the union we see the emerging narrative that it is not marketization per se that is a problem but marketization under the control of the old elite. National Solidarity's first statement of support was titled "Against *superficial* marketization, in defense of working people."[25] Solidarity in Katowice contrasted the situation of "social groups threatened with impoverishment" with the "property-grabbing nomenklatura stealing away our national wealth." In Krakow, they attacked the "party that has brought the country to ruin," and in Szczecin they demanded a "new economic, social and political system, without the nomenklatura."[26] Having redefined the moment as a political one with a clear and grand goal, national Solidarity was now able to join the strike movement. The political goal allowed Solidarity to support the August strike wave—the last time it would do such a thing for the next three years. And thanks to the specter of social unrest that the strikes represented, Solidarity was able to convince its Round Table opponents that only a Solidarity-sponsored government could bring stability.

The Solidarity political leaders won on August 12, when longtime union adviser Tadeusz Mazowiecki was appointed prime minister. Three weeks later, parliament gave his government its full support. Now the only problem for the new government was, What to do with the trade union?

Instructions for the New Era

That question, of course, had been nagging at Solidarity ever since April. For when the Round Table negotiations were completed, the issue of what to do with the local trade union organizations that had made such political success possible suddenly became pressing. The formal relegalization of Solidarity, also in April, meant that this was the moment when unions not only could, but had to be recreated, reimagined, and reconstructed. Yet just when it had both the ability and responsibility to take on this task, Solidarity was less than eager to do so. The movement's political leadership had spent the previous few years trying to get organized labor to follow its lead because it did not trust labor to do the "right" thing. Now that these leaders were finally getting the power to shape political events on their own, they wanted labor united behind them still, rather than staking out its own path. But how to build an independent labor movement that would continue to do the bidding of Solidarity's political elite? That was the question facing Solidarity now, both the few at the political center and the many factory-based activists loyal to the center's program.

The chief responsibility for dealing with this question went to those prominent Solidarity activists who had chosen *not* to enter parliament, the state bureaucracy, the media, or the burgeoning business world, but rather to work specifically as trade unionists. The task of rebuilding the unions would fall to those who consciously eschewed the political field for union work. A group of them sat down in May with the editors of the revived *Solidarity Weekly* to discuss the role of trade unions in the new era. The discussion set itself up as a contrast between two approaches: unions as co-managers versus unions as demanders, pitting Wroclaw union leader Wladyslaw Frasyniuk against Warsaw union leader Maciej Jankowski. For Frasyniuk, the new Solidarity must be the engine of economic reform. Instead of demanding pay hikes from management, Solidarity must itself become "involved in the economic activities of the enterprise." It must concern itself "not only with working conditions but also with the firm's profitability." The union must "co-govern the workplace" in order to facilitate economic reform.[27]

Jankowski proposed contestation rather than cooperation as Solidarity's new role. "Reform will not work without economic demands." And yet for Jankowski, demands were important not to protect workers but to protect reform: "It is only our economic demands that will make sure reform takes place." And the reforms that needed to take place mainly had to do with the identity of the managers. According to Jankowski, workers face problems not because as laborers they have different interests from management—here he agreed with Frasyniuk—but because Poland's managers were not yet "real" managers, its new capitalists not quite "real" capitalists. In this view, which would become a powerful internal narrative for unionists in the coming years, workers had to keep up their economic demands until "real" capitalists replaced "red" capitalists. Unions needed to be active in order to bring about "real" capitalism; then they could move to the background.

Others in the discussion located themselves within these two approaches.

No one spoke of the economic issues workers themselves were complaining about. There was no talk of forced overtime, the erosion of wages by inflation, declining safety conditions, deteriorating health care, or the continued inability of young workers to find housing. The unionists here did speak of unemployment, but only as something unavoidable. A miner said the government should ease regulation on business, while a steel unionist urged Solidarity to support management efforts at achieving greater wage differentials in order to motivate employees and keep technical engineers from leaving for private firms. So committed was this new union to market reform, in other words, that the only "bread and butter" issue anyone raised was in *support* of wage inequality, with the beneficiaries being a largely non-union group. The main conclusion of this high-level discussion was that a Solidarity trade union was still necessary, but only in order to ensure that "real" reform would be carried out.

The competing views expressed here—Frasyniuk's support for union moderation and co-governance versus Jankowski's call for militance against "red" managers—would dominate the union for a long time to come. It is striking how similar they are. The first view promotes cooperation with management in the interest of reform, the second promotes conflict with management in the interest of reform. The first assumes that managers operating in a market economy are necessarily working for a capitalist economy, the second claims that only managers with the proper pedigree can build proper capitalism. Both support the idea of cooperative union-management relations, although the second view calls for a temporary conflict due to management's political identity—but not its economic one. Neither approach sees labor as representing one particular set of interests in a conflict with another set of particular interests. As events proved, neither could thus be very useful in ultimately integrating labor into a stable liberal capitalist society.

Indeed, the only real disagreement between them concerned the question of anger. Frasyniuk, expressing the dominant liberal reformist position, sought to instill in his audience of labor activists the view that any expression of labor anger was potentially dangerous. Jankowski, articulating what would become the dominant populist yet *still* reformist position, understood what the liberals did not: that economic anger was going to emerge no matter what, so unions needed to organize it rather than ignore it. His solution, however, in that it directed labor anger at the identity of managers and owners rather than at their policies, still dovetailed with the liberals' efforts to ensure that class anger would at least not be directed at capitalist development per se.

In a prominent front-page article in the first issue of the *Solidarity Weekly* after Mazowiecki's appointment as prime minister—a period when it started to seem politically safe to some workers to defend their own particular interests now that the general goal had been secured—Wojciech Arkuszewski, another leading Solidarity activist who had stayed out of politics in order to focus on trade unionism, gave this advice to unionists: The main task of trade unions today, Arkuszewski advised, is to "help employees get accustomed to the new economic relations."[28] He continued:

> Employees will have to learn anew that their wages and jobs depend on their productivity; that their salaries are a function of the talents and capabilities of the managers, economists, and engineers; and that the general state of our factories depends on the level of the cadre governing the firm. The sooner they understand this, the easier will be the introduction of a market economy.

What were workers to do in this new era? First of all, says Arkuszewski, respect your managers. No purges. They may not be the best in the world, but there is no one to replace them. Managers and the workforce must now get along: "One side must learn to change its way of governing, while the other side must actively participate in (or at least silently accept) a policy of reductions, belt-tightening, and heightened on-the-job discipline." Arkuszewski called on workers to "actively" help impose the new market economy. The union should help managers manage, support entrepreneurs setting up new firms, encourage a new middle class to set up private schools for its own kids. The union's job was to help usher in a new property-owning professional class to run the society. Arkuszewski did not believe that workers themselves were capable of much, thus the union's job was to help others get ahead. Indeed, only by facilitating the prosperity of others, Arkuszewski suggested, could unionists gain too. Not only must unions back off, he maintained, but so should worker-elected employee councils: "Having self-management bodies elect directors has been shown to have numerous flaws." Arkuszewski urged unions to place a wager on the elite: that, he suggested, was the key to Solidarity's success.

Arkuszewski's appeal, coming just weeks after the big August strikes, was a sign of Solidarity leaders' new overarching fear: that the depth of labor anger revealed in those strikes might now be used against *them*. It was not "communists coming back"—the bogeyman of the western press—that had them worried. Those who had made pacts with the old party elite knew this was not a group that would want to stop the democratic process, or even could if it wanted to. (It might want to use its connections to profit off the democratic system, but that, of course, was simply the nature of a democracy, not a challenge to it.) Rather, the rising Solidarity elite perceived the danger as coming from below: from workers who had a different view of how economic reform should be carried out. And so in its first months of power it took a two-pronged position: it did what it could to try to suppress labor anger, and it sought to push through a radical marketization program before any organized anger might block it.

The union's first national commission meeting after the appointment of Mazowiecki was devoted almost entirely to the issue of managing the expected proletarian anger. Instead of discussing how, in these new conditions, they were going to transmit labor concerns to their former allies now in power, these unionists discussed how they could keep labor concerns from being expressed too prominently.

One way was to keep unions weak, to underemphasize the need to rebuild them. If they could not eliminate labor anger, at least they could try to deny it institutional clout. And so it was at this meeting that Walesa gave his famous appeal against the rebuilding of a strong Solidarity: "We will not catch up to Europe if we build a strong union."[29] He developed this point repeatedly in the next weeks. A strong union, he argued, would decisively oppose reform: "If we build a strong union, where is it going to be strongest? In the Katowice steel plant and other giant molochs. But something has to be done with these plants. And what strong union is going to agree to that? . . . We cannot have a strong trade union until we have a strong economy."[30]

Walesa's position was not without its critics, but we see the seeds of union decline even in those who argued that unions needed to be strong rather than weak. Warsaw union leader Zbigniew Bujak argued that only a "strong union" could ward off attacks from anti-reformers unwilling to impose the "tough economic decisions" lying ahead.[31] For Frasyniuk, only a "strong union" could persuade people of the need for reform—Solidarity must be strong so that it can "defend Mazowiecki."[32] Both Bujak and Frasyniuk had resisted entering parliament precisely because they were afraid that unions might be forgotten in the new democratic order. Now they were arguing the same things as the parliamentarians: that the union's chief role was to ensure the survival of a reform-minded government, without demanding anything in return. No corporatist negotiation of interests here. Just as in the early communist period, the new government was simply *defined* as in labor's interests.

As it happened, Walesa did not have much to worry about. The problem was not just that Solidarity was not attracting the professionals who had joined in the past. With its calls for cooperation with management, its reluctance to make economic demands, its unconditional commitment to whatever reform the new government chose to introduce, Solidarity was not attracting many blue-collar workers either. (Moreover, many local unions actually *discouraged* workers from joining: unlike in 1980, this Solidarity put political loyalty above class unity and was reluctant to admit those who had been members of the officially acceptable OPZZ unions.) At the same National Commission meeting where Walesa called for a weak trade union, Bogdan Borusewicz, the veteran activist now responsible for internal union affairs, drew attention to Solidarity's alarming organizational weakness. The union, he said, was in "a state of bankruptcy."[33] Old members were not rejoining and new ones were not being recruited. Union activists knew what the world did not: that Solidarity's victory had come about despite lack of vital signs from the union it allegedly was.

In the coming weeks, the gloomy news came in from all sections of the country. A terse news item from the Czestochowa region: "Union membership barely growing. No new cadre."[34] Bydgoszcz: down from 250,000 in 1981 to 45,000 in late 1989, and split between two rival Solidarity organizations.[35] Even Gdansk: in 1981, Solidarity counted 531,000 members; in early 1990, a fifth as many.[36] These examples illustrated a general rule: a union 20 percent its 1981 size,[37] and more declines to come. Moreover, Solidarity was hardly bringing in new members. At the Gdansk regional conference in February 1990, almost all the delegates were activists from 1980–81, "hardly any new, young faces" (and of those, hardly any women).[38] As Frasyniuk said tersely, "People just aren't joining Solidarity anymore."[39]

When they did join, they often did not pay dues. Comments about this appear regularly in the union press of 1989–90. Frasyniuk's Solidarity in Wroclaw still boasted at least 400,000 members in early 1990. But when vetted for dues-paying members only, the number dropped almost by half.[40] In the Jelenogorski region, only 45 percent of the locals sent dues to the higher union authorities. Elsewhere, the figure was usually about the same.[41]

Even veteran activists were not staying active. Many "revived" locals in 1989 did not bother to hold elections for delegates to regional conferences. Out of 1600 registered locals in the Warsaw area, less than 700 sent representatives to the regional conference in December. At regional conferences throughout the country, 20–30 percent of elected delegates did not even show up.[42]

At all levels, the union as union grew increasingly tired. Workplace activists seemed particularly demoralized. Far from excitedly engaging in rebuilding their union, many behaved as if *condemned* to rebuild the union—almost as if disappointed that they had thus far been unable to take advantage of the new situation to get out of the workplace and join the elite themselves. Most of them had seen their union activity, particularly during the underground years, as part of the struggle for political freedom. Now political freedom was here and they still had to maintain the charade. Activists accepted this notion of a "weak union" because they did not want to get involved anymore and they could not think of reasons why others should. Those others, meanwhile, could not think of reasons either. As one journalist wrote for the *Solidarity Weekly:*

> Today all of Solidarity's intellectual potential goes to figuring out the big social, state, and even international problems. Local union cells, meanwhile, are barely breathing. They're lucky if they can find one active and ambitious person who will take on all that work.[43]

Promoting Shock Therapy and Labor Passivity

Instead of being alarmed at this situation, Solidarity leaders saw it as an opportunity: to push through the radical marketization experiment, known either as "shock therapy" or the "Balcerowicz Plan" (after Finance Minister Leszek Balcerowicz), that might have had trouble passing had interests and anger already been politically organized. The new government marketed the Balcerowicz Plan as a radical break with the communist past. The centerpiece of the plan was the elimination of most state subsidies for enterprises. Firms would have to survive on their own, despite the (temporary) maintenance of formal state ownership. (The issue of actual privatization was tabled for the following year.) Firms would have to be profitable or suffer the consequences, up to and including bankruptcy. How to stay profitable was their own affair: the government hoped firms would draw up new business plans, undertake market research, reassess personnel policy, and otherwise engage in deep-seated restructuring. They could also just raise prices, although the move to a convertible currency and the elimination of import restrictions would, it was hoped, create enough competition to prevent price-gouging. All of these stabilization measures would go into effect on January 1, 1990.

The most controversial part of the plan concerned wage policy. Demonstrating that it expected resistance not from management but from labor, the government eased virtually all restrictions on managers *except* those concerning wages. Unsure that it could prevent strikes from occurring, it sought to prevent them from succeeding by imposing heavy wage taxes: any firm paying more than the officially permissible wage increase, to be determined by the state, would have to pay a tax equal to 500 percent of the "excess" wage. In other words, instead of trying to win labor cooperation on a wage policy, such as with a collaborative effort negotiated through a tripartite council (as other postcommunist East European countries, beginning with Hungary, set out to do), the Solidarity government maintained administrative sanctions instead, signaling to workers that they were not to be trusted. But the wage tax policy had counterproductive economic consequences, too. Firms that raised wages in order to compensate productivity gains or to retain skilled workers would be treated the same as those whose trade unions or employee councils[44] sought to turn all income into wages. All firms, in other words, were treated as if their employees were acting irrationally, without any evidence that employees were actually doing so.[45]

Because of the controversial nature of all these new legal reforms, the government did not want them subjected to long parliamentary discussion. Most union officials accepted this. And so the most striking thing about the public discussion of the Balcerowicz Plan is that there was not much of it. The Solidarity press wrote a great deal about the fact *that* it was coming, but not much on the details. Moreover, it never began a discussion on whether the union ought to accept this plan as its own. That was taken for granted. The plan was introduced as Solidarity's economic reform, the solution for which the people had been waiting. Solidarity would show that it, and it alone, could introduce a bold and (if only in the long-run) beneficiary economic reform. There was much here of the old Bolshevik bravado about no obstacles that the people cannot conquer. (This is why some have called it "market Leninism.")[46] Behind the bluster, however, was a deep fear that people would reject it. Imagining workers as unruly radicals with populist predilections, the national union leadership saw itself responsible for selling the plan to its members, not for negotiating any concessions on their behalf. On the few occasions when the 1989 union press criticized the Mazowiecki government, it did so not for any of the plan's provisions but for not doing enough to sell it. "There is no other way than a tough economic program," wrote the *Solidarity Weekly*, "but it is necessary to persuade people to accept it."[47]

Thus began the famous union "parasol" for market reform: Solidarity would provide cover for the government to introduce any changes it wanted. "Thanks to the fact that Solidarity is in control of the situation in the factories," the National Commission declared on November 8, "the government can realize reform in an atmosphere of political stability."[48] In the name of stability, the union chose to bow out of debate on the specifics of the plan. Even though the particular pieces of legislation that made up the Balcerowicz Plan included three bills of crucial importance to union members—concerning terms of employment, group dismissals, and the wage tax—the union declined to offer any proposals on any of them. Then it pressured its parliamentarians to accept whatever the government offered. Senator Zbigniew Romaszewski recalls that thirteen different economic bills were presented to the Sejm on December 20, to be voted on eight days later: "I am not the worst-prepared senator, but not only did I not have time to reflect and form an opinion about these bills, I didn't even manage to read them all."[49] As another union deputy put it, "The principle of consultation was violated. . . . The voice of the union was not heard."[50] The union worked together with the government to produce this silence.

The links between union and government were so strong that it became almost impossible for the union to act as an independent entity even on the few occasions when it tried. In late 1989 the union found itself unable to work out its position on an important wage indexation bill before parliament because "all its experts on this question had joined the Ministry [of Labor]." By the end of the year, about 95 percent of Warsaw's Solidarity experts had left for other work, usually in government.[51]

Having changed its view about the relationship of labor to democracy and having changed its view of democracy from one entailing broad political participation to one emphasizing elite leadership and a capitalist economy, the Solidarity leadership focused much of its energy in 1989 on making sure workers did not get mobilized as workers. It wanted a quiet and calm trade union, just as it wanted quiet supporters in general—which probably explains why it organized no public celebrations during this dramatic and revolutionary year. Not at the end of the Round Table talks, not when it won the June elections, and not even in September when it took over the government. Its refusal to publicly celebrate its triumphs reflected the evolution of the leadership since 1981, its switch from promoting labor citizenship, understood as participatory action, to promoting labor quiescence and a weakened civil society. The Solidarity leadership did not want a mobilized civil society once it took power and introduced radical market reform. Anticipating that marketization would stoke anger, Solidarity leaders sought to ward off society's ability to forcefully express that anger. Thus, it did not even want local Solidarity unions to get too big. Solidarity leaders now considered labor an obstacle to reform and a danger to democracy. For democracy they now understood not as a "self-governing republic," to use the phrase from the union's first National Congress in 1981, but as a liberal market economy, and in a quasi-Marxist way they saw labor exclusively as a threat to a market economy and not, as the western capitalist experience has shown, its stabilizing, democratizing agent. There were, of course, exceptions. Not all democratic intellectuals close to Solidarity supported this emerging anti-labor consensus. People such as Ryszard Bugaj, Barbara Labuda, Karol Modzelewski, Wlodzimierz Pankow, and Jozef Pinior wrote powerfully-argued appeals for an alternative road. Tadeusz Kowalik, an economist who served as adviser to both the 1956 and 1980 workers' movements, has tirelessly promoted social democratic options in countless articles up to the present day. These were important voices, even prescient ones, but precisely because they were dissenting voices—kept out of elite Solidarity circles and mostly off the pages of the former Solidarity press—they are not the ones to consider to understand what happened to the union in this crucial period.

The specific way that 1989 played out in Poland thus had important long-term implications. First of all, this was the time when the professional, intellectual leadership of Solidarity introduced policies as well as a political style that bolstered its own emerging class interests and pushed labor to the background. The class divisions that never manifested themselves previously in Solidarity now started to become clear, at least to those at the head of the movement. It is important to avoid a Machiavellian interpretation of these developments. To say that the Solidarity elite hijacked a workers' movement in order to introduce a bourgeois society, as some claim[52] is far too simplistic, for it was not so intentional as this. After all, the adoration of the working class in 1980 was real. Moreover, the statist nature of the communist system meant that intellectuals often felt themselves to be similar to workers, and their desire for greater autonomy from the state certainly dovetailed with the desire of workers for independent trade unions. Many of the union's intellectual leaders sincerely believed that creating a new dominant class, in which they themselves might be key players, was in the long-term interests of workers. (They tried not to think of the obvious analogy: that just like the communists before them, they alone knew what was in labor's interests, and so were justified in deceiving workers because "in reality" they were only helping them. Still, they genuinely believed this to be so.) Finally, the bulk of the country's trade union activists were complicit in this market turn. Workers accepted and believed in their leadership, as demonstrated by their remarkable quiescence in the face of these painful reforms. So although 1989 saw the emergence of clear class divisions within Solidarity, it is important to keep in mind that this was far from obvious at the time. Indeed, it is precisely the ambiguity of what was happening that is the key to understanding subsequent developments.

This change in political style had important implications for long-term political stability as well. For Solidarity's general lack of interest in trade union matters had two consequences: it led to a breakdown of genuine small-*s* solidarity and to the failure to create any kind of collaborative neocorporatist bargaining regime able to manage the upheavals of the future. The first consequence can already be seen in the chaotic strike wave of August 1989. When official Solidarity did nothing to counter the hyperinflation introduced by the last "communist" government, it triggered a free-for-all: whichever sector could mobilize its workers to demand a compensatory wage increase went on strike and won, and whichever could not, did not, and so won nothing. This breakdown of solidarity would have profound impacts both for labor's ability to organize collectively and for the government's ability to broker agreements. It meant that dispossessed workers would be more open to the appeals of illiberal, non-economically based solidarities and that future governments would have a harder time getting labor to work together.

In the end, the great mistake of the Solidarity leadership was its fear of anger, its tendency to see the class anger of labor as the primary threat to democracy. For Solidarity's unwillingness to recognize, much less mobilize, workers' anger only led to the mobilization of that anger under a different leadership. The result, as will be demonstrated in subsequent chapters, was not only a profoundly weakened labor movement but also a steady deterioration in the authority of the liberal elite.

3

Market Populism and the Turn to the Right

In this chapter we will see how Solidarity's national union leaders, because they sought to capture popular anger but refused to channel it along class lines—either by building up strong organizations of labor or by mobilizing around issues of distribution—helped push politics in a decisively illiberal direction. They were aware of the anger very quickly, and they experienced a powerful dose of it during a railway strike in the spring of 1990. But in their eagerness to protect radical economic reform, they kept trying to divert economic anger toward political targets. And they succeeded. Unwilling to proffer economic solutions to economic grievances, Solidarity directed social anger onto substitute targets instead, thus legitimizing illiberal, politically exclusionary ideas.

It should be noted that the meaning of "Solidarity leaders" in this chapter has changed. In the previous chapter, the term referred to the movement's leaders in 1989, meaning the liberal intellectuals who enjoyed the support of Walesa. They had become the leaders by virtue of Solidarity's decision, in the preceding years, to adopt an elite-based strategy oriented to negotiating a settlement with the ruling Party. The strategy had worked; these leaders had come to head the government and dominate the new public sphere. Success, however, meant that Solidarity became a trade union again. Of course, the centrality of Solidarity to the entire political transformation meant that those veteran oppositionists not part of the dominant liberal group sought to use Solidarity as the vehicle for *their* assent to power. For that reason, many Solidarity leaders were also would-be political actors (and would continue to be till 2001, when the turn away from politics, described in chapter

6, finally occurred). But this book focuses on labor, and after 1989 the leadership of Solidarity is above all the leadership of a trade union, however much it engaged in politics. "Solidarity leaders," in this chapter and hereafter, refers to the leaders of the trade union, not the government, and I will show how Solidarity's engagement in politics ended up damaging labor profoundly.

Few people opposed the introduction of the Balcerowicz Plan in early 1990. As a plan introduced by a popular government to make things better, when few believed things could get any worse, most people were easily persuaded that it was "necessary," even if they voiced their approval in lifeless monotone. Only 9 percent of a national sample opposed the plan in mid-January, whereas 42 percent supported it and 40 percent weren't sure.[1] Yet things hardly augured well for the future. Over three-fourths of the population regarded their economic conditions as bad by the end of January 1990;[2] as the weeks went by, conditions only got worse.

Walesa had sold "shock therapy" to workers by claiming that hard times would last for three months. It was clear very soon, however, that the decline would last much longer than that. After one month of reform, real wages declined by over 30 percent, accompanied by a new round of near hyperinflation and a sharp increase in families living in poverty.[3] The coming of spring brought no improvement. Instead, macroeconomic shocks gave way to microeconomic ones, when firms, especially those outside the major cities, saw that budget constraints had truly become hard (subsidies were not forthcoming) and began to introduce painful restructuring plans.

The social response was quite visible to Labor Minister Jacek Kuron, the only unionist-turned-minister who regularly met with working people in the first months of the new regime. In his peregrinations to sell the Balcerowicz Plan to the people, Kuron was astonished to find a wall of "anger and aggression." Hate mail and threats directed at him in the past, he said, had been professional. Now it was emotional—and real. People really were doing worse than twenty years earlier, he realized.[4] Polish scholars studying the social mood found the same thing: "Reading the newspapers, watching TV, participating in public meetings, or even just listening to the 'voice of the street,' one gets the impression that Poland is a country full of frustrated people—people pushed to the margins, ignored, manipulated, and deprived of all dignity."[5] One could see this anger in the April 12 interview Walesa gave on television, taking questions live from people on the streets. "Nothing has changed! Why don't you do more for the people?" demands one young man. "Everything is worse than it was a year ago," another chimes in. Walesa responds only that things take time.

Solidarity's initial response was both to ignore the anger and to defend the economic changes against it. When workers begin to express dissatisfaction, the union's job, according to Frasyniuk, is "to explain to them that there is no other way: there must be profitable firms and there must be a market, and only then can we fight for wages."[6] These coolly rational statements were already ringing hollow to many. Gdansk's union weekly found local workers increasingly distrustful of Solidarity, unsure of its new role. "It defended me in 1980 when I set up a union committee," said one forty-one-year old construction worker. "But when I went to them for help this time, they told me that I have to suffer for the sake of reform." A 51-year-old teacher said she had no idea what Solidarity's "current activity has to do with its name. Whatever happened to the idea of caring for the weak?"[7]

As long as there were no major protests, however, Solidarity preferred to disregard the growing dissatisfaction. At its Second National Congress in April 1990, the union all but ignored the crucial economic issues of the day. Walesa had billed it as the congress that would set Solidarity the union apart from Solidarity the government, but nothing of the kind took place. Walesa spoke out strongly against wage demands and rejected a resolution that would prevent parliamentarians from holding union posts. I attended this congress, as I had the first one in September 1981, and was startled to find the union spending far more time discussing its position on abortion (fiercely against) than its position on market reform (for, with moderate reservations).[8] I did not yet know this was a sign of things to come.

Ignoring Anger: Lessons of the Railway Strike

Just days after the Congress had ended, the union's complacency was interrupted by a railway strike, giving a concrete presence to the growing anger that everyone feared. As the first major labor protest of the postcommunist era, the railway strike illustrated the pitfalls not so much of the government's program as of Solidarity's unquestioned support for it. Far from a "militant protest against economic reform," which is how the new media presented it, the strike was a protest against the way railworkers had been punished for their *lack* of militance. As such, it illustrated the problems Polish industrial relations faced after the collapse of collective solidarity.

During the strike wave of August 1989, rail was one of the few manufacturing sectors whose workers did not join in. That strike wave was a free-for-all, neither sponsored nor coordinated by national Solidarity. Those who went on strike won a wage increase from the still-communist government, while those who did not won nothing. At best, they got a compensatory wage hike only after the new government came to power. Railworkers received an increase only in October 1989. The problem, however, is that the Balcero-wicz Plan set September wage rates—those prevailing when the Solidarity government was formed—as the base for determining acceptable pay increases. That is, firms were allowed to raise wages according to a multiple of the September base, and raising them more would incur the steep wage tax. Those workers who had not joined the strikes thus paid a price for their restraint.

There were moral issues involved here too. Strikes have their own rituals, countries their own strike repertoires, and occupations their own special aura. The role of shipworkers, for example, in the building of the modern Polish labor movement is well known, like the role of auto workers in the United States or miners in Great Britain. For reasons having to do with official industrial policy, the diverse skills of its workforce, the "buying off" of miners, and the presence of social movement organizers, shipworkers on the Baltic coast were at the vanguard of the struggle for independent labor unions in the 1970s and 1980s. Railway work, however, has a long and complex history in Poland, as well as a deep and patriotic legacy that has given it a special place in the country's labor movement—although never at the head of a protest movement. In short, railworkers were accustomed to having their demands supported by others, whether the state or other workers, because rail work in Poland had been seen as the apotheosis of patriotic duty.[9]

This high social prestige, bringing with it a deep ethos of service, dates from Polish independence in 1918, when integrated rail travel was one of the first ways Poland manifested a territorial integrity after more than a century of partition. With industry still underdeveloped and oriented to pre-independence markets in the now neighboring countries, rail transport brought Polish markets and regions together before production did. Railworkers were one of the most organized groups in interwar Poland, and the communist authorities then added privileges to this high status, including a guaranteed average wage higher than the national average, personal coal allotments for each employee, and free rail travel for employees and their families. All this encouraged railworkers to think of themselves as servants of the nation, and to expect that they would be protected by the nation in return. The former meant that they would never go on strike; the latter meant that they should never need to. The arrangement worked to expectations in 1980, when Gdansk rail workers declared solidarity with the strikers but—like hospital and urban transport workers and others whose services were indispensable for the daily life of the community—refrained from a work stoppage. Gdansk workers defended them at that time; these were the solidarity strikes that gave the union its name. After the declaration of martial law, railworkers returned the favor: much underground material was smuggled into the country thanks to the willingness of railroad employees to look the other way.

But now things were quite different. Fellow workers did not defend them in fall 1989, and the Solidarity government did not defend them the following spring. Whereas their pay had customarily been pegged in relation to other industrial sectors, their restraint in the fall had caused their wages to fall to about 80 percent of the national average, and the new government's wage policy would only cause the gap to widen. It was as if the rules of collective action had changed and railworkers alone had not been informed. It was a sign of the general breakdown of solidarity, in both senses of the word, that in 1989 the railworkers' ethos had come to haunt them. And so they commenced protest action in April 1990 with a single key demand: that their wages be pegged at 110 percent of the national average of other state-owned industrial sectors. In this way, they argued, wages would be worked out through bargaining in other sectors, and railworkers would not be penalized by their traditional restraint.

Solidarity responded to this first postcommunist labor action by expressing sympathy for the railworkers' plight but opposing any strike action and by trying to get the workers to demand enterprise restructuring rather than higher wages. Instead of demanding a wage increase or a change in the September tax base, the employees should insist on getting rid of the old *nomenklatura* and holding elections for all managerial personnel.[10] The national leadership, in other words, wanted the railworkers to fight for what the leaders believed to be the key issue, not for what the workers believed to be the key issue. Indeed, after the first protests, national Solidarity went on its own to the prime minister and secured an agreement for new elections to rail supervisory positions, the resignation of the director, and a one-time-only triple bonus payment to employees. When the latter rejected the agreement, saying it did nothing to resolve either the September tax base issue or the 110 percent guarantee, relations between the center and the strikers quickly deteriorated. In order to dramatize their situation, nine employees in the depressed northeastern city of Slupsk began a hunger strike, a traditional tactic from the country's repertoire of protest. The group was supported by the Solidarity cell at the Slupsk station, but union support stopped there. Solidarity's regional office branded the strike illegal, and the strikers in turn announced that Solidarity had "lost touch with the ranks and had stopped caring about the working and pay conditions of railway workers."

At this point tensions escalated. Railworkers throughout the country sent delegates to Slupsk, some to begin hunger strikes of their own, others to take part in the official negotiations that they expected would soon begin. The government, however, refused to meet with them. Labor Minister Jacek

Kuron said he would negotiate only with official union representatives and therefore not with the strikers of Slupsk, who had lost their union backing. On May 18, Slupsk railworkers stopped trains for two hours. Two days later, rail traffic was blocked in the entire region.

Solidarity now condemned the strikers as provocateurs, agents of OPZZ or of the small militant offshoot union "Solidarity '80."[11] But this only exacerbated the conflict. "We, the employees of the Bialogard station," read one typical railworker petition a few days later, "announce that we break from the leadership of the Solidarity railworkers union."[12] When the protesters called on the leaders of all the country's unions to come meet with them in Slupsk, only OPZZ and Solidarity '80 sent representatives. Solidarity seemed on the verge of being pushed to the side by labor anger.

But it was not yet the time for this. Although the public tended to support the strikers' demands, it was not ready to countenance mass action against the new government. Protests were beginning to interfere with preparations for the country's first free local elections, and Solidarity used this to press its advantage. "It is not accidental," said the union, using the Bolshevik language it had previously enjoyed mocking, that OPZZ was involved in strike actions just a few days before the elections. In reality, OPZZ was barely involved, and only became involved because Solidarity officials had disowned the strike.[13] But the accusation had an impact, and the strikers were soon isolated. The resolution took a few days. Walesa finally traveled to Slupsk—arriving near midnight, in order to dramatize his authority—and told the strikers that their cause was just but that their actions were weakening democracy; they must trust in Solidarity to represent their interests in negotiations with the government. The strikers asked only that he return in two weeks to tell them what had been won.

In the end, national Solidarity got the agreement *it* wanted: elections to supervisory positions and a commitment to hasten restructuring of the giant firm. As for the strikers' demands, the government agreed to adjust the base calculation for the wage tax, but refused any percentage guarantee. By the end of the year, railway workers' wages hovered at 92 percent of the relevant average. Protests did not resume.

Organizing Anger: Walesa Runs for President

When Solidarity first began losing its clout among the railworkers, union vice president Lech Kaczynski traveled to Slupsk and made a telling confession. "I would like to re-emphasize that the task of the union is to represent the interests and standpoints of employees, not the government," he said, as if reminding himself above all. It was wrong for the union "to keep playing the role of co-employer." And "that is the role," he acknowledged, that Solidarity had been playing.[14]

This first brush with grassroots economic anger had shown Solidarity that it could not rely solely on a moral appeal to enforce social peace. Nor could it count on simply telling people to follow its lead. Ignoring the public's genuine dissatisfaction with economic developments was a recipe for losing public support. The rail strike had been an indictment not of market reform but of Solidarity, for leaving workers no way to negotiate reform for themselves. Instead of ignoring anger, the union would have to organize it. Thus began the push towards political illiberalism as the way to capture labor's emerging class anger.

Walesa's campaign for the presidency constituted the opening salvo in this new approach. No election was scheduled, but Walesa, who had declined to enter parliament and whose only formal position was president of Solidarity, now insisted on one, against the advice of his former advisers now leading the government. On this point Walesa was certainly right. The Round Table provision assigning the presidency to the former ruling Party had become anachronistic in light of the fall of the Berlin Wall and the collapse of the entire communist bloc. It was not the fact of Walesa's campaign but rather its nature that signaled the new illiberal approach, specifically Walesa's identification of a new enemy: not just the communism of the past but also the political liberalism of the present, the latter personified by the prime minister (Mazowiecki) whom Walesa himself had named the previous year.

Walesa explicitly organized around class issues. He charged the Mazowiecki government with carrying out policies that hurt workers in particular. He criticized the wage declines, the collapse of industrial towns, the growing impoverishment existing side by side with growing wealth. Although previously an uncritical supporter of the Balcerowicz Plan, the *Solidarity Weekly*, firmly under Walesa's control, began writing about how workers were suffering "disproportionately," and called for action to counteract this tendency.[15] But though Walesa identified the problems as economic, the solutions, he claimed, were purely political. The proffered enemy said to be responsible for these economic problems was not the government's economic program but its political one. The Mazowiecki government was said to be too moderate, refusing to oust "communists" from positions of influence; too elitist, dominated by "egg-head" intellectuals rather than common people; too internationalist, forgetting its obligations to serve the "Polish nation"; and too secular, insensitive to the Christian imperatives the "nation" allegedly wanted. The problem, in other words, might be the deleterious effects of *economic* liberalism, but the *cause*, Walesa argued in this emerging new narrative, was *po-*

litical liberalism. Change the political priorities and the economic problems would disappear. Walesa never made clear how challenging political liberalism would alleviate the ills of economic liberalism, but then that was precisely the point: economic anger was to be transformed into political anger, and it did not matter whether the proffered solution would work.

Although Poland's new capitalism obviously lay at the heart of the economic problems Walesa was talking about, "capitalism," in this new narrative, emerged not as the problem but as the solution. Walesa blamed the Mazowiecki government for preventing "real" capitalism from taking root, with "real" capitalism identified as the kind that helps working people. And so he demanded the "acceleration" of market reform in order to bring "capitalism" about faster.

Walesa's approach here is consistent with what Kurt Weyland has called "neoliberal populism," a phenomenon increasingly common since the early 1990s, in contrast to the left-leaning populism widespread in earlier times, particularly in Latin America.[16] By stoking anticapitalist anger but stifling the emergence of an anticapitalist discourse, Walesa helped promote a political environment in which labor's real opponent could not be named, necessitating the creation of substitute targets. Walesa did occasionally promise that economic benefits would accrue from his proposals, but most of all those proposals stressed combat over stability, identities over interests, emotions over reason. He broke with Mazowiecki in order to promote a "war at the top," he proclaimed. He promised to be a "president with an axe" and to take action against these enemies—actions whose result, he said, would be a financial bonanza of 100 million zlotys (about $4000) for each Polish worker. He said he would push through a program of "de-communization," or lustration, with little regard for civil rights. He would break with those intellectuals who had broken their alliance with workers and were pursuing policies bad for the "Polish nation." And in demonstration of his sound Christian nationalist credentials, he did not even shy away from anti-Semitic rhetoric. "I am proud that I am a Pole," Walesa told one press conference, "but if I were a Jew I'd be proud that I am a Jew,"—implying that those who support Mazowiecki should admit they are Jews.[17] Walesa was certainly no anti-Semite; his long cooperation with Jewish Poles, such as his close ally Geremek, and his regular criticisms of anti-Semitism amply demonstrate that. But he was willing to introduce this element into the political struggle in order to capture the votes of those who were dissatisfied with current events and wont to blame "aliens" [*obcy*] for their economic afflictions. Anything to keep people from blaming the new economic system.

In reality, there were hardly any important differences between the two sides. Both Mazowiecki and Walesa (or the liberals and nationalists, as they began to be called) favored privatization, weak trade unions, greater managerial authority, and rapid development of a market economy. For all his criticisms of secular liberals, Walesa was strongly supported by the influential network of secular liberals from Gdansk, one of whom he would soon appoint as the new prime minister. The root of their conflict was how to get to this promised land and what to do about the labor unrest that both sides saw as the great obstacle. Mazowiecki's supporters hoped to defuse unrest by getting Solidarity to vouch for government policies, so they blamed Walesa for "stirring up the masses." Walesa's supporters, more realistically, understood that they had to mobilize anger before they could defuse it. As key Walesa associate Jaroslaw Kaczynski later put it, "For us, the crucial question was who would articulate and use politically the protest against all the painful aspects of the economic reform."[18] So where Mazowiecki and the liberals thought class anger could best be derailed by denying it, by packaging painful neoliberal policies in patriotic slogans that all politicians would agree to support, Walesa and the nationalists (conservatives) believed anger had to be confronted head on and captured in order to protect economic reform. That such a diversion might also help bring Walesa's team to power was no doubt an added incentive. Part of the story here, after all, is Walesa and Kaczynski deploying feigned class anger as a ruse to gain labor support for their own political ambitions, since both felt threatened by the degree to which Solidarity's former liberal leaders were consolidating their own hold on power. But as future events would demonstrate so vividly, since both groups would go on to hold power in the coming years, both sides were in full agreement on the need to pursue radical marketization policies that would marginalize labor, and to do so with only minimal input from the dispossessed. They disagreed chiefly on how to handle the social anger that their policies inevitably generated. One side was "liberal" and one "nationalist" because of their views on what to do with that anger. In the end, by proffering a non-economic attack on the economic policies harming workers, the union president opened a Pandora's box that would reappear in Poland many times in the decade to come.

The Anticommunist Substitute for Socialism

Economic policy under President Walesa was no different than it had been under Prime Minister Mazowiecki. Despite the rhetorical drubbing of Mazowiecki's strategy, Walesa kept the author of that strategy, Finance Minister Balcerowicz, in place. For prime minister, Walesa chose the free-market liberal Krzysztof Bielecki. Even the much-criticized wage tax remained in place.

But precisely because of the continuation of this economic program, anger soon needed a new home. Walesa had succeeded in capturing economic anger in 1990, but by becoming president he had lost his oppositionist mantle. Of course, people were willing to give him the benefit of the doubt. And opinion polls revealed most workers to be moderate supporters of economic liberalism, far from the radicals eager for a fight that liberals usually imagined them to be. The problem, though, was that Walesa had become president at a moment of renewed economic decline. Firms were having an even more difficult time than in 1990, for several reasons. First, the price increases that had originally bailed them out no longer sufficed, undercut by declining demand and increased foreign competition. Second, exports to the West were hurt by the stabilization of the zloty, as well as by Western Europe's maintenance of severe import restrictions despite Eastern Europe's having almost completely opened up its own markets to the West.[19] Finally, the exports to the East that had been keeping many firms afloat came crashing down with the collapse of the Soviet Union. (Loss of the profitable niche export market to Iraq due to participation in U.N. sanctions was another significant blow.) Thus the year 1991, which people hoped to be a year of rebirth, was experienced by most simply as Year Two of a devastating economic crisis.

Pressure now grew on the trade unions—that is, on Solidarity—to do something about the situation, or at least to make some noise. The offshoot Solidarity '80 trade union, formed by Walesa's right-wing populist rivals before Walesa himself made gestures in that direction, was beginning to poach Solidarity members by denouncing the effects of the Balcerowicz Plan (and by suggesting it was a plot by the West against the Polish nation). And although OPZZ was much less combative, its members and leaders having been reared in an ethos of compliance, it too started responding to the pressure from below. So when Solidarity announced after Walesa's election that it was distancing itself from politics, its members seemed to approve. Delegates to the union's national congress in April 1991 rejected Walesa's hand-picked successor and instead elected Marian Krzaklewski as new union president. Krzaklewski, an engineer from Silesia, had campaigned on a program to stay out of politics and be a "real unionist." As we shall see, Krzaklewski ended up doing neither of these things. His declaration on behalf of "real unionism" foundered on his own loyalty to rapid marketization, and by the middle of the decade he had politicized the union even more, making it the basis of a right-wing political party. But in 1991 Krzaklewski well understood the need to speak to labor discontent.

Strikes grew in 1991, most originating as wildcats. The number was still small, much less than the extent of the economic crisis would suggest—the official total was 450 for the year, compared to 205 in 1990. Moreover, reflecting continued belief in market ideas, most of them were framed not as opposition to marketization but as opposition to conditions preventing effective marketization.[20] In the first half of 1991, strikes tended to occur in small but competitive state-owned firms, where workers objected to the wage tax, which, by restricting pay increases even for higher productivity, prevented a healthy restructuring process by driving the best workers to seek employment elsewhere. (The Bielecki government had abolished the tax for private and privatized firms.) In the second half of the year, strikes broke out in large manufacturing firms threatened with sudden collapse due to the sudden demise of the Soviet Union. Workers in these firms demanded new subsidies not because they felt that the government should bail out uncompetitive firms but because extraordinary international circumstances jeopardized the survival of their firms, which were just beginning their restructuring.

Despite the rational grounds for these strikes, Krzaklewski's national Solidarity regularly opposed them as "contrary to economic reform." Although factory Solidarity cells usually participated in the strikes, they did so mostly in order to maintain their own credibility and keep the protests in line. Despite the ultimate presence of union officials in many of these strikes, it would be a definite misreading to see these actions as inspired by the union. The union did not want to mobilize workers but rather to control them, and this often required union officials to lead protests so as to avoid the charge that they had sold out.

While Solidarity's hegemony could still limit workplace unrest, the deepening economic crisis and the increase in strikes, most of which ended in failure, meant a definite increase in politically available anger. But where would it go now? Walesa had refused to form his own political party, the union liberals around Mazowiecki refused to organize workers, and the former communists were still too discredited to be much of an alternative. The fragmentation of the political scene meant that anger had no natural, institutionalized home. A year earlier, Walesa tried to stem class anger by running for president. The question for the union in 1991 was how to stem it now.[21] With its increasing signs of unrest, the membership seemed to be pressing for some sort of class-based mobilization. Solidarity leaders, however, even under Krzaklewski, were unwilling to go there. The union elite needed a new narrative that could explain the economic problems *without* criticizing marketization. Fearing that labor anger might soon be directed at emerging capitalism, it needed a different enemy instead. It soon found one—through the narrative of lustration.

That narrative was developed originally not by the union but by the government of Jan Olszewski, whose five-month tenure as prime minister in 1992 proved to be a turning point for Solidarity. A lawyer who had played a key role in drafting Solidarity's charter in 1980, since 1990 Olszewski had worked closely with the Center Alliance, the conservative Solidarity successor party set up by the proponents of Walesa's presidential run, the elite rivals of the dominant liberals. Their aim was to take power away from the Solidarity liberals in parliament now that Walesa had taken it away in the presidency. Slogans deployed for the cause included calls for a hasty transition to an "independent Poland" free of all "communist influence" and able to pursue its own road to "real capitalism." Heading a weak coalition of five self-proclaimed right-wing parties, Olszewski claimed to be opposed to the rigors of shock therapy, and insisted on the removal of Balcerowicz as finance minister. His main emphasis was not on economic change but political change, focused around a vague program of "de-communization." Prime Minister Olszewski painted himself as the master "de-communizer" and offered radical lustration as the new and only remedy.

At the heart of this narrative was the contention that "good" capitalism was endangered by "bad" communism. All of the country's ills resulted from lingering communist influence. Indeed, Olszewski claimed that Poland in 1992 was *still* a communist country—and that his government would be the first to do something about it. He drew special attention to the lingering old-boy party networks still running the banks and to the presence of communist-appointed officials still holding middle-level positions in government ministries. With McCarthyite verve, he charged that communist agents were present at all levels of power, economic and political. And they had to be identified and purged, he said, because failure to do so would leave the country open to blackmail and sabotage. Olszewski supported the free market but claimed that in Poland it did not exist: the market was run by communists, and it was these bad individuals, not the turn to a market economy, that had caused the economic hardships angering workers.[22]

For all the moral force of the lustration narrative, with its emphasis on punishment for crimes, it is noteworthy that morality always played a secondary role for Olszewski. He focused on economic themes instead, which explains the support he would get from labor. The main reason for de-communization, according to Olszewski, was not to punish past perpetrators but to defend workers by taking the economy out of the hands of those ruining and corrupting it. He offered a discourse that attacked the actually-existing market economy in the name of an idealized one. "The invisible hand [of the market]," Olszewski famously said, referring to Adam Smith's metaphor for capitalism, was "simply the hand of the swindler plundering public funds from the state treasury." The remark outraged liberals, who thought it would undermine support for the market economy. But the line is better interpreted as an attempt to *maintain* support for the market in face of the increasing real opposition it was facing, by locating the desired "real" market economy still in the future. Olszewski lauded free markets and privatization—provided they were "done right." By blaming communists for the hardships of capitalism, the myth of "real capitalism" could be preserved intact. In this way he could both mobilize class anger and channel it onto non-class targets. He aimed to turn the already burgeoning economic anger, about which the liberals were doing nothing, into anger directed at political enemies instead.

The strength of this approach stemmed from the fact that there was no other pro-market ideology able to attract voters. Market ideas were popular even as market realities were not, and de-communization offered an explanation that allowed people to hold onto their pro-market beliefs and oppose market results. The "Olszeviks," as liberals dubbed them, playing on the rhyme with "Bolsheviks," did not gain strength because of some imagined worker susceptibility to "irrationality," to cite the usual argument of liberals (and not only those in Eastern Europe).[23] Rather, they gained because they offered a non-socialist ideology able to explain economic woes. Liberals were saying that transition was a difficult time and that workers would just have to suffer. Socialists were beginning to make their classic economic critique, but as a result of the communist experience, that narrative could not yet be accepted. Political illiberals filled the gap: they offered a critique of capitalism that nevertheless left capitalism intact.

This explains the schizophrenic nature of Olszewski's government, which has bewildered most observers. It came to power promising an end to the Balcerowicz Plan, yet soon ended up reproducing it. It railed against IMF austerity measures, and then meekly agreed to all of its conditions. The about-face on labor issues was even more extreme. Olszewski's labor minister began his tenure apologizing for the "arrogance" of previous governments, but when teachers started protesting, his minister of education waved his cane and threatened to draft legislation taking away their right to strike.[24] Most observers highlight one or another element of this behavior, as they try to show that the government was "really" pro- or antimarket, left or right. Both aspects, however, were of a piece: Olszewski merely chose to defend the market by criticizing it. He protected it from incipient labor antagonism by criticizing it on non-economic grounds. This saved the market by diverting the anger directed against the market onto political targets instead. It was a right-wing movement *because* it sought to organize economic anger against political targets. "Communists" as the enemy easily turned into "others" as the enemy, meaning "non-Catholics" or "non-believers," even though Olszewski himself was no Catholic fundamentalist. It did not take long before "liberals" became the enemy as well, identified with the "left" because of their secularism. Anyone could thus become a target. As the economic situation deteriorated, people were invited to come up with their own enemies. In this way, politics fed into conspiracy theories. Workers wasted their anger on illusory targets, thus helping create an illiberal polity protecting only the interests of the emerging new elite.

Like other potential organizers of labor anger, Olszewski wanted to make sure that anger would *not* be mobilized against the new economic system, because he too supported that system. But as a smart politician, he knew that social anger had to be tapped, not ignored. His solution would not address the source of labor's anger. Instead, workers would be left with a system in which imaginary enemies would be punished while the uninclusive market economy and its weak trade unions that provoked the anger in the first place would continue intact. They would, in other words, buy into an illiberal solution themselves.

This was the government, and the narrative, to which Solidarity now gravitated. For national union leaders it was a continuation of previous governments, slightly adjusted to the new times. They saw it as a suitable complement to Walesa's presidency, despite the strong mutual dislike between the president and the new prime minister. Olszewski and Walesa both curried favor as defenders of the "little" people against the "red barons," and were much tougher in bluster than in policy. Olszewski's criticisms of neoliberalism went further than Walesa's, but this was necessary as a way of recapturing the economic anger that Walesa had mobilized a year earlier but which, given Walesa's unwillingness to form a party, was once again up for grabs. Moreover, the combination of militant rhetoric with actual capitulation followed the familiar post-1989 pattern. Olszewski's effort to direct economic anger safely against defeated opponents dovetailed with Solidarity's and Walesa's own strategies.

In the end, the union did sponsor some large protests during Olszewski's tenure. But far from symbolizing a new era of union militancy, the protests followed Olszewski's narrative in seeking to direct economic anger onto political others. In April 1992, in the face of a budget proposal full of large spending cuts (contrary to Olszewski's campaign promises but in line with demands of the IMF and western creditors,)[25] Solidarity organized its largest demonstration since 1989, about 50,000 strong. While ostensibly a response to the economic hardships,[26] the slogans were directed almost entirely at the "traitors and thieves" in parliament.[27] With Olszewski supporters leading the way, Solidarity submerged anger about rising unemployment (identified by two-thirds of the population as the country's leading problem) or the continuing drop in real wages into demands that "communists and criminals" be thrown into jail. This is perhaps better than blaming "the Jews," but the principle of diverting economic anger is the same.

The Olszewski government collapsed suddenly in June 1992 as a result of its handling of the lustration issue. Internal Affairs Minister Antoni Macierewicz had distributed to parliament an alleged list of "communist collaborators" that included the names of dozens of leading parliamentary officials closely connected to the old Solidarity opposition, and even Lech Walesa himself. Within days, the various former Solidarity parties united to oust the government. But while Solidarity's deputies voted to oust Olszewski, the union's national congress a few days later showed that the stylized Olszewski anger had left its mark on union activists. To Krzaklewski's surprise, congress delegates acted as if all the country's formidable economic problems had boiled down to what to do about the traitors in their midst. They believed in the "Macierewicz list" and had faith in the restorative power of a healthy purge. When Walesa came to address the congress, delegates jeered him. Because they could not attack him on economic grounds, lacking the language or the "frame" in which to do so, they mocked him instead as a simple communist agent. With rage etched palpably on their faces, national union representatives styled themselves grand inquisitors protecting the Christian commonwealth against the evil and profane. To viewers on television, it seemed that the revolution had begun eating its own. For the first time in his career, Walesa did not know how to respond.[28] Muttering à la Nixon that "I am not an agent," he quit the session, saying this was no longer his Solidarity. The delegates voted to censure him.

A Militant Interlude

At this point Solidarity changed course, but only for a short time. Union leaders seemed struck by the depth of the anger they were facing. They knew that they had helped promote it by latching on to Olszewski's anticommunist critique. But they also knew that they had nothing to offer this anger, nowhere to direct it. With membership declining, unemployment growing, and workers still unaware how they might emerge from the crisis, the substitute targets offered to deflect economic anger now threatened to derail the union entirely. And so the leadership tried to rein it in. Its parliamentary officials brokered a new governing coalition to replace Olszewski. This coalition, under new prime minister Hanna Suchocka, brought together the liberal and nationalist factions of old Solidarity that had been feuding since 1989. The Solidarity union tried to revive its image as underwriter of reform.

Yet it appeared that it might be too late. For this effort to restrain anger only seemed to unleash more of it. That there was now no prominent group seeking to capture class anger only gave workers a real opportunity to organize it along economic lines, for the first time since the fall of communism. It came with the strike wave of the summer of 1992, just after the fall of Olszewski.

The strike movement was directed equally at the government and at Solidarity. While never anything close to a general strike, this was the first time that large numbers of workers in different plants had gone on strike against the wishes of Solidarity. The movement began in the key industrial sectors of the economy—auto, aircraft, coal, copper—and spread to the public sector and even the farms. Industrial workers demanded pay increases, debt reduction for their firms, and abolition of the wage tax. Farmers staged blockades on behalf of cheap credit and high tariffs. Health and education employees sought cost-of-living increases and wages pegged to the national average.

Each of these strikes revolved around economic issues. Both moribund and prosperous firms joined in. At one end of the spectrum was the aircraft manufacturing plant in Mielec, whose workers struck when they did not receive wages for the third consecutive month, despite a workforce half as large as in 1989 and wages less than half the national average. At the other end were the strikes in Polish Copper or the Fiat plant in Tychy. At Polish Copper, the country's largest industrial firm with over 40,000 employees and one of its most prosperous, workers walked out after rejecting a small pay increase negotiated by Solidarity, claiming that the firm was doing well enough to afford more. Workers also opposed Solidarity in Tychy, where the FSM automotive plant had recently been taken over by Fiat. Where the union sought a moderate pay hike, employees demanded a monthly salary pegged at 10 percent of the cost of the Cinquecento car they were producing, certainly not unreasonable by western standards but nevertheless constituting more than a threefold increase over the current pay scale. It was not only the wage demand but the action itself that ran counter to Solidarity's ethos, which strongly opposed mobilization against private employers. The 1992 strike, which lasted about two months, was the first and remains one of the largest strikes against a private employer since 1989.[29]

When Solidarity could not control the movement, it tried to isolate it, but that only gave the small new militant class unions a chance to grow. Solidarity '80 emerged as the chief beneficiary of Solidarity's moderation. Founded as a militant-nationalist offshoot by former union leaders whom Walesa had cut out of the loop, Solidarity '80 had turned into the one organization regularly seeking to mobilize class anger. Like Olszewski, Solidarity '80 identified ex-communists and new capitalists as the same thing, but whereas

Olszewski, like official Solidarity, used this as a rationale for protesting only "red" influence in politics, Solidarity '80 saw its role as defending labor against communists *qua* capitalists in the workplace.

With Solidarity seeking to marginalize discontent, particularly after the lustration fiasco, Solidarity '80 was able to step in and organize along class lines. It was particularly successful in the Silesian manufacturing plants. Solidarity '80 organized the auto strike in Tychy in July, despite having only 160 members out of 7000 total workers. By early September, membership jumped to over 2000.[30] Such developments brought OPZZ in too. By late August, Solidarity '80 joined with OPZZ and a few smaller unions to create a national strike committee with a list of twenty-one demands. This nasty touch—the original Solidarity strikers in 1980 had also presented twenty-one demands to the Party, and the phrase had served as the union's virtual trademark—led Solidarity to see the strike exclusively in political terms. Guilt by association: the role played by its old adversaries convinced Solidarity that the 1992 strike wave was "revenge for 1980 and 1989" and that "with such an alliance there is nothing to negotiate."[31]

In the end, the strike wave never got beyond a limited scope. Most of the strikes did not even have the support of a majority of the plant's workforce. As a result, they subsided by early September without any significant victories. In several cases, the militant unions accepted the moderate settlements that Solidarity had earlier negotiated. Yet the strike wave was a crucial turning point for Solidarity. For the first time, its calls for moderation were no longer tantamount to a back-to-work order. Moreover, it lost many of its local activists. Workplace militants grew tired of being the continual voice of reason and getting little from government or management in return. In some factories, the entire Solidarity local simply transformed itself into Solidarity '80.[32] The honeymoon with shock therapy was over. Economic frustration had reached a point where it could no longer be tempered by appeals to "wait just a little longer."

It was at this point that Solidarity made its biggest, though ultimately ephemeral, about-face. No longer plausibly able to divert class anger, and clearly unable, as the strike wave had shown, to ignore it, Solidarity finally made that anger its own. For six months, from December 1992 to May 1993, Solidarity acted as a militant trade union fighting for labor's economic interests.

Its first act was the organization of a massive miners' strike in December 1992. Since 1989, Solidarity had strongly supported the "reform" of the coal sector, aimed less at marketizing the industry than eradicating it. For example, despite the fact that coal was one of the country's best earners of foreign currency, the government imposed limits on exports, which increased indebtedness in even the better mines, thus increasing the pressure for layoffs. As one Katowice scholar put it, "Social acceptance for such restrictive policies was made possible by Solidarity's role in helping introduce them."[33] But with its control of the mines threatened by the strikes of the summer, Solidarity took a different tack and organized the largest single walkout of the entire postcommunist era. This is said to have been the largest mine strike in European history, encompassing 320,000 workers in sixty-five mines over three weeks.

Soon after, in early 1993, Solidarity brought hospital workers and teachers out on strike, sectors that had always refrained from striking in the past, but whose anger at declining conditions and broken governmental promises was now eating away at Solidarity support. A 1989 law guaranteeing health and hospital workers an average wage of 106 percent of the national average had been systematically violated by every Solidarity government ever since, even after the highest judicial body required the government to enforce it. By 1993, average public sector pay hovered at about 75 percent of the national average. And unlike in the manufacturing sphere, no prospect of insider privatization shares hovered on the horizon to sweeten things up. In the "every sector for itself" ethos of the post-1989 years, it was the reluctance of nurses and teachers to protest that led to their dramatic decline, and many blamed Solidarity for allowing it to happen. And so the union now sought absolution, organizing a series of mass protests, demonstrations, and then strikes, culminating in a walkout of over half a million teachers and health care workers in May 1993. (To maximize pressure, teachers chose exam week for their strike.)

At the same time, Warsaw Solidarity leaders began a series of protest actions, culminating in a one-day general strike on May 20. Among their demands were a moratorium on price hikes for fuel, an extension of unemployment benefits in particularly hard-hit regions (benefits the Suchocka government was planning to cut), and an end to rampant labor law violations.[34]

This sudden militant phase led Solidarity into direct conflict with the government it had consistently upheld since 1989. But this time the union did not turn back. When the government said pay hikes would break the budget, Solidarity parliamentarians fought to revise the budget. When the budget passed anyway and the government's Solidarity-affiliated ministers refused to change it, Solidarity parliamentarians, under orders from the trade union, tendered a vote of no confidence. This was not a bluff. When the vote came, the Suchocka government fell by one vote. Solidarity had pushed an economic fight to the point of ousting a government of pure Solidarity pedigree. The parasol had finally folded up.

Ex-Communists Come to Power

President Walesa dissolved parliament and called new elections. The subsequent electoral victory by the former communists proved just the thing to drive Solidarity away from its budding class agenda and back into a frenzy of lustration.

The 1993 parliamentary elections gave a solid victory to the two "successor" parties from the old regime. The Democratic Left Alliance (DLA), the successor to the old ruling Party, emerged as the big winner, with 20.4 percent of the vote, up from 12 percent two years earlier. Second place, with 15.4 percent, went to the Polish People's Party, the successor to the compliant farmers' party of the communist years. Because of a new electoral law designed to promote large parties and prevent the fractionalization that had debilitated the previous parliament, these proportions translated into 37 and 29 percent, respectively, of the new parliament's seats, giving these two parties a nearly veto-proof two-thirds of the Sejm.

What hurt Solidarity was not so much the victory of its former opponents but the effect this victory had on the political opposition. Representatives of the old Solidarity opposition entered parliament only through Mazowiecki's liberal Democratic Union (third place, 10.6 percent of the vote), and partly through the Union of Labor (former Solidarity social democrats), the Confederation of Polish Independence (nationalist), and the quirky Non-Party Bloc to Support Reform.[35] The important bloc of post-Solidarity Catholic and conservative parties, however, including Olszewski's, all failed to pass the five-percent threshold, as did the Solidarity trade union itself, whose list of candidates came within half a percentage point of admission.

Altogether, about a third of the ballots were cast for parties that did not win any seats. Since these were mostly conservative parties claiming affiliation with Solidarity, this created a large extra-parliamentary opposition of disgruntled former Solidarity activists. And this now became the union's new focus. As suddenly as it had begun fighting for labor's economic interests only a year earlier, it now stopped. Instead of representing workers, the union now turned to representing these disgruntled and newly isolated Solidarity political activists who found themselves excluded from a parliament dominated by their historical enemies. If the right-wing parties had won the election, Solidarity might have continued its focus on economic issues, might have been forced to pursue the trade union role it was just beginning to inhabit. But the failure of those parties suddenly left a huge hole on the political right, and Krzaklewski now identified a new opportunity.

The union's first actions after the elections already suggested the right-wing turn it would take, and it took these actions even though they clearly conflicted with the economic interests of its members. For example, when incoming DLA Labor Minister Leszek Miller asked if he could meet with Solidarity to discuss areas of possible cooperation, Krzaklewski refused, on the grounds of Miller's "communist" affiliation. Aware of his party's weak legitimacy in militant labor circles, Miller had hoped through these negotiations to preempt future political crises, which meant that Solidarity was in a position to secure the kinds of concessions it could not gain from former Solidarity liberals. But Solidarity refused even to try. Even after Miller bent protocol in the union's favor by offering to travel to Gdansk himself rather than have Solidarity send representatives to Warsaw, the union still declined.

If the victory of the left had initially left Solidarity both outraged and disillusioned, the reality, once it set in, seemed to give the union a new vitality. It seemed to cure it of its identity crisis by giving new life to an old narrative. Once again, the union knew what to do: it had to fight the communists. And Solidarity leaders seemed mightily relieved to be able to turn back to political contention as their *raison d'être*. They had never really felt comfortable contesting economic issues and never wished to be perceived as antireform, a role they had been pushed into by a rank and file upset at the privations of neoliberalism. With an "ex-communist" government in place, the enemy changed back: it was not the new but the old, not a market economy in which labor was uncertain of its interests but a "communist system" in which labor supposedly had no interests. The left's victory resolved Solidarity's identity crisis by pushing it away from the union it was becoming and back to the political organization it always preferred to be. The union and its right-wing political allies would now try to make this new narrative stick.

Of course, Solidarity hoped to be able to mobilize labor opposition to the new government by appealing to economic concerns as well. The problem was that the DLA refused to play its part. For the irony was that the ex-communist government was the most favorable one labor had had since 1989. It demonstrated this through a number of measures in the first months after coming to power.[36] For example, the DLA had vowed in its campaign to abolish the detested wage tax, and its very first piece of legislation fulfilled this promise. Although the bill called for the tax to be abolished in a few months' time, state firms acted as if it had been abolished already, and so wages, with the government's support, rose significantly in the DLA's first months in office. As for public sector wages, which had provoked Solidarity's mortal conflict with the previous government, parliament voted a pay increase in January 1994 and promised a second one in June. While still rejecting the old guarantee of a wage equal to 106 percent of the national average—which, with industry no longer governed by the wage tax, was almost impossible to reinstate in any case—the government did commit itself to regular public sector wage hikes that would exceed the rate of inflation. When Solidarity nevertheless initiated health sector strikes late in the year, the government responded by offering more money in return for a no-strike clause, which contributed to making 1995 and 1996 years of remarkable labor peace.

The health deal had been negotiated in the new Tripartite Commission. This itself was an important DLA innovation. First proposed by Jacek Kuron as part of the Pact on State Enterprises negotiated with the trade unions in early 1993, legislation bringing the commission into effect was one of the new government's first orders of business. The commission was established as a forum for regular interaction of competing economic interests, labor consultation on proposed social policy, and sectoral collective bargaining. Demonstrating a desire to reach out to his opponents, Labor Minister Miller persuaded Andrzej Baczkowski, a prominent Solidarity unionist and former underground leader from Lublin, to stay on as deputy minister in order to serve as chairman of the Tripartite Commission. (Baczkowski agreed despite considerable opposition from the union.) Mutually acceptable wage increases negotiated at the Tripartite Commission were supposed to replace the wage tax, and the new government proved more conciliatory on wage increases than the Solidarity governments had been. It also put more trust in the employee councils, trust that paid off: contrary to the fears of neoliberals, wages did not zoom out of control after the abolition of the wage tax in April 1994.[37]

In the three years to follow, the DLA government passed much other labor legislation. It passed debt relief for firms, gave free shares for employees of privatized firms, and required all firms to set up their own social funds. It finally revised the old Labor Code, bringing it up to date with existing conditions. (It was a sign of the prior lackadaisical interest in labor issues that, until 1994, trade unions were operating with a collective bargaining law dating from 1974.)[38] In 1995, the government revised the 1990 privatization law to include a number of significant labor-friendly measures, such as allowing more free shares for employees, extending share giveaways to farmers and fishermen, encouraging employee buyouts, and allowing some corporatized firms to remain state-owned. It backed off on calls to eliminate the guild-like privileges of low-status professions, such as mining or teaching. It made a special effort to improve conditions for retirees by increasing pensions to their relative 1989 levels (which no other group of workers had yet achieved), including retirees in firm share distribution, and defending their income-enhancing small private plots against urban renewal and highway construction plans.[39] The government also took action against abuse in the private sphere. It closed the loophole allowing firms to withhold benefits by hiring employees on recurring "temporary" contracts.[40] And it at least paid more lip service to issues of health and safety.

All in all, this was not the anti-labor government that Solidarity had expected, and even hoped for. As one conservative writer put it, expressing his own political frustrations, the DLA government had "ended the conflict with the public sector, . . . proved quite conciliatory in tripartite negotiations over wage increases," and did other things such as maintain regional structural adjustment funds that the Suchocka government had tried to cut.[41] And this is what put the union in such a difficult position.

To be sure, the DLA's administration was no labor panacea. In general macroeconomic policy, the government differed little from previous ones (the exception being special subsidies for agriculture, necessary to the DLA's coalition partner). Its neoliberal wing controlled the finance and privatization ministries, pushing to limit expenditures and speed privatization. It was strongly committed to the new private sector (as the latter knew, giving it strong electoral support) and to the new styles of that sector, such as greater wage differentiation, individualized bonus payments, and the exclusion of unions. Its budget fell easily within IMF guidelines, and except for some radicals within the DLA coalition, there was none of the verbal abuse heaped on the IMF or international institutions that had been common in Olszewski's circle.

The DLA was able to make the small but meaningful changes that it did for three reasons. First, economic growth finally resumed after four years of decline. GDP in 1994 finally surpassed 1990 levels, and in 1996 it even surpassed 1989 levels. Second, the IMF, satisfied with the record of previous governments, no longer had final veto on the budget. And third, there had *always* been a little leeway in the budget. Solidarity governments had refused to share this with labor in order to demonstrate who was in charge,[42] but the DLA government, not burdened with having recently led a genuine democratic workers' movement, could afford to be more forthcoming.

This was no anticapitalist party. It sought not to empower workers as much as to make capitalism acceptable to them. Its chief aim was to smooth the social acceptance of market reform through small material and symbolic concessions. According to Zbigniew Siemiatkowski, a key party spokesman and future minister of internal affairs, the party's aim was to do in Poland what the Spanish social democrats had done in Spain.[43] This did not mean mimicking Spain's unemployment rate, which at well over 20 percent far exceeded Poland's (though Poland matched Spain by 2003), but in making sure that even if such rates were attained, workers might still feel included by having a party in power that they trusted.

The key difference with previous governments is that while those appealed to workers as citizens, this one sought to treat workers as workers. It saw them as neither potential political rivals nor potential entrepreneurs, which is how many Solidarity activists saw themselves, but as permanent subordinates in a market economy. It wanted to talk with unions about issues that bothered them, and it expressed its interest in resolving conflicts through dialogue. But it never acted as if organized labor was its equal, and it was this that Solidarity could not tolerate.

Solidarity's Response

Solidarity might have responded by treating these economic concessions as a labor victory. But that would have required seeing itself as a class actor, representing labor interests rather than reform in general. This it was unable to do. OPZZ, with strong official representation in the DLA coalition,[44] did react favorably to these developments. But since OPZZ was traditionally and congenitally a quiescent movement led chiefly by mid-level supervisory personnel, its comportment mattered little for social peace. In the end, Solidarity treated the left's victory as itself the problem, regardless of what that government did in power.

Solidarity thus responded to the new government by declaring its total opposition. Instead of resisting strike calls from below, as it had done in the past, Solidarity now tried to organize as many strikes as it could. This was not easy. The abolition of the wage tax had eased the most immediate source of labor dissatisfaction, and the subsequent rise in wages, without strikes, meant that many workers believed conditions might now get better. Efforts to mobilize specifically political strikes against "the communists" also failed to gain support.

In the end, Solidarity had no choice but to wait for unrest to arise on its own. This happened in early 1994, with a strike by the traditionally militant brown-coal mines of Belchatow, where workers were resisting the establishment of a holding company to manage several money-losing mines. The holding company was a familiar strategy in the mining sector, imposed by previous governments on coal mines in Silesia. Miners themselves usually opposed it, seeing it as a sign of impending layoffs, but Solidarity officials tended to support it as a rational way to restructure the industry. This time, however, since it was the DLA pushing the proposal, Solidarity sided with the miners. It joined the strike and quickly tried to expand it. Within weeks, Solidarity was challenging the government on a wide front, threatening general strikes in sectors such as energy and fuel where it had almost always condemned strikes in the past.

Like its previous (unanswered) strike calls, this one too ultimately ended in embarrassment for the union, as well as an exacerbation of internal rifts. This story I can tell from personal experience. When Krzaklewski, the Solidarity leader, was calling for a nationwide strike in support of the miners, I happened to be doing research and interviews in Mielec, site of the giant WSK aircraft manufacturing plant. Mielec workers, who rarely strike—their most prominent one, in 1992, occurred because workers had not received *any* wages for several months—earned on average about one-fourth of a miner's pay and were not inclined to support this walkout. But the plant's Solidarity local was told by the national authorities to prepare for an imminent strike in solidarity with the miners. Dutifully but without enthusiasm, the local leaders went about all the preparations, informing members, preparing leaflets, arranging with management so as to minimize disruption to the plant. Two days before the scheduled action, the miners abruptly settled. The national union was caught by surprise, but bigger damage ensued at the local level. Mielec activists and rank and file alike were furious to have been mobilized on behalf of others doing far better than them, only to be ungraciously "switched off" when the miners won theirs, leaving Mielec laborers in an even worse comparative position than before. Such was the self-destructive illogic of Solidarity's militant anticommunism.

Even with ex-communists now running the market economy, the union was careful not to indict capitalism itself. An interview in the *Solidarity Weekly* with a sympathetic right-wing economist provides a good insight into Solidarity's new narrative. According to Adam Glapinski, minister of industry in Olszewski's 1992 cabinet, ongoing economic problems such as low wages and enterprise indebtedness were signs not of capitalism but of lingering communism. Still-communist bankers were lending money based on old personal contacts rather than on a firm's creditworthiness, and the recipients were using that money to help themselves rather than the firms. "The secret police or Central Committee folk [working in the banks] gladly take treasury funds to give credits to their buddies, without worrying about whether they'll pay it back. In the end it's the budget that pays," and everyone else suffers.[45] Thus, says Glapinski, workers can improve their conditions not by building stronger unions but by removing the communists. For it is not capitalism, he stresses, that is responsible for hardship. Embedded communist networks means that "there is still no capitalism in Poland!" Workers and right-wing economists must thus unite to fight for capitalism together. Solidarity must "join with anti-socialist economists who defend private property and the market" and together fight for "real" capitalism—the "democratic capitalism that we have fought for ever since 1980."

Here we have the rationale that came to dominate the union: in a "real" market economy, workers are treated fairly and are rewarded for their work, while in the "false" market of the present it is the old elites, not "real Poles," who benefit thanks to their connections.

Turning to the Right

When class conflicts become impossible, implausible, or impractical, trade unions will seek other grounds to justify their existence. With the faux radicalism of 1994 unable to mobilize supporters, and the union unwilling to see itself become a "mere" trade union, Solidarity turned to a succession of other causes. Determined to oppose the governing party no matter what, Solidarity from 1994–97 reconstituted itself as a self-proclaimed "right-wing" political organization committed to anticommunism, "honest" capitalism, and an active Church presence in politics. Workplace issues were defined as secondary to political ones as the union initiated a series of high-profile confrontations over a succession of non-economic issues.

For example, there was the fight over the new constitution.[46] Due to the illegitimacy of the first parliament (1989–91) and the divisiveness of the second (1991–93), it was only during the DLA administration that parliament finally got around to drafting a new constitution.[47] Despite the fact that the parliament allowed non-parliamentary social groups to present their own drafts for consideration and eventually integrated many of the extra-parliamentary opposition's specific points, Solidarity denounced the process and the final document continually from conceptualization to final approval. In late 1994, when the Constitutional Commission had basically just begun its work, Solidarity together with much of the Catholic Church already called for the constitution's rejection. The problem was not something specific to the text. Departing far from the principles of a liberal democracy, Solidarity and its allied parties saw this not as a constitutional debate but as a moral battleground, the place to define to whom the country belonged. Railing against the "communists" and their supposed "atheization" of the country, Solidarity presented its own draft constitution. But even though the Constitutional Commission accepted some of Solidarity's proposals, such as including a reference to God in the preamble, still the union denounced the final result as a "godless," "heathen," and "evil" document. The language is significant. For Solidarity, the problem with the constitution was not that it was anti-worker but that it was anti-Christian. Solidarity latched onto the words of Pope John Paul II who, intervening in the debate, wrote that the constitution's refusal to acknowledge "a dimension of sanctity to social and public life" was tantamount to "the atheization of the state and has little in common with ideological neutrality."[48] Essentially, anything short of the proclamation of Christian "natural law" was presented as a dangerous threat to the nation's soul.

Having failed to organize workers around phony economic issues in 1994, the union now turned decisively toward organizing along nationalist and religious lines. In 1996, with strikes at their lowest since 1989, the union made the campaign against abortion the center of its program. The DLA, belatedly making good on its electoral promises, had finally gone ahead with a bill restoring abortion rights, which the previous parliament had taken away. Solidarity leader Marian Krzaklewski seized on this as proof of the left's evil, and declared the continued delegalization of abortion to be the union's greatest interest.

Political opportunity, in the form of an ideological hole that needed to be filled, also pushed the union to the right. In late 1995, two years after the DLA won control of parliament, its leader, Aleksander Kwasniewski, defeated Lech Walesa in the presidential elections, securing a solid majority in the second round of voting. The right now seemed to be leaderless and hopelessly divided. Krzaklewski had come to power in 1991 promising to turn the union *away* from politics, but this gaping hole on the right kept luring them back. The small Christian nationalist parties were distrustful of the union, but they kept losing. The brand name of Solidarity was the only hope they had. The union's leaders, meanwhile, seemed relieved to be moving away from tedious union work into the more high-flown world of politics. Since 1989, the union had been a stepping stone to political and economic power, a source of political capital as effective for upward mobility as the familiar former *nomenklatura* status. And with Krzaklewski leading the way, Solidarity's new leaders now followed suit. In July 1996, five years after telling the union conference that elected him that now was the time to move away from politics, Krzaklewski announced the creation of Solidarity Electoral Action (SEA) as an electoral vehicle for taking state power. SEA originated as a diverse coalition of some thirty self-proclaimed "right-wing patriotic" political groups and organizations under the unquestioned leadership of the Solidarity trade union, committed to a program of "Christian values" and anticommunist lustration. (At the extreme end of the SEA coalition, forty candidates and subsequent parliamentary deputies were endorsed by the radical right "Radio Maria" radio station, which actively supported the erection of crosses at Auschwitz and ran shows calmly discussing whether those who support abortion rights could still be considered Poles—the consensus was no.) Other parts of the SEA platform called for health and pension "reform" (the latter entailing the privatization of social security) and, as the only one specifically economic plank, "universal privatization," or a broader distribution of privatized public property. But as was clear from the identity of its main allies as well as its campaign propaganda over the next year, Christianity and anticommunism were SEA's main selling points.

"Regional SEA circles will be organized by the regional union chairpersons," declared union vice president Janusz Tomaszewski.[49] In this way, Solidarity sought to turn local trade unions into the political arm of this incipient party. Local leaders were often upset by this, but the national leaders seemed to welcome this turn away from union affairs. Solidarity's rejection of unionism for politics had been growing for the past two years. In 1994, when the national Tripartite Commission had finally been established, Solidarity virtually ignored it, using its sessions to demand bilateral negotiations over unspecific issues (the aim being to marginalize OPZZ) rather than to negotiate concrete policy. In 1995, several top union leaders active in an AFL-CIO supported program on member recruitment dropped their work at once when political opportunities opened up.[50] Most Solidarity leaders just did not want to deal with the tediousness of real unionism.

Solidarity's post-1993 focus on "fighting communists," together with its increasingly strong rejection of political liberalism (for allegedly allowing communism to return), led to the emergence of strong extremist tendencies within the union. The most prominent of these was the Christian-nationalist faction led by Zygmunt Wrzodak, Solidarity leader in the powerful Ursus Tractor Plant in Warsaw. Wrzodak brought to the union the vision of the prewar *Endecja* party, for whom liberals, foreigners, and Jews were the root of all evil. He combined populist, Proudhonian faith in small enterprise owned by workers with a conviction in the need for a strong state run on Christian principles in order to protect "the nation" against being bought out by its enemies. And the enemies—defined always as "aliens," or non-Poles—were everywhere: they were the communists, capitalists, Russians, Americans, Europeans, foreigners, and Jews. In 1994, Wrzodak was given a regular column and a monthly insert in the *Solidarity Weekly*. By 1995, he was organizing militant union demonstrations in Warsaw, provoking the first violent clashes of the post-1989 era, in which the government was denounced for selling out the interests of the nation. At one anti-government rally in March, Wrzodak supporters chanted "To the Gas!" as the names of government leaders, none of whom was Jewish, were read from the podium.

Krzaklewski criticized Wrzodak as extreme, even "proto-fascist." Yet he regularly played on the same themes, though without the aggressiveness or open bigotry. Nationalist, anticommunist, masculinist (anti-abortion rights, family wages for men), and "tough on crime" themes were all indispensable elements of SEA's program. Meanwhile, Krzaklewski watched as the union became a bastion of political illiberalism. Its national newspaper, *Solidarity Weekly*, came at times to resemble little more than a Catholic nationalist tabloid, publishing fundamentalist pastiches, antiliberal diatribes (including translations of Rush Limbaugh), and even thinly veiled anti-Semitism.

All this does not mean that the union entirely ceased to talk about economic issues. It was, after all, still a trade union with an almost exclusive working-class base. The point, however, is that it presented labor problems almost solely as *moral* problems. Solidarity continued to appeal to workers, but the source of their ills, the union stressed, was not capitalism but the identity of the present capitalists, not the poor protection of workers but the imaginary non-Christians making all the laws, not new managerial strategies minimizing employee participation but "communist" managers doing bad deeds. In its effort to maintain its support, Solidarity continued to try to organize class anger, but in its continued commitment to direct that anger away from the market, it offered substitute targets instead. In this way, Solidarity became an agent of illiberalism and a danger to an inclusive democracy.

Answering Objections

I should take a moment here to compare my account of postcommunist Polish labor with that of Ekiert and Kubik, whose 1999 book, *Rebellious Civil Society*, deals with some similar issues but comes to very different conclusions.[51] To read their account together with mine is to get two very different pictures of Polish trade unionism after 1989. For Ekiert and Kubik present a picture of Polish unions as strong and decisive, forcefully articulating and publicly manifesting through strikes and demonstrations a defense of workers' fundamental economic interests. Indeed, they argue that without Solidarity's leadership, there would have been little labor protest at all. My view is quite different: that Solidarity did its best *not* to organize workers around economic interests, and that they came to head strikes mostly in order to maintain their own control of the labor movement, and more often than not to squelch economic unrest rather than promote it.

How are such different interpretations possible? One key reason is our different methodologies. Ekiert and Kubik ground their work in a database of protest actions from 1989 to 1993 as reported in the Polish press. This means they rely on press accounts of who organized protests and what the protests were about. Since Solidarity's name was indeed frequently mentioned in the press as the organizer of a protest action whose participants made economic demands, we get a picture of a militant union committed to organizing workers.

My account is more ethnographic, based on spending a great deal of time visiting Polish factories and talking to unionists, frequently in factories where there had been recent unrest. This provides a very different picture from press accounts. I would find that indeed Solidarity had been at the head of this strike or that protest action, but the factory union leaders regularly explained to me that they were simply responding to rank-and-file frustrations—frustrations they didn't share, since they tended to support the government's marketization program and believed throughout the 1990s that the reforms needed more time to work. (Statistical data confirming this account of trade unionists is discussed in chapter 5.) They generally tried not to organize actions, they explained to me, but when they did, they did so more in order to maintain their authority inside the firm than to project power outside it. As often happens with ethnographic research, then, I came up with a much more complex picture than one can get from the press.

A case in point is the highly publicized strike in the WSK aircraft manufacturing plant in Mielec in 1992. Having already suffered widespread layoffs with many more sure to come, and with the remaining workers having not been paid anything at all in several months, thousands of employees went on strike and marched downtown to demand payment of wages and government intervention to protect their jobs. The press presented this as a sign of the new labor militance threatening the country. When I went there and asked the plant's Solidarity officials about the strike they had led, they smiled: "Yes, we read about us leading that strike, too." It was, they said, the last thing they wanted to do. The workforce and the city were suffering real hardships, but such, they thought, was the price that had to be paid for reform. "But the workers didn't want to hear this—even after we explained it to them," complained Artur Olinowicz, the local Solidarity vice president. He continued:

> They kept saying someone's got to do something. They wanted some big strike action and a march, but we didn't like the idea. But when we said so, this almost got us lynched. We then said we need to go through all the formal conditions for a strike, including a referendum. But people cried, "What are you waiting for?" and threatened to go it alone. We wanted to solve the problem with methods stated in the trade union law, a method more civilized than "the streets." But the people wouldn't be swayed, and they dragged us along. And in the end, it's better we led the strike than Solidarity '80. We're more responsible than they are.[52]

I return to the Mielec union in more detail in chapter 5. But it was far from an anomaly. In the giant steel plant of Stalowa Wola, the automotive plant of Starachowice, or the mines of Bytom, Solidarity unionists repeatedly told me how they supported market reforms and kept coming into conflict with the rank and file, which did not. A Warsaw Solidarity official attending the Harvard Trade Union Program in 1991 told me with all sincerity that Solidarity's main goal had become to keep workers from protesting. (As noted, survey data confirming that such attitudes were widespread follows in chapter 5.) The point, in any case, is that strikes "led by Solidarity" are not necessarily evidence of strikes organized by Solidarity. The union needed to do something with the anger emerging from below, and sometimes strike actions and protests were the best way to let the rank and file safely blow off steam.

Ekiert and Kubik's claims about labor leading protests in Poland lead them to a broader conclusion, namely that people protested because political agitators pushed them to do so, not because the economic situation was bad. Their aim here is to debunk the "deprivation" theory of collective action, according to which people protest when conditions drive them to do so. In postcommunist Poland, they say, it was otherwise. Political protest was driven not by socioeconomic mechanisms but "by the *political calculations* and *understandings of reality* of protest leaders and organizers." That people felt they needed to protest "was influenced by the protest organizers' framing more than by the changes in the economic situation."[53] (Their argument here is oddly similar to that offered by the ruling party in 1980: that the strikes leading to the creation of Solidarity happened not because workers had real grievances but because political agitators won them over.)

Their evidence for these claims is thin. Workers' families in 1993, they say, earned 67 percent of what they earned in 1989 compared to farmers' families who earned only 64 percent, but workers protested more than farmers, ergo worker agitators and not socioeconomics must be the key factor. Losing a third of your real income in four years, in other words, is apparently not a sufficient reason to be angry enough to protest, say Ekiert and Kubik. So if workers do protest, that must be because union agitators make them. And we know this because those who lost slightly more than one-third of their income protest less![54] (In this account, long traditions of labor protest and the greater availability of resources in factories count for nothing.) Other evidence they offer appears even weaker. In 1994, they note, health and education workers protested less than they did in 1993, despite the fact that the wage gap between them and industrial workers had widened. While deprivation theory *could*, they say, explain why health and education workers protested heavily in 1993, the fact that they protested less in 1994 tells us that "deprivation," or economic conditions, must not be the key factor.[55] They do not mention that in 1994 the DLA government finally sat down with health and education workers and agreed to raise their wages, though that seems a more compelling explanation for the decline in protest actions.

Finally, they point to minor signs of economic recovery in 1993, and then claim that the rise in protest incidents that year despite such improvement demonstrates that economic conditions were not driving the discontent. The problem, however, is that the "recovery" figures they cite are so insignificant that it's hard to imagine anyone aside from professional social scientists being able to notice. "In January 1993 unemployment stood at 14.2 percent; by May it increased merely by 0.1 percent to 14.3 percent! In . . . April, compared with March, unemployment went down slightly (by 6,234 persons); it decreased even more between April and May (from 14.4 to 14.3 percent)."[56] Can one really expect citizens to see such developments as compelling evidence that they should no longer protest? Can we really say that those who continue to protest in the face of such "robust economic recovery"[57] must be doing so for reasons *other* than a sense of deprivation?

The biggest problem with their approach, it seems to me, is its very narrow understanding of deprivation. The transformation of labor relations from the period of late state socialism to primitive capitalist accumulation can surely not be measured by income alone. What Ekiert and Kubik fail to take into account is the whole panoply of factors involved in constructing a class society—the subtle humiliations, the change in power dynamics, the shifts in prestige and symbolic representations, the overwhelming assault on dignity. "There were always many poor people in Poland," wrote the conservative historian Bohdan Cywinski in 1994. "In early communist times, almost all of us belonged to that group. But one was poor differently at that time. With much more dignity than today."[58] Being poor—which many of those people who lost a third of their real incomes now were—had become a shameful thing in this new world. Cywinski was pointing to what Richard Sennett has called the "hidden injuries of class."[59] This is central to the meaning of deprivation.

So when Ekiert and Kubik argue that since GDP rose in 1992–93, the higher protest rates then as compared to 1990–91 suggest that something other than deprivation is at play, they do not seem to grasp the extent to which such statistics fail to convey what is happening in people's lives: the confusion and uncertainty, the fear of losing one's job, the worry that trade unions are no longer defending you, the way management is transforming industrial relations in an individualist and hierarchical direction with trade unions meekly going along, the experience of private firms in which conditions are awful and regulation is nonexistent.[60]

In a word, they miss E. P. Thompson's point made a long time ago about the economic growth of early nineteenth-century England: "By 1840, most people were 'better off' than their forerunners had been fifty years before, but they had suffered and continued to suffer this slight improvement as a catastrophic experience."[61] My point is not to label postcommunism "catastrophic," but to remind readers that even growth can be experienced as a shattering violation, even a desecration, of accepted values, ushering in fear, insecurity, anger, and, yes, a sense of "deprivation" to those who live it as the designated subordinate class.

Class formation here means the manufacture of new kinds of workers, new kinds of humans, new kinds of what Pierre Bourdieu calls "habituses." As Elizabeth Dunn documents in a wonderful book on the transformation of the labor process in one Polish factory taken over by an American multinational, "market reform" is not just about cutting state subsidies and letting market logic prevail, but also about creating new ideas and expectations and legitimating new patterns of inequality. It's not even necessarily about efficiency. Dunn shows how management insists on beating the old values and practices out of workers even when those old styles would be more efficient for the firm. The new capitalist firm insists that "its employees become privatized individuals," no longer working together to solve problems but acting only as individuals with itemized tasks, knowing how to follow orders and to act out their new roles.[62] Success comes to be based more on acting than on merit: One becomes successful "because one can display the attributes of upper-middle class standing, not the reverse."[63] For workers, meanwhile, pay, bonuses, and quotas all become private and secret, as the effort to break solidarity becomes paramount. As Dunn puts it,

> These managers tried to use merit bonuses and individual quotas to increase workers' productivity and flexibility by setting up competition between individuals. Permanent, full-time shop floor workers saw this as divisive and counterproductive, since it would make it impossible or impractical for them to help one another, break the community apart, limit interchangeability, and impede the smooth flow of work. Danka, a worker with fifteen years of experience, told me that once individual merit bonuses were put into effect, mutual aid among workers would end. "Then nothing will get done around here," she snorted.[64]

Dunn shows the detailed reality behind the numbers, demonstrating that market transformation can provoke protests grounded in a sense of deprivation even in times of statistical economic growth.

Finally, in line with their portrait of Solidarity as a forceful defender of labor interests, Ekiert and Kubik claim that Solidarity never did erect a parasol over the government, pointing to the toppling of the Suchocka government as proof. My account, however, indicates a definite Solidarity parasol—not necessarily over any particular government but over the basic market reform program, which the union never did anything to challenge. The parasol at first embraced the liberal Mazowiecki government, an intention made clear by the logo chosen for the union's National Conference in April 1990—a giant umbrella. But union leaders, with ears closer to the ground than their predecessors who had gone off to parliament, recognized better than the liberal parliamentarians that defending fundamental policies required a strategy of opposition as well as one of assent. Governments cannot be defended *ad infinitum* when their policies are alienating huge numbers of people. But one can keep the policies from being thrown out with the governments that introduce them by developing a narrative that converts anger at the policies into anger at something other than the policies, such as the identities of those who implement them. And as we've seen in this chapter, that is precisely what Solidarity did: channeling anger at nascent capitalism into a 1990 election campaign against political liberals, or into a mid-'90s campaign for lustration and Christian values, up to and including demands for a Christianized state.

The point is not that there was some kind of conspiracy here, with trade union leaders sitting around thinking of ways to pull wool over workers' eyes in order to bolster capitalism at any cost, inventing illiberal narratives to help them carry out this mass duplicity. The point is simply that this is what Solidarity did, this is what its actions entailed, with most union leaders pushing such policies because they actually believed in them. As chapter 5 will show, Solidarity leaders at all levels actually believed in capitalism, and most, no doubt, in "Christian values" too.[65] They believed that they were doing good for workers by getting workers not to challenge capitalism. They believed they were acting in the interests of their members who did not understand their interests as well as they, the leaders, did. And so, Solidarity as a trade union continually pushed policies that could capture class anger and divert it onto non-economic others. It continually pushed measures that sop up emotions while leaving overall economic policies intact. The protest actions of 1992–93 were a partial exception to this pattern, but only partial. For example, although Solidarity did organize a massive miners' strike, it settled without having won much at all, after accepting long-term restructuring plans that made massive layoffs inevitable.[66] Even the vote of no confidence in the Suchocka government—did this signal some dramatic new role for Solidarity? Hardly. In the end, Solidarity demonstrated that it was more concerned with the government's identity than its policies. For when a government more sympathetic to trade union concerns replaced the Suchocka administration, Solidarity proceeded to reject its every concession and to promote completely extraneous substitute solidarities instead. Indeed, so deeply did Solidarity ignore basic labor issues during the 1990s that Poland would enter the European Union in 2004 labeled a potential "Trojan Horse" for industrial relations because of its extreme managerial, anti-corporatist characteristics.[67] All this indicates that there was quite a parasol indeed.

Ekiert and Kubik are not the only ones to offer English-language readers the picture of a tough Solidarity forcefully defending the economic interests of Polish labor. Maryjane Osa, using Ekiert and Kubik's 1989–93 database, and Jonathan Terra, in a more comprehensive study covering the entire 1990s and comparing Polish and Czech labor outcomes, see union strength evident in the fact that Solidarity sometimes won economic concessions.[68] Osa writes that labor protests led to occasional wage increases and to promises of better working conditions (although why the second item constitutes a victory rather than a stalling tactic is never made clear), while Terra points to frequent union participation in economic policymaking as evidence that Polish industrial relations have been a model of "inclusion." But these do not seem to me very convincing arguments. Of course unions, when they did lead protests, sometimes won wage increases, and Solidarity certainly did work with government restructuring commissions. But the first claim, given the overall fact of dramatic real wage decline, seems to treat any activity on the part of trade unions as proof of forceful representation, while the second mistakes participation for resistance. Yes, Solidarity was very active on the economic and political fronts in postcommunist Poland. Historical legacies and the weakness of the party system kept it in the center of public attention for years. But to look at the record overall is to conclude that Solidarity acted chiefly to smooth the introduction of a neoliberal economic system by diverting labor anger onto "safe" targets, jeopardizing political liberalism instead. As far as its power in the workplace (discussed more fully in chapter 5), the most that can be said is that Solidarity helped negotiate the terms of labor's capitulation.

4

How Liberals Lost Labor

"Liberals are useless when it comes to symbols, and just as useless when it comes to arguing with the irrational in general."
—Christopher Hitchens, "Waiving the Flag," *The Nation*, July 21, 1997, 8.

How did it happen that by the middle of the 1990s, the Solidarity labor movement came to be dominated by a political right that made issues like the fight against legalized abortion or in favor of a religious preamble to the constitution the centerpiece of its activities? How could a movement that had been marked by openness and an eager embrace of the modern world have retreated into such a sectarian cocoon? How did a union that still represented millions of workers end up with a national leadership that spent far more time denouncing political liberals than worrying about secure contracts for members or unionization drives in the new private sector? How, in short, could liberals have so quickly lost their control?

The aim of this chapter is to look at how the new political groups emerging from Solidarity dealt with the economic anger that resulted from the introduction of a capitalist economy, and how their handling of that anger affected political outcomes. My interest here is in the political legitimation of the new market system. Instead of looking at how the capitalist transformation was carried out, I explore at how it was politically managed.

The evolution of Solidarity in this rightward direction was by no means inevitable. And indeed, the argument of this chapter is that far from gravitating there naturally, Solidarity was pushed there by its former leaders—those once wedded to anti-politics who had come to embrace a liberal polity and a market economy. The illiberal turn of much of the labor movement should be seen not as a sign of a primeval and inexplicable irrationalism of the masses, as liberals have been prone to explain their decline, but rather as the result of being abandoned by the liberals who once had such influence over them.

The problem was not just liberal policies or politicians but the whole progressive edifice founded on "reason." By presenting their policies not so much as "good" ones but as "necessary" ones, not as "desirable" but as "rational," liberals left their supporters no acceptable way to protest or express dissatisfaction. By insisting on the glib globalist mantra that "there is no alternative"—in this case, no alternative to the exceedingly painful measures they were administering—liberals labeled all resistance as irrational and illegitimate. The story of the first postcommunist years in Poland is the story of Solidarity unionists wrestling precisely with this proscription on anger, ultimately finding it unfeasible and even incoherent. By decrying all opposition as dangerous and populist, and labeling themselves the only voice of reason, liberals *pushed* opponents into the illiberal camp, for that became the only space opponents were permitted to inhabit. By the end of the decade, the more anti-liberal the candidate, the more authentic his oppositionist credentials seemed, a dynamic that eventually led to the watershed 2001 elections in which the flagship liberal Freedom Union party was voted out of parliament while the two most extreme right-wing parties became key figures in the parliamentary opposition. The 1990s is thus the story of liberals with ideological and organizational hegemony squandering their assets and producing precisely the kind of opposition they were supposedly trying to thwart.

A few words on terminology. The main focus of this chapter is the group of activists and politicians I call liberals, who played the key role in Solidarity's leadership up to 1989 but who lost control and influence soon after. Of several imprecise terms, it seems the most apt. Interestingly, this group has never quite known what to call itself.[1] The one label it did adopt in the mid-1970s, "secular left," it soon disowned, due to the nationalist right's eagerness to pounce on it as "proof" of the group's anti-Christianity. Its activists then took to calling themselves the "democratic opposition," but this doesn't work either, since after 1989 they were no longer in opposition and everyone now claimed to be a democrat. And so they began to call themselves "liberals." But this term is not very precise either, as it includes a wide range of political actors. The term is often used, particularly in Europe, to refer to pure *economic* liberals who care little about individual political rights. (Chilean dictator Augusto Pinochet has often been a model for this group of liberals.) But the group under discussion here believed simultaneously in both economic and political liberalism. Like economic liberals, they have tended to think, at least since the mid-1980s, that private property and a market economy are the foundations of political freedom, but unlike pure economic liberals, they have been unwilling to sacrifice the latter to get the former. They believed that both must, or at least should, go together, and that this combination lies at the heart of progress and democracy.

When I use the term "liberals," then, I am referring to the consistent defenders of both economic and political liberalism, those who seek the emergence of a modern market economy (even if they differ over the level of regulation) but not at the cost of violating the democratic rights of any person or group. In Eastern Europe it describes groups such as the Freedom Union in Poland, the Alliance of Free Democrats in Hungary, and the Civic Democratic Alliance in the Czech Republic. All of them entered the post-communist period with great moral and political authority, which they soon squandered. A key aim of this chapter is to understand why.

If the decade of the 1990s shows the liberal mismanagement of anger, it is also marked by the nationalist right's brilliant deployment of anger. In a series of moves marked both by genuine concern and cynical calculation, right-wing nationalists who had been marginalized in 1989 remade themselves into defenders of labor and critics of the new class inequalities. For while "democratization" and "marketization" were the frames through which Eastern Europe was viewed in the West, the fate of labor and the emergence of new inequalities were the central issues on the domestic front. Liberals had the dominant political control of the labor movement in 1989 but lost it by ignoring and even denigrating nascent class anger, while nationalists and right-wing populists strategically sought to make that anger their own. In other words, within the broad Solidarity camp it was only the right, paradoxically, that allowed Polish workers to think of themselves as workers. While liberals insisted that workers think of themselves as rational citizens instead, giving them little choice but to accept "necessary" economic reforms, the nationalist and religious right urged workers to think of their own deteriorating conditions and offered them a narrative in which to understand their ills as the consequence of Poland abandoning its moral, national, and religious foundations. Even the former communists held back from such class-based appeals, as they were busy trying to rebuild themselves as a viable national and cross-class party. In the end, workers turned to the right because only the right appealed to them as workers, because no one else offered such a clear narrative validating the class experiences they were having.

The first point that needs to be dispelled is that there was some natural or inevitable predilection for Solidarity to embrace the right. Of course, its enemy's identification of itself as the left would tend to nudge the union toward the other end of the spectrum. But that had been the case in the early 1980s without producing such a reaction. Indeed, self-defined right-wingers in the early 1980s continually expressed their exasperation with Solidarity. For the pro-market right, the union was too enamored with self-management and social welfare, too skeptical of capitalism and markets, too interested in collective action over personal responsibility, too focused on civil rights instead of property rights.[2] For the traditional right—religious and nationalist rather than pro-market and anti-statist—Solidarity's conservative bona fides were dubious. Workers might go to mass and paste posters of the Pope on factory gates during strikes, but they were too independent, too distrustful of authority. For the traditional right, the problem was not that Solidarity promoted civil society (participation) over bourgeois society (private property), as it was for the pro-market right, but that it seemed to use religion and nationalism instrumentally. Witold Gombrowicz once wrote that the Catholic Church is but "the pistol with which [Poles] like to shoot Marx,"[3] and traditionalists saw Solidarity's use of religion in the 1980s the same way. Lech Walesa might never leave home without a pin of the Virgin Mary faithfully attached to his lapel, but why did he pick for his advisers activists such as Michnik and Kuron, who explicitly identified with the "secular left"?[4]

The doubters were correct: Solidarity had historically been dominated by the left—the "anti-political" and liberal left—and this remained true particularly in 1989, when the Round Table accords and the subsequent elections were dominated almost solely by this tendency.[5] By 1989 this was no longer an economic left; after all, it avidly embraced the market economy. (For many of its adherents, this meant that it should no longer be considered on the left at all. Jacek Kuron, for example, complained that people still called him a leftist because of this past. "I would like to belong to the left very much," he said, but "I cannot build capitalism proclaiming that I am [on] the left.")[6] It was, however, very much on the left in terms of the other dimension of the left-right split: not the rejection of capitalism but the rejection of nationalism, clericalism, and authoritarianism. Theirs was the old Enlightenment leftism of reason versus faith, progress versus tradition, and one of the important things the postcommunist world showed was precisely that these old conflicts had not been resolved by communist modernization.

What did this liberalism entail? It meant opposition to lustration, which liberals saw as a violation of due process and a surrender to an irrational politics of revenge. It meant resistance to legislation enforcing Christian morality on the populace. Wary of nationalism, liberals promoted universalism, which they understood as embracing "the West"—primarily the EU and NATO—on whatever terms it offered. They saw it as their mission to take Poland out of the cocoon in which, they believed, it had been embedded since 1945. Contrary to what western radical leftist critics maintained, however, this liberalism did not just mean accepting global capitalism and American hegemony. It also came to mean promoting gender equality and minority rights, or at least recognizing that such values were now a requisite part of the (pro-western) world order. It meant anti-racism (defense of Roma and immigrant rights, opposition to anti-Semitism) and, for most, an acceptance of gay rights. It meant the embrace of NGOs and other aspects of what westerners now called "civil society"—a concept, paradoxically, taken from an earlier East European opposition and stripped of its radical participatory ethos before being re-exported back to the East.[7] Basically the whole panoply of contemporary western human rights norms was embraced by this group, and it was precisely for this reason that they still constituted a political left.

The crucial point, however, is that this group now tied the defense of political liberalism to the triumph of economic liberalism. All the grand ideals of human rights and civil society, they believed, depended first and foremost on the eradication of state ownership and government subsidies and the introduction of a capitalist economy with hard budget constraints. Political liberalism simply seemed secondary now. As Jerzy Szacki puts it, "political liberalism has aroused incomparably less interest than economic liberalism and has incomparably fewer dyed-in-the-wool supporters."[8] Many were saddened by the pain inflicted on society by the Balcerowicz Plan—unlike contemporaneous Thatcherites and Reaganites, they did not see suffering as a moral good—but they "knew" they had to inflict that pain nevertheless. The very term "shock therapy" captures the combination of pain and salvation that its proponents were convinced it would provide. Thus did political liberals come to define their economic program as the only rational, correct, and legitimate one, the program that underpinned all others. And thus did they come to see critics of the plan not as reasonable people with different views but as misguided people with wrong views. This was their fatal error. For while their forceful and passionate commitment to market reform kept most unionists loyal at the outset, the continued popular dissatisfaction with the *effects* of shock therapy, together with the continued denigration of opponents as "irrational," ended up driving much of labor straight into the arms of anti-liberals like Wrzodak and Lepper, who did not mind being characterized as irrational. If stigmatizing opponents to the Balcerowicz Plan as "irrational" initially helped marginalize opponents, it ended up boosting those who were proudly irrational and illiberal, as they alone came to be seen as the most consistent opponents of shock therapy.

In the end, then, instead of seeking to incorporate anger, the liberals preferred to ignore it, and to mock it when it appeared. For them, any challenge to capitalist modernization was not just undesirable but impossible, so they couched their rejection of the right, which challenged the Balcerowicz Plan, not in the language of political debate but in the language of science. But instead of marginalizing the right, they succeeded chiefly in driving their own critics *toward* the right. The liberals got it wrong: it is not capitalism but the way capitalism is *challenged* that underpins democracy. Political liberalism is endangered by tying it too closely to economic liberalism. The liberals in power endangered their cherished political liberalism precisely by defining economic liberalism as its sole, rational foundation.

The Liberal Campaign Against Labor and "Labor"

Although the new postcommunist elite sought to create both a democratic polity and a capitalist market economy, it saw only the second of those aims as especially difficult. Democracy it understood mostly as calling off the cops, which the last communist government had already done. By the time the new leaders came to power, the free expression, freedom to form political parties, and fair elections that they understood as the basis of democracy had become reality. Formalizing the institutions to regulate political competition would take time, but after the fall of the Berlin Wall, no one seriously thought that was in jeopardy. Building a capitalist economy, however, was another matter. This required the transformation and privatization of thousands of individual firms, unemployment and short-term impoverishment for millions of citizens, and the creation of a whole host of specific economic institutions (capital markets, stock markets, commercial banks, contract law) to enforce new notions of property rights.[9] Toughest of all, it required the creation of a new propertied class. As reform leaders pointed out at the time, radical economic reform was being carried out in the name of a class that did not exist. The task was to create the class that would be both the beneficiary of the new capitalism and the social base for its continuation. But how to create a solid pro-capitalist constituency in a country that had just experienced a labor uprising? How to promote a capitalist class in a country where labor was so dominant?

Let's begin by looking at the liberal intellectual elite that dominated the initial postcommunist period, with a leadership consisting of Tadeusz Mazowiecki, Bronislaw Geremek, Jacek Kuron, and Adam Michnik. This group would go on to become the leaders of a specific political party—first called Civic Movement, then Democratic Union, and finally Freedom Union—but in 1989 they were much more than that. To note that this foursome constituted the country's prime minister, parliamentary leader, most popular politician, and editor of the main newspaper, respectively, is still to miss the extent of their influence. They were, at the time, Lech Walesa's closest advisers. The first two had extensive connections with liberal Communist Party circles, and Mazowiecki with the Church as well. The latter two were the most prominent figures of the political opposition, the ones whose inclusion in the Round Table negotiations (against Party objections) Walesa insisted on as a condition for his acceptance. They constituted the heart of Solidarity's negotiating team and the locus of formal political power afterwards. They had close connections with the West, supported by liberals, social democrats, and conservatives alike. Michnik would soon break from formal affiliation with this group, but mainly so he could better promote its basic political line in his daily, *Gazeta Wyborcza*. Together with other prominent liberal activists, such as Helena Luczywo and Seweryn Blumsztajn, Michnik turned the paper into an informational powerhouse of uncommon clout. As the paper of record *and* the chief forum for intellectual discussion, all with a reader-friendly prose and layout, it is like the *New York Times*, the *New York Review of Books*, and the *Daily News* rolled into one. And in the early postcommunist years, it vigorously promoted the liberal line of this dominant political formation.

By the fall of 1989, then, this liberal group controlled the government, had good links with the existing (communist) elite, had good relations with the Church, had close ties with the West, were revered by the broad ranks of the Solidarity opposition, and were treated by Solidarity unionists as the chief voice of "our" side. They had power, name recognition, an identifiable program, and control of the media. It was they who sponsored Leszek Balcerowicz and persuaded Walesa to approve. The liberals saw their chief political task as ensuring a stable social environment so that the economic reforms could take place. Their aim was to use the broad support they enjoyed to promote the social peace that would allow painful economic changes and unpopular capitalist class formation to occur.

As for popular discontent, liberals saw it as their role to channel it *away* from the new market economy that would cause it. Anticipating considerable opposition to economic reform, they saw it as their responsibility to divert the emerging anger away from its natural target. But where to direct the anger instead? Who or what would be the acceptable "other" now? The liberals proposed three answers, or three "enemies": the old regime, no one, and labor.

The old regime was the first target. It was also the easiest. Polish society had just completed a long struggle against the communist system, so it was easy to persuade people that any short-term hardships could be ascribed to its misrule. The opposition had been saying for years that the economy was in terrible shape and required a fundamental upheaval. Moreover, unlike in neighboring Czechoslovakia or Hungary, regular people *perceived* the economy to be in terrible shape and did not expect sudden improvement. So when the liberals promulgated the Balcerowicz Plan of shock therapy, they told everyone that it was going to be very painful because the communist system had destroyed the economy. You have a right to be angry, liberals instructed society, but only at the old regime that caused this mess, not the marketization policies that were, they said, fixing it.

Directing anger at a nonexistent enemy was similar to directing it at no one. And indeed, this was where the liberals really wanted to direct discontent. For as good liberals, they feared passion, believing in progress instead.[10] Progress for everyone, they believed, was obtainable, but only through the calm and rational measures that they were pursuing. Universalized good was thus possible, but only if society shed its anger and united behind benevolent liberal leadership. Thus they saw anger not as an inevitable product of modern class society but as a false consciousness that must be jettisoned in the interests of progress. They sought to quiet anger, not manage it.

The notion that passion could only derail reform was made quite explicit by parliamentary leader Bronislaw Geremek. Because the government's economic program "necessarily causes impoverishment," he said, it requires complete social acceptance, "the loss or even the weakening of which" would inexorably lead to a breakdown. Thus, reform can succeed only if there is a "political cease-fire." Conflicts were dangerous because they "inevitably lead to the demise of social peace, with all its consequences."[11] For Geremek, therefore, passions had to be kept at bay, anger had to be banished, and everyone had to rally behind the cause he represented. In a passage harking back to Michnik's mid-1980s cautions against the "petty satraps" of Solidarity, Geremek cited "Stalin, Mao, Robespierre, Mussolini, and Hitler" as examples of political leaders who had tapped popular anger.[12] To thwart such demons, the liberals would do their best to build a Solidarity without passions, under their control.

It is in this context that we can understand the liberal resistance to lustration. They wanted passions invested in building a new society, not in locating responsibility for the old. They had suffered as much as anyone from communist-era repressions. Kuron and Michnik each spent several years in jail. But they also recognized that they had been given a once-in-a-lifetime opportunity—to govern without opposition and with a popular mandate to create something new. This was a moment to put interests before passions.

So Prime Minister Mazowiecki pronounced a "thick line" separating past from present, saying his government was interested not in what people had done in the past but what they were doing now. For the liberals, this revolution would be consecrated with elections and parliamentary procedures, not bloodletting.

The problem, however, was that liberals saw *any* show of emotion as having the potential to lead to bloodletting. Thus they explicitly refrained from sponsoring the kind of cathartic, symbolic break with the past that occurred in Hungary with the reburial of Imre Nagy and in Czechoslovakia with the public proclamation of Vaclav Havel as president, not to mention East Germany and Romania. They simply did not believe that passion could serve anything other than irrational causes. And unlike postcommunist liberal elites in neighboring countries, this group believed that it was *able* to repress that passion because it already controlled a mass movement. It did not have to win over labor, but only avoid losing it.

The fear of anger made liberals particularly fearful of strikes. Even though the strike was the quintessential form of popular protest in this particular revolution—the reason that the liberals were in power in the first place—all strikes after 1989 were denounced by liberals as a dangerous transgression, creating conflict and animosity when unity and good will were needed.

And so we see here the identity of the third enemy proffered by the liberals: labor itself. In the end, the liberals needed some "other" against which good citizens could be instructed to define themselves. The "old regime" was of limited usefulness, precisely because it was the *old* regime. "No one" may have been their desired enemy, but it was politically useless: parties need an "other" against which to position themselves. And so labor gradually emerged as the liberals' enemy of choice. In targeting labor, liberals saw themselves following their much vaunted ethic of "living in truth." For they earnestly believed that the consolidation of a capitalist economy *required* the marginalization of labor. Combining Cold War anticommunism with the assumptions of postindustrialism, they wanted to build a world in which entrepreneurs were the hero and labor played a minor part. They knew it would not be easy. In contrast to the postindustrial economies of the West, the East was still very much mired in an industrial economy. And even more daunting than labor's impressive numbers was its symbolic power. The fact that a trade union had brought down communism gave the concept of labor an undeniable discursive swagger, which was completely at odds with the liberals' socioeconomic project (as well as with the nascent globalist one). For the liberals, therefore, there were thus two new enemies: "labor" and labor. The first meant that the pervasive culture and discourse of class had to be transformed. Workers had to be demoted in the public consciousness from puta-

tive universal to mere particularity, of no special interest to those not working in factories or aspiring to stay there. The second meant that the *reality* of
a large labor force had to be transformed too. It meant something had to be
done with the factories and the people working in them, and that people had
to accept this. In fact, workers did little to challenge the neoliberal reforms
that hurt them so profoundly. But the liberals operated with the *a priori* assumption that workers would be the chief force resisting capitalist formation,
and they believed that this resistance had to be nipped in the bud.

The pages of *Gazeta Wyborcza*, which expressly saw itself as the carrier of
modern liberal values to a backward society, are a good place to observe the
emergence of this new antilabor ideology, to observe the liberals' construction of a dangerous labor "other." The article by Grzegorz Gorny on a small
miners' strike in January 1990 is representative.[13] The strike began just two
weeks after the introduction of the Balcerowicz Plan and ended within a few
days. As usual, Solidarity did not support the strike, which made it easier for
Gazeta, still claiming to be the Solidarity newspaper, to be unsparing in its
attack. But what is most striking about the piece is not its disapproval but its
derision, its eagerness to present the strikers as unruly and unreasonable
characters with whom "modern" citizens have nothing in common. For the
previous decade, pro-Solidarity intellectuals had always emphasized the conditions that led workers to strike. Even when they disagreed with a particular action, they took care to stress the moral and material underpinnings of
the action and the dignified humanity of the workers. Gorny, however, says
nothing about the conditions that led to this strike. Nothing about the speci-
ficities of the location (Walbrzych), where mining was in a particularly pre-
carious position because of its low-quality brown coal; nothing about the
wage dispute or the plans to shut down the mine. Coverage of such a strike
by one of *Gazeta's* predecessor *samizdat* publications would have noted that
it was not labor's fault that the coal was so poor or that their labor had become expendable. It would have noted how the labor force had been specially
lured to the formerly German outpost of Walbrzych after 1945 to work and
to sacrifice. It would have explained that the entire country had relied on coal
revenues during the 1970s to keep it from bankruptcy, resulting in seven-day
workweeks and a record number of accidents.

But the earlier sympathetic accounts, it now turned out, belonged to the
rhetoric of the glorious struggle—what Milan Kundera calls the "Grand
March"[14]—no longer operative for liberals in 1990. Gorny focuses not on
the problems of workers but on problem workers. He presents strikers as hot-
tempered and irrational, hostile to voices of reason. These were not the good
Solidarity workers we knew in the past, but the "new radicals" Michnik
warned us about. The only good ones here are the union officials who try to

calm the passions. "I told them their cause was just," the local Solidarity leader is quoted as saying, "but that a strike was not the way to go." The union's regional leader chimes in: "We recognize the validity of the strikers' demands, but do not support striking as a correct form of protest." As for the strikers themselves, we are told they tried to bring vodka into the mine. As Gorny knew, there was no better charge with which to discredit workers. In 1980, Solidarity's decision to ban alcohol from strike sites was presented by intellectuals as proof that this was a new, mature, and responsible labor movement, one with which reasonable oppositionists should join. Accusing workers of bringing alcohol to a strike site was a way for Gorny—and *Gazeta*—to suggest that labor no longer deserved the same sympathies. Significantly, Gorny did not even know the charge to be true. The accusation, he tells us later in the piece, was based on an overheard conversation in which one strike leader told another to reinforce gate patrol. "So people won't leave?" asks the other. "No, so they don't bring in vodka." Gorny follows this with more insinuations of labor irrationality, as when the strikers, not believing that an agreement had been signed, jeer a union official who tells them it had. "Down with Solidarity!" Gorny has them chanting, and then something much nastier: "*Chuje!*"—cocksuckers. Gorny concludes by telling us the official was right about the signed agreement, though he does not tell us its terms or whether local miners had any input.

The importance of the piece lies precisely in its tone and style. The author and the newspaper do not tell readers much about this strike, but convey the theme that workers must be restrained if rationality is to triumph. The irrationality of the rank and file is conveyed even by Gorny's use of quotations: moderate union leaders are quoted by name, but strikers are anonymous, their comments are often lumped together. It is unclear who says what, and we have the sense that there are a mass of people all shouting. We never hear the internal logic of anyone who is angry. The angry are robbed of their dignity. We get a sense of a herd, not of a group of rational individuals. Gorny himself misses the significance of the one time where their anger sounds not wild but poignant, when they turn to the *Gazeta* reporter himself and cry, "You've forgotten about us!" In January 1990, workers do not yet want to believe that those who had protected them in the past are no longer ready to do so. They say they still support the Mazowiecki government, and are angry at *Gazeta* for making them seem antireform just because they are on strike. "We want to help the government, and you lie!" they tell Gorny. "Who would you be without us?" This is one of the first signs of the disintegration of the labor-intellectual alliance that would so profoundly shape the politics of the coming decade.

The point is not just that the Walbrzych miners were slandered. Perhaps they were indeed unsympathetic characters. The point is that Solidarity intellectuals had never publicly presented labor this way before. Part of the reason we know good and uplifting stories about workers in 1980–81 is that only the Party wanted to publicize the nasty ones. Any manifestation of populist demagogy or irrational collective action, which did sometimes happen in late 1981 when hope was wearing thin, Solidarity's intellectuals generally refused to publicize; on the rare occasions they did, the events were characterized as "provocations," as if Polish workers could not generate excess but were only, at most, susceptible to it.[15] But if in 1981 liberal intellectuals had no desire to wash dirty linen in public, after 1989 they seemed determined to hang it in the town square. When they spoke about workers now, they seemed to want to talk about nothing other than how irrational and illiberal they were. They highlighted unsympathetic stories of workers acting contrary to new market norms but, as the prominent industrial sociologist Wlodzimierz Pankow later put it, "ignored the thousands of examples where trade unions, as well as the enterprise councils under their control, pressured management to bring about real reform of their firms, and often took the initiative in drawing up the reform programs themselves."[16]

Instead, the themes of labor danger and irrationality peppered the pages of newspapers. At one point in 1990, *Gazeta Wyborcza* editor-in-chief Adam Michnik, no longer a Solidarity member, wrote that the unionists taking part in a certain strike were betraying the ideals of Solidarity—as if workers were so dangerous that it was not enough for liberals to have taken over labor's political leadership but ought to run the trade union as well. And this problem was hardly confined to *Gazeta Wyborcza*. In her content analysis of Poland's two leading political weeklies, Wieslawa Kozek points to a consistent pattern of maligning and disparaging unions, and not just in the articles themselves. Most of the *titles* of *Polityka* and *Wprost* articles on labor in the 1990s emphasized dysfunctionality, as if trade unions did nothing but make unreasonable demands, sabotage negotiations, occupy buildings, and contribute to the economic decline even of healthy enterprises. Accompanying photographs are "full of negative associations," the rank and file depicted as dangerous and aggressive, their leaders as disheveled and isolated. Almost all the articles concern conflict with management or government; almost none are about successful collective bargaining.[17]

In 1990, workers were afraid, and scared people often act badly. In the past, those who acted badly were protected by those who didn't need to act badly, because both were united against the Party; in this new age, the scared people who acted badly were vilified for their bad actions by those hopeful about the future. Those who hope that things will improve by the workings of the system are always threatened by the anger of the frightened, since that anger threatens to upset precisely what makes the hopeful hopeful. And so the "calm hopeful" seek to protect their interests by organizing anger against the angry. They make the "fearful angry" the target of disdain. Hence the nastiness of the reports on labor actions of the time. The same intellectuals who whitewashed workers in 1980 did whatever they could to muddy their names ten years later. For they now saw both "labor" and labor as the obstacles to building the new order, the obstacles to reason and progress.

Ignoring Anger, Producing a Political Right

In her work on the sociology of emotions, Arlie Hochschild speaks of the connections between status and the right to anger, between class and the perceived rationality and legitimacy of perceptions. Her basic argument—that people of lower classes and lower status are accorded less "right" to their emotions, rendered less able to have their anger and frustrations accepted as legitimate—is, I think, central to understanding how liberal hegemony can backfire, as in Poland.

Hochschild often expresses the issue in gender terms: "When a man expresses anger, it is deemed 'rational' or understandable anger, anger that indicates not weakness of character but deeply held conviction. When women express an equivalent degree of anger, it is more likely to be interpreted as a sign of personal instability. It is believed that women are more emotional, and this very belief is used to invalidate their feelings."[18] Liberal comportment in Poland, beginning in the mid-1980s, suggests that this is a good analogy to their own relationship to labor. We can recall Michnik's abusive characterization of union activists (1985), Solidarity's refusal to countenance early unionist attempts to go legal (1987), the distrust of strikes in 1988–89, the disparagement of strikes in 1990, the reluctance of the post-1989 liberal press to discuss labor hardships, the fear that labor expression of economic anger would only promote "social explosion," the refusal of political liberals to seek labor votes, even the changing iconography of the labor hero from manual laborer in 1980 to laborer-as-businessman in 1989—all of this speaks of the conviction that workers' anger is not to be trusted, that their emotionality always verges on the dangerous.

Hochschild argues that this denigration of the emotions of the weak leads to a belittling of their rationality as well. "The lower our status, the more our manner of seeing and feeling is subject to being discredited, and the less believable it becomes. An 'irrational' feeling is the twin of an invalidated perception. A person of lower status has a weaker claim to the right to define what is going on; less trust is placed in her judgments; and less respect is accorded to what she feels."[19] Here Hochschild calls attention to how easy it is for elites to disregard the complaints of the powerless, to stigmatize *a priori* their demands as but an understandable but thoroughly impeachable response to their loss. Polish liberals' continual disregard for the perceptions of those whose struggles had elevated them to power seems a case in point.

What the Polish experience suggests, however, is that such a strategy of marginalization and condescension is politically both naïve and counterproductive, bound to lead ultimately to the liberals' own decline. In the first place, this approach gave labor no role to play except that of cheerleader for the elite. A sub-elite of factory-level Solidarity officials would help bring change to firms, but everyone else was to do nothing except go to work and support those on top creating the new class society. Second, it left workers no legitimate way to express their anger, and not even any legitimate reason to feel anger. According to the guardians of reason, one was allowed to be upset about the past, but not about the present.

As we saw in the previous chapter, the depth of the economic recession made this approach politically unsustainable. Though not yet clear to the liberals, who were busy governing the country and believing that their Solidarity origins guaranteed them continued rank-and-file support, this soon became clear to Walesa and some of his allies, chiefly Lech and Jaroslaw Kaczynski, twin brothers long active in Solidarity politics but outside the liberal network then in power. And so Walesa declared a "war at the top," a political struggle aimed at toppling the liberal leadership he had earlier put in place, while the Kaczynskis formed a new party, the Center Alliance, focused around a Walesa run for the presidency. Whereas the liberals sought to wish anger away and mobilize everyone behind "reason," these others—let's call them "conservatives"—recognized that reform could succeed only by capturing rather than avoiding anger, by "articulating and using politically the protest against" the pain.[20] They were conservatives precisely because of the price they were willing to pay: to preserve economic liberalism, they proposed limitations on political liberalism. That is, they recognized that anger stemmed from economic reasons, but offered political palliatives as analgesic. Claiming that the economic problems were the result of a weak and "talkative" parliament, the continued domination of "communists," and a lax moral environment, the conservatives offered a program based on political authoritarianism, restrictions on unpopular groups and views, and the legislation of moral values. But theirs was not, the conservatives stressed, an antireform program. On the contrary, they presented their program as one of *accelerated* reform; they wanted a *faster* transition to capitalism. Their aim, in short, was to preserve economic liberalism at the cost of political liberalism, and to propel themselves to power in the process.

The conservatives made their political appeal directly and specifically to labor. Unlike the liberals who ignored workers, the right saw them as its chief social base. Walesa in early 1990 fired a Mazowiecki supporter as editor of *Solidarity Weekly* and installed Jaroslaw Kaczynski, who promptly filled the union paper's pages with attacks on communists and liberals, exposés of corruption, and paeans to the Church. Under Kaczynski's stewardship, *Solidarity Weekly* wrote a great deal about enemies and very little on trade unions. One irate unionist wrote a letter asking why the paper never printed information about workers' basic rights, such as how to combat layoffs.[21] The answer, of course, was that the conservatives identified labor's enemy not as an economic but as a political other. Workers, they said, had a right, even a responsibility, to be angry. But that anger needed to be directed at former communists allegedly still running things and at the governing liberals allowing communist control to continue. Far from targeting capitalism, the conservatives said labor was hurting because there wasn't *enough* capitalism, or because the existing capitalists were really communists.

For economic liberalism, this strategy had the merit of diverting potential anger onto safer waters. For political liberalism, the consequences were quite detrimental. First, the conservatives deployed a vindictive style that had always been lacking in Solidarity—hurling invective at everyone associated with the former Party and claiming that by negotiating the Round Table accords the liberals were complicit with the old regime. Second, their proposed target was completely off-base. Persecuting "communists," after all, was not going to help labor. The new market society imposed new dynamics of stratification based on controlling assets rather than political titles, and, as discussed in chapter 1, former dissidents (including the Kaczynskis) had become prominent in the new elite.[22] Conservatives were offering only a "symbolic appeasement" unable to produce any "appeasement in fact," and such a combination, as Piven and Cloward show in their classic book on protest movements, leads to anger "escaping the boundaries [of] political norms."[23] In Poland, this meant promoting a witch-hunt mentality in which economic problems came to be seen as the result of bad individuals, not bad contracts or systemic inequities. Labor was being mobilized not to seek economic redress of economic problems, but to seek retribution against imagined scapegoats. It was being mobilized, in other words, to challenge economic liberalism through political illiberalism.

Liberals initially responded to the challenge by complaining about it and urging the conservatives to stop "destroying our unity." Instead of the formation of several Solidarity parties, they wanted there to be only one, under their control. Only when Walesa and the conservatives refused to abide did they form their own organization, the Democratic Union. But if liberals were angry with the conservatives, they were disappointed with workers. The difference is telling. You cannot be angry with those who do not know what they're doing, and the liberals believed, as in Hochschild's account, that workers really did not know what they were doing, but were only falling victim to political demagogues seeking to arouse their emotions. The theme of disappointment, tinged with fear, emerged even more strongly in the aftermath of the 1990 presidential elections. Walesa defeated Mazowiecki so soundly in the first round of voting that second place was actually taken by Stan Tyminski, a successful and shadowy émigré businessman from Canada with close ties to the former secret police who argued that if everyone wanted a market economy so badly, they should vote for the one candidate who personally knew something about it. Tyminski got his strongest support among the heart of the new working class, workers between the ages of 18 and 29 without college education living in small and medium-sized cities. Indeed, this group he won outright, beating Walesa.[24]

Rather than take this group as a challenge—how to win their votes?—liberals chose to present them simply as a threat. They portrayed them as part of what is often called "Poland 'B'"—the "other" Poland—inhabited by those who don't read books,[25] or as budding fascists,[26] or as an incurable "homo sovieticus."[27] Even liberal sociologists wrote this way, leading one to caustically remind her colleagues that democratic participation does not require a university degree.[28] Liberals acted as if the population were not worthy of its leaders. It was as if they wished to do what Bertolt Brecht had ironically advised the East German Communist Party forty years earlier: dissolve the people and elect another.

In the event, the liberals took their 1990 defeat as a chance to show their mettle. If people rejected sound policies, the liberals would demonstrate their honor by continuing those policies anyway, magnanimously disregarding the people's judgment in order to best serve those same people. While some argued that they would ultimately be rewarded electorally for their perseverance, others argued that this did not matter. They were doing good for Poland, and if the voters disagreed, well, the voters would get a good system anyway. With aristocratic élan they argued that they did not need the people's applause. And indeed, a curious thing began to happen: they started explicitly shunning applause. They began to equate popularity with "populism"—the derisive term with which they now dismissed criticisms from both left and right—and took their own *lack* of support as the surest sign of the justness of their cause. They argued, both to themselves and to a highly receptive media, that since the reforms were "painful," people naturally rejected such reforms, and as the chief messengers of reform, they would naturally meet rejection by the people as well. Their loss of support came to be treated not as a cause for alarm but as a sign of authenticity. Just as the old Polish gentry once saw business as defilement, their intellectual heirs now saw politics as defilement. Governing, of course, was fine: they considered themselves preeminent leaders, and they were happy to ally with anyone who recognized and utilized their expertise (except "ex-communists," even though they increasingly had most in common with them). When it came to such matters as gaining a base and winning elections, however, they kept a correct gentlemanly distance.

In September 1993 I had an instructive conversation with Piotr Morel (not his real name), an official of the Democratic Union in the city of Rzeszow. A parliamentary election campaign was in full swing, and the votes of depressed industrial communities like Rzeszow and its surroundings would be crucial in deciding the outcome. (Deputies were elected in province-wide slates, so the Rzeszow organizer was responsible for the towns and cities nearby, such as Mielec.) But when I asked Morel what he was doing to win the votes of laborers frightened about their future, he responded simply, pleasantly, and without hesitation, "Nothing." I pressed him. Surely the party must be trying to do something to convince such voters that the Democratic Union represented their interests. But he looked at me as if I was quite dense. "The fact is that we *don't* represent their interests," he replied. He continued:

> We don't have anything to offer them. For things to get better, these people are going to have to suffer even more. We don't like it, but there's nothing we can do about it. And nothing we should *try* to do, because that will only postpone the improvement. We believe in honesty. Our role is to tell it like it is. If this wins their votes—well, we hope so, but that's not the point. There's nothing else we can do. We tell them things will get worse for them. Because that's the truth.

It is worth lingering a moment over these comments. On the one hand, note the compulsive desire to be "honest" and "tell the truth," mantras liberals repeated over and over in the early 1990s, as if a hangover from the "anti-political" days of "bearing witness" and "living in truth." Yet the injunction to be honest was actually quite duplicitous—or perhaps self-duplicitous, it is hard to know which. Before I go deeper, however, one point: my argument does not concern whether or not there "really was" an alternative to shock therapy. That is simply the wrong way of posing the question, both because there was no single "shock therapy" anyway (as Orenstein shows, Poland changed course on many specific policies),[29] and because that turns a political issue into a technocratic one. Rather, my point is that the liberals' approach betrays a fundamental misunderstanding of what democracy is and how best to consolidate it, and that it was intellectually dishonest as well. In the end, their approach was disingenuous, ineffective, and detrimental to the consolidation of the liberal *politics* that they also represented, the promulgation of which was potentially their chief contribution to the creation of a just postcommunist polity.

In the first place, then, Morel's comments about honesty forget that parties are about saying, not just doing. Liberals claimed they could not appeal to labor because they could not deliver the goods. But parties gain an electorate not just by delivering goods but by expressing concern, and by offering symbolic concessions that convey that concern. Sometimes the liberals did seem to understand this, but never in relation to labor, suggesting an element of duplicity in their alleged frankness. (The liberal government of early 1993 offered to revise the budget in order to keep a small agrarian party in the governing coalition, while insisting to the trade unions that "honesty" and "responsibility" for the budget prevented them from making *any* budgetary adjustments to pay for public-sector pay increases mandated by law.) In this sense, Morel's claim that the only thing the Democratic Union could honestly "offer" workers was additional suffering was in part just a ploy aimed at keeping labor from making demands.

Second, Morel's comments show how "honesty" and "truth-telling" were consciously equated with the liberals' particular partisan program. Whatever they say is by definition the difficult truth, and others who have different opinions may be pitied, but not taken seriously. The stance presumes that they alone know what's right. To claim that they're the ones "telling the truth" is to claim that anyone telling a different story is not telling the truth. This endows them not just with a smugness but with an unimpeachable defense of smugness: all we're doing is telling the truth. That they're willing to suffer electoral defeat for this only makes them seem all the more heroic.

And yet they did, of course, hope to get electoral *reward* for this, suggesting another level of duplicity. "Honesty" and "self-sacrifice" simply became the icons of their partisan identity. Telling people life would get worse and demonstrating a readiness to perish politically rather than "lie" were the themes they hoped to ride to power. Yet here their approach also betrayed an ignorance of electoral behavior and psychology. People rarely vote for parties that claim to be better than them. And while one might admire a group willing to sacrifice itself, why should anyone want to see such a group come to power, where the aim is not to be honest but to improve lives?

Finally, of course, the liberals were not losers at all. They were the beneficiaries of transition, the new elite, and they knew that. Their power stemmed chiefly from their social, educational, and political capital, easily transferable to the economic arena (if not necessarily into economic capital) by making them good professionals and desirable consultants.[30] And so their willingness, even eagerness, to perform the role of those who would give up their power in order to serve the cause of reason was itself a disingenuous act, based on denying the real sources of power in the new era and ultimately aimed only at enhancing their influence by adding electoral office to their asset base. That it was also an ineffective act was clear to everyone but themselves, although with the steady drop of poll numbers they eventually had to face facts too.

Why this liberal cynicism (and eventual self-destruction) was a problem for *democracy*, however, is that the liberals were the most consistent defenders of tolerance and mutual respect—that is, of politically democratic principles—within the old Solidarity camp. By squandering their moral and political authority, by adopting such a hostile attitude to their labor base, they *created* a base that came to identify political liberalism with arrogance on the one hand and economic liberalism on the other. As in Yeltsin's Russia, where free-market policies succeeded in turning the word *demokrati* into a synonym for crooks, liberals in Poland ended up producing a substantial Solidarity electorate ready to accept the view, from emerging right-wing parties, that an open and mutually respectful civil society was merely a cover for economic oppression. Their fatal flaw, so dangerous to the political principles they held dear, was to really come to believe that liberal democracy could be grounded solely in private property, that "bourgeois society" was the sole foundation of "civil society." This new view, of course, was in direct contradiction to their profound democratic insight—the insight, developed in practice from about 1976 to 1981, that made Solidarity possible in the first place—that civil society could be built without reference to both state and market. Moreover, the new view had dramatic political repercussions. With it, the liberals handed their opponents a foolproof mode of attack. By now identifying a democratic civil society with an inegalitarian capitalist society, they enabled the political right to stifle the former by presenting its attempt to do so as merely an attack on the latter. Liberals thus helped the right win labor support for its campaign against inclusive liberal democracy.

The liberals were also wrong to think that market capitalism in Poland was ever really jeopardized. Contrary to what they believed, the liberals were hardly the indispensable key to its consolidation. Other political groups pretended to be opposed to it, but this was either an organizing strategy or a temporary conviction of which they would soon be disabused, meaning it would *then* become an organizing strategy. The key question in the early postcommunist years was not whether capitalism would emerge but what kind of capitalism it would be.[31] In what capacity would labor be incorporated? In what kind of polity would it be embedded? Other groups, in other words, came to recognize that the fight over the market was really a political fight. Only the liberals persisted in their rather quaint but ultimately destructive belief that the market had to be established first, without political conflict. Only they believed that political conflict would be damaging to the market. In the end, only they misunderstood the importance of anger. They did not accept the key role played by anger directed *at* the market in *consolidating* even a *liberal* market society. And this misunderstanding ultimately allowed the right to organize that anger for illiberal ends.

In the end, the liberals never did what every democratically successful bourgeois or social democratic party has always done, which is to challenge capital (or the new elite) on at least a symbolic level. They never understood that, as Luebbert has shown, only those parties that incorporate labor have a chance of succeeding, and that there can be no political stability without such incorporation.[32] Instead, they stuck to "reason" and "responsibility," ignoring the importance of symbols and emotions, and in this way brought about their own downfall.

Geremek cited "Stalin, Mao, Robespierre, Mussolini, and Hitler" as those who tapped class anger. But why not George Meany, Ramsey McDonald, or Jean Jaures? Why not Walter Ruether, Willy Brandt, or FDR? Why not all the leaders of trade unions and socialist parties that helped integrate the working class into liberal democratic systems? In the end, the liberals were so afraid of anger that they would not even speak of interests. They were so afraid of the language of interests that they convinced themselves that people didn't need such a language, either. That is, they really *did* seem to believe it was "dishonest" to appeal to labor's interests. They supported democratic capitalism but did not seem to understand that democracies flourish precisely when conflict revolves around the class interests that capitalism creates. Shunning all this, the liberals spoke only of reason. And in this way they allowed the anger that would emerge to be pitted against "reason." In this way, they helped create the right they feared.

Generating the Irrational

It is unnecessary to say much about the liberals' specific political missteps. Their steady erosion leading to their ouster from parliament altogether in 2001 speaks for itself. In 1991, for example, fresh from being defeated by Walesa, the parliamentary liberals became the strongest supporters of Walesa's prime minister. They defended virtually all his unpopular decisions without regard for electoral consequences. When the Democratic Union pulled in 12.3 percent of the vote in 1991, just edging out the ex-communist Democratic Left Alliance for first place, they interpreted the result as a resounding victory, ignoring the fact that the overwhelming majority of the 1989 Solidarity electorate had gone elsewhere.

In 1993, the liberal vote dropped to 10.6 percent, about half the total of the resurgent DLA. Instead of assessing the reasons for the continuing loss of their old social base,[33] the liberals consoled themselves for being the largest "post-Solidarity" party. (This was a fluke brought about by the fragmentation of the right: about a third of the popular vote, and a majority of the old Solidarity vote, was cast for parties unable to pass the five-percent threshold.) They then made things worse by merging with the small Liberal Democratic Congress, a new party that, like the conservatives, favored the imposition of liberal economics even at the expense of liberal politics. Its difference with the conservatives was its more overt anti-union stance, manifested in its calls to curtail labor rights in the workplace, to limit the right to strike, and to give government special powers to impose such restrictions regardless of parliamentary will. The LDC, in other words, represented the modern right, in contrast to the traditional right. Whereas the traditional right wanted to divert labor's anger, this modern liberal right sought only to suppress it. The LDC's modernizing ethos appealed to the political liberals of the Democratic Union, thus leading them to favor a merger. The resulting new party, Freedom Union, moved even further away from political liberalism and toward a market fundamentalism that would erode what remained of its labor base. Apart from the small Union of Labor party, Solidarity supporters were now left with no consistent politically liberal defenders.

The Freedom Union consecrated its market fundamentalist image by electing "shock therapy" architect Leszek Balcerowicz as its leader. Balcerowicz was perhaps the most polarizing individual of the period, his name a veritable lightning rod sure to attract discontent. Moreover, he was a poor public speaker and an inexperienced politician, his battles to that point having been won behind closed doors. Yet the liberals treated this very colorlessness as an asset. Balcerowicz would represent the cold rationality of the liberal agenda, the self-conscious eschewal of anger. Party leaders did not mind that many voters associated him with economic disaster. As a young aviation worker told me at the time, "Balcerowicz is the embodiment of why so many of us tell sociologists that we were better off under the old system." Balcerowicz served as a sign that the FU would be the party of rationality, not of popular opinion, and the party faithful stayed with him even as the FU continued its slide.

Though the party improved slightly in the 1997 elections, a result of being in opposition during the previous four years, it was easily defeated by the conservative Solidarity Electoral Action coalition. Included as junior partner in the subsequent government, the liberals entered their period of rapid decline, as the FU willingly shared responsibility for an austere and corrupt SEA administration in return for having Balcerowicz serve as the government's chief economic minister. Some party activists began sounding the alarm, recognizing rather belatedly how far from its base the party had strayed. We used to have ideas, passions, and a vision, veteran oppositionist and leading FU parliamentarian Jan Litynski wrote to his comrades. We believed in universal human rights, protecting the poor, a secular education. But we've given all this up in order to control the Finance Ministry. The ex-communists became the party of the poor, the right fought and won Christian public schools, and we're afraid even to fight for the rights of women. "When people hear us, all they hear is technical language, devoid of emotion," he complained. We speak in "the soulless voice of the technocrat." No wonder we're losing, he concluded: "We've become the party of the rich and contented."[34] In 2001, the Freedom Union did not even pass the five-percent threshold necessary for parliamentary representation.[35]

With liberals fixated on minimizing conflict, afraid to offer even symbolic support to the discontented, no wonder so many voters went to the conservatives, with their religious and nationalist bromides for class anger, or to the ex-communists, who at least had the political sense to express concern and to say that economic adjustments could always be made. By the mid-1990s it was precisely the ex-communists of the DLA who were the most politically astute liberals. The problem is that polling data demonstrated that there was a solid bloc, at least a third of the electorate, that would not vote for them no matter what. This group looked to Solidarity for guidance—meaning, by now, to one of the political groups that had emerged out of Solidarity. But with Solidarity liberals doing nothing to capture economic anger, there was no "pro-Solidarity" way to be angry at the effects of market reform *except* through the right-wing narrative. Workers turned to the right because liberal unionists were not offering them a class narrative for the class experiences they were having.

As it happened, the moderate conservatives were unable to hold onto them either. By 1995, the pro-labor extremist right wing had begun to grow, focused around people like Zygmunt Wrzodak, the populist-authoritarian Solidarity leader at the Ursus Tractor Plant in Warsaw, and Andrzej Lepper, the pugnacious champion of small farmers. Their extremism consisted less in the policies they advocated, which were never very coherent, as in their slogans and style. Both loved to revel in irreverence, thumbing their nose at "respectable" society. They denounced the rule of law, mocked parliament, and called for massive purges of "crooks" throughout society. Wrzodak red-baited liberals, hurled invectives at foreigners, and called for a pure Catholic Poland. He is known for his openly anti-Semitic remarks, his favorite charge against liberals being that they are secret "Judeo-communists." Lepper, founder of the Self-Defense Party, embraced a more secular rage, decrying liberals, parliaments, foreigners, and the European Union. Yet Lepper compensated for his religious deficiencies by being the more flamboyant and politically astute of the two. A cross between Robin Hood and Mussolini, combining the latter's bullying swagger with the former's celebration of banditry for the people, Lepper would go on to become the second most popular politician in the country, according to opinion polls conducted in 2004.[36]

It is easy to condemn these extremists, who took the conservative backlash far beyond anything the Center Alliance ever proposed. But the important question is why this extremist, outlandish style of opposition got the support that it did. In 2001, both Wrzodak's and Lepper's parties (League of Polish Families, and Self-Defense, respectively) were voted into parliament with nearly 20 percent of the electorate between them. By 2004, opinion polls gave them about 30 percent. That such openly and eagerly irrational approaches garnered the support they did suggests that the very concept of reason had been compromised. The elite had denigrated popular opinions as "irrational"—or, to use Hochschild's terms, accorded less respect to the feelings of those with lower status—so many of the objects of their scorn responded by coming to see "reason" as but a marker of class privilege.[37] If it was going to be a codeword that only economic liberals were allowed to own, then they could reject it without remorse.

My own experience in the country at the time, and my countless conversations with those who saw themselves as the "losers" of the transformation, supports this view of the "irrational" becoming a kind of safe haven, a location from which one could not be captured by liberal discursive hegemony. I think here of the many workers I interviewed in the mid-1990s, the ones who so admired the liberals for their heroic work in building Solidarity but were so disappointed that the liberals no longer admired them. Or even more, that the liberals and their press seemed to castigate them whenever they tried to make their voices heard. Their strikes would be written off as adventurism even before anyone knew what they were about. At best, they were treated as ignorant people who simply did not understand that things were going well and that there was no alternative. At worst, they were treated as enemies who had to be kept isolated. Their anger and frustration, in short, were marked off as dangerous, irrational delusion. Small wonder that workers felt betrayed.[38] Liberals had gone from lionizing a "new working class" in 1980 to libeling it a decade later, as if they had never listened at all.

The result was that workers themselves no longer had a language with which they could get their concerns heard. If they spoke the usual language of Solidarity—that they just wanted a "normal" society, which they understood as one that included them—the liberals would say that official policies were leading precisely in that direction. If they said they wanted progress *and* a change in economic policy, liberals would explain that progress required *maintaining* economic policy and trot out citations from the West to clinch their case. The people I spoke with did not agree, but they had been pounded down by the rhetoric of rationality and could not come up with a response. They were not, after all, the equals of the liberals, either in formal education or in contacts with the West. Few workers are. And those few who were, well, they tended to be economic liberals themselves.

And so, unable to challenge shock therapy on "rational" grounds, many workers found themselves pushed to challenge it on the only grounds that seemed available: "irrational" ones. Solidarity unionists who used to loyally follow their liberal intellectual leaders now began to see that embrace as a trap. They began to see rationality itself as a trap. In this context, embracing extremism made a certain sense. With little discursive space to be both "rational" *and* critical of neoliberal economic policy, it was easier to dispense with the rationality than the need to voice their concerns.

When those with power define their knowledge as rational and label critics of their way of thinking as irrational, those without power who still want their criticisms to be heard have no choice but to embrace "irrationality." That becomes the only way to remain a player.[39] The constant berating of skeptics of the Balcerowicz Plan as irrational and illiberal led, in other words, to a split in Solidarity. While most union leaders were pushed back to the reigning orthodoxy, as evidenced by the strong pro-market attitudes of union leaders even in 1994,[40] those who still maintained their opposition were driven to exaggerate their irrationality, leading them to reject political liberalism along with economic liberalism. For irrationality provided the only space free from the smothering embrace of the liberals. Those who accepted reason and moderation could not escape co-optation by former Solidarity leaders, now uncompromising economic liberals. Those who rejected such values had the turf all to themselves. (Which meant that they also got free publicity for their views, otherwise hard to come by for activist groups in an era of legality. In authoritarian times, the mere act of protest suffices to attract attention, but in democratic times it takes more than that. There are, in other words, higher resource requirements for publicity in democracies. Breaking with "rationality," in a context in which everyone else has embraced it as part of the new consensus, was one way for new activists to attract attention.)[41]

In my conversations in the late 1990s with laborers (or farmers, or the unemployed) who were newly supporting extremist politics and politicians, what stood out was the way they felt they had regained their dignity. They no longer felt like objects of condescension. They had—there is no other way to put it—a bounce in their step that labor supporters of market rationality distinctly lacked. Having departed from the camp of "reason," they were finally free. Free to criticize. Free to have their own view of things without fear of reprimand. Once they had stepped "beyond the pale," once they were excluded from "reasonable" discussion, they no longer had to worry about what others thought. (As I show in chapter 6, something similar happened in 2001 with the factory union activists who had supported pro-market policies out of loyalty to national Solidarity. They too talked of being "liberated" when Solidarity finally withdrew from direct political involvement.)

These were people who resented not so much the decline in living standards but the stunning abandonment to which they were now subjected. They experienced the economic decline as particularly painful because their previous defenders now justified it as beneficial and in their interest. In other words, more than the economic hard times, which they had known to expect, it was the *existential* hard times that had them reeling. "In the past, when things were bad, I could go to the Party secretary and perhaps get a little help," one young Mielec woman, expecting to lose her job, told me in 1994. "Afterward, Solidarity protected us. But now that Solidarity's won, no one's interested in us any more." Labor and the poor had lost its dignity, even its nobility, which, however bogus, was not completely bogus, and was able to provide some solace under the old regime. No wonder so many became simultaneously nostalgic for the old regime and amenable to right-wing calls for moral rectitude.

Thus the curious paradox: unlike in established market societies, where strike leaders usually come from the left, they were far more likely in postcommunist Poland to come from the right. By the late 1990s, fundamentalist Christian organizations, associated with the Radio Maria radio station and the *Nasz Dziennik* newspaper, supported strikes far more than the ex-communist left, which had also embraced neoliberalism. Dissenters from the neoliberal orthodoxy found illiberals leading the way.

In the end, then, Polish workers turned to the right because the politically dominant liberals would not offer them a way both to express their discontent and remain loyal. By doing nothing to keep labor with them, by seeking to banish anger rather than to organize it, and by so vociferously claiming the language of rationality only for themselves, liberals had no chance to maintain their preeminence. And when liberals abdicated their responsibility to organize labor, conservatives and extremists stepped in, appealing to labor's class experiences and proffering non-economic enemies as the target. Paradoxically, the old Solidarity leaders stopped allowing workers to think of themselves as workers, insisting they think of themselves as citizens instead. But because this meant accepting passively the "rational" and "necessary" economic reforms, it was not a program able to capture labor support. A political group refusing to try to organize discontent only leaves that discontent politically available to others. The nationalist and religious right thus had an opening, and they played it well. Liberals pushed workers away, and conservatives pulled them in. (The DLA pulled too, but had little success with Solidarity activists raised on anticommunism.) This right spoke to labor's economic anger where the liberals would not. And even though it offered a phony non-economic solution ("symbolic appeasement"), this was enough for those many Solidarity stalwarts who would not embrace the ex-communist left. Solidarity workers turned to the right because the liberals pushed them there.

A Czech Comparison

This liberal combination of neglect, scorn, and incompetence would not have been able to so affect labor were it not for certain factors within Solidarity itself. For in a sense, Solidarity was set up to be manipulated in this way, both by the era in which it formed and the enemy against which it formed. A comparison with the post-1989 Czech unions is instructive here. While certainly no formidable power, the latter never had the kind of fawning relationship to liberal politicians that marked Solidarity. For whereas Solidarity defined itself in the struggle against communism, independent Czech unions emerged only in late 1989, at the time of nascent capitalism. Unlike in Poland, Czech labor activists had no historical, institutional, or personal ties linking them to the new government. They could not easily be persuaded to toe the neoliberal line, and their need to build up an organizational identity in fact prohibited them from doing so. As a result, whereas Polish unions simply sanctioned the Balcerowicz shock therapy package, Czech unions helped negotiate market reforms themselves, winning concessions (such as fewer layoffs, resulting in unemployment levels lower than anywhere else in Eastern Europe in the early 1990s) that their Polish counterparts could not, which in turn made workers less susceptible to the pull of right-wing parties anxious to channel class anger along other lines.[42]

What this brief comparison suggests, similar to the argument in chapter 1, is that it's best for labor (and for democracy) for unions to mobilize in opposition to economic liberals, not together with them. Better to deploy economic anger not only against the old regime but also at the new one. Better to be a negotiator in the transition than a too-willing accomplice. Better to have a liberal opponent and not a liberal ally. Unions mired in a close alliance with economic liberals, or that too eagerly accept market logic, will not be able to play their crucial democratic role as organizers of class discontent. Poland's economic liberals certainly did their best to push labor to the right, but with its overly close alliance with the liberals and their ideology, Solidarity was ready to be pushed there. Why this was so is the subject of the next chapter.

5

Communist and Postcommunist Experiences of Class

In the summer of 1994, I visited the manufacturing city of Starachowice. A city of some 60,000 residents, it boasted one large factory, the Star auto plant, which had employed some 24,000 workers in the 1970s, down to 18,000 in 1989. Now, five years and several rounds of layoffs, early retirements, and industrial restructuring later, it was left with only 5000 employees and more layoffs scheduled soon. There were 14,000 unemployed in the city, making for an unemployment rate of about 45 percent, but this did not include the 6000 people whose unemployment benefits had already expired. Inside the plant I met with two Solidarity officials, the vice president of the union at the auto assembly plant and the head of the union at the old parts division. (Like most other large manufacturing plants, Star had been broken down into several formally independent companies as a prelude to full-scale privatization, and each company now had—or, in some cases, did not have—its own trade unions as well.) When I asked them about the situation, they first spoke in a resigned way about the bad economic conditions for their workers and the city and then unleashed a torrent of angry words filled with attacks on "the communists." These were familiar comments to me, but when one went on to tell me about his "right-wing" views I affected surprise, interjecting that many people see trade unions in their very essence as leftist institutions. "Yes," he responded at once, "as unionists, we *should* be leftists. But after forty-five years of oppression by red barons, we can't be. So you're right: we should be leftists, but we aren't."

What the Starachowice leaders were saying is that postcommunist Polish labor ought to have a sense of themselves as a class, as a group with distinctly different interests from other groups, but do not. They were confirming, and themselves simultaneously pondering, the surprising fact that Polish trade unions have hardly been the forceful defender of labor's class interests that so many expected them to be. Unions have been active on the political scene since 1989. But their chief roles, particularly in the early years, were to promote market transformation at the firm level and to serve as political stepping stones for a new elite at the national level, not to defend labor interests in the workplace. Labor may have been expected to be militantly class conscious, but that has not been the case. It is the aim of this chapter to explain why.

What is "class consciousness"? I understand the term to mean only the self-perception that workers have interests distinct from those of other economic groups, and that they need to utilize the means at their disposal in order to realize those interests. Class consciousness means labor thinking of itself as representing a *particular* social group, not a universal one. (The Starachowice unionists understood this exactly. As one of them made clear later in our conversation, "We should be leftists, but we're not" meant, "We should be defending our workforce against this rising new elite, but we're not.")

This notion of class owes much to the work of Victoria Hattam.[1] For Hattam, working-class consciousness entails the recognition of labor's position as the subordinate class in a relationship between labor and capital. It is based on a recognition of weakness, not of strength. Hattam develops her approach in the context of American labor history. She distinguishes between two different discourses adopted by American labor to make sense of its predicament and to frame its collective strategies for improvement. A premodern discourse, one that she attributes to the nineteenth-century Knights of Labor, divided society into producers and nonproducers, with the former comprising both skilled labor and small capital and the latter including unskilled labor and finance capital. This way of thinking, central to much of nineteenth-century American radicalism, was based on the belief that it was possible to maintain artisanship and small manufacturing and thereby avoid the modern factory system with all the denigration and disempowerment of labor that it entailed. A countervailing discourse, emerging in the fledgling American Federation of Labor at the end of the century, was built on a very different foundation: that artisans had lost their struggle to control the labor process and that the factory system was unavoidable. Labor, in this view, had been defeated by capital. It was now a systemic subordinate, structurally unable to regain its position of dignified controller of the work process.[2] The task for a labor movement, therefore, was to gain for workers the best deal possible within a bad arrangement. Anti-producerist partisans of this new class consciousness, such as the AFL's Samuel Gompers, believed that "the world had changed in important ways, and unless workers realized their new position, they would fail to secure their interests in the modern industrial economy."[3]

It is the latter discourse that underpins a class consciousness able to secure gains for labor in a capitalist context. It is the recognition of marginality, not the presumption of strength, that allows labor to defend itself against the attacks of nascent capital. Class consciousness entails the recognition of labor's subordination, and thus of labor's particular interests in a system skewed against it. It starts not with the conviction that labor can and ought to topple capitalism. Rather, class consciousness starts when workers give up illusions about imminently eradicating capitalism and devote their efforts to getting a better deal within it. Workers, in this view, become class conscious when they organize as workers, not when they pretend they are something else.

What the Starachowice unionists, like so many other Solidarity activists in Polish manufacturing towns, told me is that they were unable to see themselves simply as workers. They kept believing they were something else. They saw themselves alternatively, and in no particular order, as citizens, liberals, Poles, Christians, and men. Everyone, of course, has multiple and "cross-cutting" identities. The point, however, is that "worker" was a secondary identity for them *even* in their role as unionists. It is this that demands explanation. For it is this that explains why Polish unionists have acted so weakly as unionists, despite their considerable post-1989 travails.

Why this weak post-1989 class identity? I give a historical answer in this chapter, focused on the sui generis way in which communism shaped class identities. In short, my argument is that communism gave workers a simultaneously exhilarating and debilitating notion of class, leading workers' movements to be extremely powerful and yet not, ultimately, concerned with the particular interests of workers.

It was exhilarating in that workers began with a sense of themselves as privileged actors and rightful rulers, members of the class that legally ruled. They didn't believe they did rule, but they could always use this abiding fiction to serve their own interests.[4] Because of this myth, workers were allowed more latitude in voicing their opinions, thus making their voice the one that could not be openly suppressed. Because of this myth, workers were the only ones who could appeal for a greater share of the pie and claim that they were thereby serving universal rather than particular interests. Because of this myth, all protest during the communist years had to be framed within the left-wing paradigm as a benefit to workers. "Worker" simply carried a clout that no other identity could match.

But it was this very exhilarating concept of class that simultaneously made it so debilitating, as well as uniquely inadequate for the postcommunist market economy. For since to be a worker meant representing universal interests, it did not mean representing labor's interests per se. Because labor was a universal category, it could not be a particular one. This had powerful political implications. For since workers were the only ones allowed to speak out,[5] any group that wanted to speak out had to claim that they were workers. In the end, the fact that all movements against communism had to pose as movements in defense of workers—that is, as movements aimed at truly realizing communism's aims—only meant that the real interests of workers *as workers* were always occluded, always subordinated to general interests. And when "general interests" came to be interpreted as promotion of a market economy and creation of an entrepreneurial class, labor rather naturally became subordinated to that. In other words, the same universality of class that made all East European uprisings seem like "real" workers' revolutions—and that made western leftists so sympathetic and envious—left workers unable to articulate their own particular interests as workers.

Labor, we might say, was too strong to recognize that it was weak. And its failure to recognize its weakness prevented it from developing a sense of its own particularity, and kept it from undertaking effective action to defend its particular interests. This points to a fundamental difference with capitalist economies. It is not that the concept of class comes to workers naturally in capitalist societies. On the contrary, there are numerous other paradigms that compete for workers' allegiance, most notably *capital's* universalist paradigm, according to which profits for the boss (or shareholders) are beneficial to everyone.[6] The point is that trade unions, in capitalist society, by the very fact of arising, necessarily introduce a moment of particularity. Trade unions challenge the classless ideology of capital with their assertion that the capitalist workplace and society are spheres of competing interests. A trade union in capitalist society *constitutes* labor's assertion of particularity, of having discrete interests because of its role in the production process, of representing a class other. By challenging capital's claim to represent everyone's interests, trade unions inexorably introduce the concept of class.[7] This, after all, is why both I and my Starachowice interlocutors could understand that trade unions "ought" to be leftist.

But such assumptions do not hold in communist society. The concepts and experiences of "class," "worker," and "trade union" mean something very different than they do in capitalist society. And so if we are to understand the roots of postcommunist labor's weakness, the causes of its inability to assert its particular interests, we must look at the meaning of class in the communist context. My claim is that labor came to adopt a concept of class based in the communist experience, which made it particularly vulnerable in conditions of a capitalist experience. Communist class practices produced a specific way of behaving, and a specific type of collective action, that led labor away from the class consciousness necessary to protect it in the future market economy.

In the rest of the chapter, I shall explore the impact of the past on practices and ideas in the post-1989 era. I will show why political movements in communist society had to manifest themselves as workers' movements, and explore the implications this has had on workers ever since.

The Communist Construction of Class

Theoretically, the nature of the problematic legacy that the communist experience left for labor can best be stated in paradoxical Marxist terms as follows: Polish labor acted as a class-for-itself, but it never constituted a class-*in*-itself. On the face of it, of course, this makes no sense. Class-in-itself refers only to the objective group of industrial workers; it would seem to exist necessarily. In the Marxist paradigm, only class-for-itself is a contingent category. It applies when labor appears on the political stage aware of its clout and asserting its long-term interests. The Marxist project is aimed at turning the dormant in-itself into an active for-itself. To have a class-for-itself without a class-in-itself thus makes no sense in Marxist theory. But that is because Marxism, like most social science, speaks to the experiences of *capitalist* society. The paradox does, however, capture the special nature of communist society, where the objective parameters of the working class were always unclear, but where political opposition could only be expressed in the name of that class. The result was a concept of "working class" that did not refer to workers per se.

The objective parameters of the working class become blurred when a self-proclaimed working-class party comes to power and nationalizes all property. At once, virtually all citizens become employees of the state-owner, deprived of control over the product of their labor, and thus, objectively, part of the working class-in-itself.[8] More important, everyone can claim subjective membership in the working class as well, as "worker" becomes an honorific, the equivalent of the liberal democratic "citizen." Both these facts determined the historical outcome that all grand opposition movements in postwar Eastern Europe were framed as workers' movements. It is not only that the ruling Party, because of its ideology, was vulnerable to movements framed this way. (As Lawrence Goodwyn laconically puts it, the "official ideology did not make it operationally simple for party functionaries to oppose workers on theoretical grounds.")[9] The important point is that communist property structures *pushed* opposition to be framed this way. Any intellectual interested in organizing political opposition could claim to do so on behalf of workers—*and* be convinced that he was sincere. And insofar as opposition movements were about securing greater freedom, not changing property structures—a topic both politically off-limits and existentially irrelevant, since there was no private property to begin with—workers could go along with all such opposition movements and treat them as their own.

We see this in the long legacy of opposition movements in Poland (and elsewhere in Eastern Europe). Each was portrayed internally as a movement on behalf of labor, but inexorably came to focus on political demands not strictly related to workers. This was quite clear in 1956, for example. When the army quelled the original labor upheaval in Poznan in June, revisionist intellectuals took their place and presented their own movement as in the interests of Polish workers. No doubt it was. The point, however, is that the revisionist movement did not concern itself with the particular workplace issues that had galvanized the workers in June. Those workers, in Poznan, had originally organized themselves due to anger over new piecework and production norms that led to wage losses and a deterioration in job safety.[10] The revisionists organized around the calls for political freedom and enterprise self-management—important issues for workers too, but neither of them speaking to the concerns for which Poznan's workforce sought redress. Significantly, even when the self-management movement spread across the country, it never became strong in Poznan.

Such was the general pattern in the communist era: whenever labor mobilization became politically institutionalized—meaning whenever protests took place not just in the workplace or on the streets but also in institutions with access to the media, becoming a legitimately accepted challenge to the Party—labor interests took a back seat to universal ones. This is perhaps most clearly borne out in the Solidarity movement of 1980–81. A lot has been written about whether the union was created by workers or intellectuals,[11] but posing the question this way misses the point. Solidarity was undoubtedly *created* by workers, who went on strike in August 1980 and stayed on strike until the authorities acquiesced to the existence of an independent union, something intellectuals thought the Party would never allow. But once the union was formed, it quickly lost its labor focus.[12] It was a working-class trade union but a universalist political movement, always emphasizing civic rights over labor conditions. Ideologically and politically, Solidarity followed the path laid out by opposition intellectuals, pushing for an open civil society, not for labor empowerment.

This does not mean workers gained nothing. Thanks to the existence of an independent and very active union, flush with revolutionary success, workers immediately secured greater clout at the workplace. Here, Solidarity was able to push through numerous changes beneficial to workers, such as close observance of safety rules, favorable adjustments in production norms, fair distribution of benefits, and, of course, protection of workers involved in political activity. But at a national level, where the ideas and the future of the union would be shaped, the leadership regularly abandoned class issues for civic ones. If organizations are shaped by their founding circumstances and styles, as institutional theory tells us, Solidarity was shaped as an organization that cared not so much about benefits for workers as about the secure existence of an open public sphere.

My point is not to criticize Solidarity's choices. It made perfect sense to insist on the right to organize as *the* central issue; since recognition of that right required systemic transformation, it made sense to emphasize political issues as well. Workers, as citizens, had interests that extended beyond workplace concerns. Many highly skilled workers, moreover, harboring ambitions of leaving factory work, valued their autonomy and dignity more than money and social benefits.[13] Nevertheless, by regularly subordinating class demands to civic ones, Solidarity confirmed, and institutionalized, a pattern whereby labor did not engage in public political action over labor concerns. Produced by communist structures themselves, this pattern would have profound implications for the future. For it meant that post-1989 trade unions, unlike those that emerge in market societies, were formed without a class-specific identity. By articulating the democratic demands of all, they largely ignored the specific demands of labor. This was not such a problem in the communist era, when workers had privileged systemic claims on the national income, and had hidden, non-political ways of defending their interests. But it would be a major problem in the postcommunist era, when the new capitalism legitimated vast inequalities and workers were left with no privileged claim whatsoever. In the future, in other words, labor would need a strong organization fighting for its *own* interests. By setting itself up as an organization committed to universal interests only, Solidarity adopted a strategy and policy that left it vulnerable precisely when success was achieved.

The point, then, is that when labor conflicts in the communist era entered the *public sphere*—the space where civic, economic, and political issues are discussed openly by independent organizations representing differing sides[14]—universal as opposed to labor-specific issues always took priority. "Labor" was a powerful identity in the communist era, but when deployed in the public sphere, it did not and could not refer to labor alone. Workers were able to have great clout, but they exerted that clout only on behalf of all, not on behalf of themselves. Without accepted class *divisions* to appeal to (that is, without a clear sense of the boundaries of "class-in-itself"), workers could only use the language and imagery of class to promote policies that did not benefit them in particular. Labor, in short, did not and could not defend itself through politics.

The Hidden Mechanisms of Labor Influence

How then did it defend itself, if not through politics? What *were* the mechanisms through which labor improved its conditions in the communist era? Unlike workers in market societies, who bettered their lives by organizing unions and movements, workers in communist societies improved their lives thanks both to the communist system itself and to "hidden bargaining" in the workplace. The Party provided benefits without workers demanding them, and workers were able to change policies to their benefit without political mobilization.

As for the Party providing benefits, it must be remembered that Eastern Europe's ruling communist parties were workers' parties too. Before coming to power they recruited heavily among workers, fought for better working conditions, staged militant strikes, and led struggles to build trade unions. Coming to power changed a great deal, in the way that power always transforms the aspirations and programs of social movements, and turned many "proletarian power" communists into "state power" Stalinists, treating workers as fodder for long-term development strategies. But many communists always had misgivings about Stalinism,[15] and when Stalin died, "revisionism" emerged, and draconian Stalinist-era laws maximizing workloads and criminalizing absenteeism gave way to that most benign of communist methods for holding onto power: the social contract. The unwritten pact this phrase denotes, in which the Party promises labor an increasing standard of living in return for political quiescence, came about not only because of labor protest but because it better fit the sensibilities of those who had become communists in the first place: to aid the oppressed, not to become oppressors themselves. In the post-Stalinist period, ruling communist parties tried to recapture some of their roots as working-class organizations by passing beneficial social welfare legislation and becoming increasingly sensitive to consumer needs.

What is most important about post-Stalinist policies from the point of view of the labor movement such policies produced is that they were done *without* negotiations with independent trade unions, *without* direct public pressure exerted by labor representatives. Indeed, the most significant (but least noted) aspect of the whole "social contract" paradigm is precisely the passive nature of the transaction. Labor wins benefits *but does not have to fight for them*. A look at the historical record clearly demonstrates this. In contrast to students of social policy in the West, one cannot identify, in the communist era, a political constellation or "class coalition" forcing the state to pass specific pieces of social welfare legislation. Unlike historians of pluralist polities, we cannot point to the social protests, press campaigns, political discussion, parliamentary debate, declarations of trade unions, or protocols of meetings between unions and government in order to learn what kind of pressure led to what kind of beneficial outcomes. When communist governments expanded old-age pensions or improved workplace disability insurance, they did so on their own, because they believed it was necessary. They may have been responding to perceived pressure, but the point is that it was *perceived* pressure, not the direct pressure that access to the political public sphere allows in liberal democratic systems.

Take, for example, the important changes made in bonus policy in Polish enterprises. Originally intended to be allocated according to individual performance and percentage of plan fulfillment, by the 1970s bonuses were essentially converted into de facto pay supplements guaranteed to all. This constituted an important benefit to laborers. Yet it did not come about as a result of unions formally expressing such a demand to management or the state. There were no formal negotiations between conflicting parties, no model collective bargaining agreement establishing such a pattern. Rather, the government began implementing this policy without workers having to fight for it openly. This pattern prevailed throughout the bloc. Soviet labor got greater access to consumer goods during the Brezhnev era, as did Czechoslovak labor after 1968, and Bulgarian labor got more enterprise self-management in 1982, also without organizing politically for such results. Workers in the communist era defended themselves in *informal, non-public* ways. They secured economic gains without public political conflicts.

If repression blocked workers from entering the public political sphere, concessions convinced most that they didn't need to be there. Indeed, ruling communist parties always added concessions to repression in order to win workers back. For one of the features of the communist system was that it *needed* to seek working-class support. Party leaders could not behave like military dictators in Latin America or Greece, who responded to labor militance by ignoring labor's needs, introducing pro-business policies that led to drastically deteriorating working conditions, enhanced inequality, and a rapid erosion of social benefits.[16] Military juntas have usually sought to penalize workers and favor the middle class and bourgeoisie. In communist society, however, there were no other classes to favor. In the absence of elections, and with an official Marxist ideology, there was no way for the party to legitimate its crackdown on workers *except* to try to improve conditions for workers.

The peculiar way that the labor-state relationship played itself out thus dissuaded workers from believing they needed a formal political presence to help their specific class interests. They might come to believe they needed a political presence to defend and demand *other* values, such as autonomy, dignity, and democracy. But their experiences led them away from recognizing that they needed such a presence to insure benefits like higher wages. They did not need politics to defend their interests as workers. (Of course, when the Party grew unable to fulfill its end of the social contract, things changed. It was food price hikes and other austerity measures in the 1970s that led Polish workers to finally demand their own union, Solidarity. But things had not yet changed much: they used that union, as I have shown, to fight more for civic rights than labor benefits.)

While the communist system could not allow formal, public bargaining with independent unions, it did allow labor a voice in various informal ways. This is what has been called "hidden bargaining."[17] If the ideological origins of the Party led to the social contract that benefited labor, the economic foundations of state socialism caused the hidden bargaining that also benefited labor.

Labor's hidden clout derived from the system's endemic labor shortages, which resulted not from physical scarcity (even though communist labor participation rates were the highest in the world), but from management's chronic need for resources with which to fulfill the plan. As is well known, it was difficult to fire workers in state socialist economies. For some managers, however, it was more difficult to *hire* them. For far from wanting to fire laborers, managers had a stake in hiring as many as possible. Wages were a "free" resource paid by the state, and managers always wanted extra workers on hand in order to increase the likelihood of fulfilling the production plan, on which managerial earnings and promotion depended. Moreover, in a system that saw bigger firms as better firms, having more workers meant having more clout, more "political capital," which could be used to extract extra subsidies from the planners. This led to the tight labor markets that gave workers their informal leverage.

This leverage derived first of all from the right to switch jobs. Individual workers left (or threatened to leave) when a different employer promised an apartment, access to scarce goods, or higher pay. Since wage guidelines were centrally imposed, managers eager to retain workers devised innovative ways to influence take-home pay levels, such as transfer to a new job characterization or manipulation of piece-rates. Piece-rates—or the payment of workers according to the number of tasks done rather than the number of hours worked—for example, were set at the enterprise level and so might be adjusted artificially in order to increase the effective wage of certain categories of skilled workers, and used either to lure them away or to keep them from leaving.[18]

While skilled workers were best positioned to benefit from this kind of bargaining, even unskilled workers found themselves the objects of recruitment. For supply shortages and bottlenecks meant that management sought to have on hand as many laborers as possible when supplies finally came in. Even firms whose workers often found themselves with nothing to do tried to bring in more, for managers never knew when the extra hands might be useful. It is this situation that probably led to the change in bonus policy. Since piece-rate adjustment would not satisfy those whose labor was frequently left unused anyway, managers needed to offer such laborers a share of firm revenues regardless of individual output. Or perhaps the change in bonus policy followed from workers grumbling about unpaid bonuses due to supply bottlenecks causing output decline that were no fault of their own. In a system that sought to identify labor grievances in order to prevent them from taking dangerous form, such a complaint would naturally move its way to the top, with both enterprise and local Party authorities pressuring higher-ups to do something about it.[19]

Firms, in other words, were an arena of constant bargaining and negotiation between workers and management, all of it kept hidden from the public eye. And it was only here, in this informal sphere, and not in the political public sphere, that labor could win concrete economic benefits.

The upshot of hidden bargaining is that workers did not need to organize politically along class lines in order to win economic improvements. Rather, the state socialist system allowed for gains to be won precisely through the *eschewal* of political mobilization; this is what the social contract was all about. Labor needed class mobilization in order to fight for universal interests, not particular economic ones. So when it did organize publicly, or politically, it did so to fight for non-economic conditions. This made its alliance with intellectuals more natural—and also more debilitating for a future labor movement that would have to organize publicly to defend its *own* interests.[20]

The Cold War's Construction of Class

Internal structural factors are not the only ones that shape experiences and understandings of class. International contexts matter too. I'd like to briefly explore four factors connected to the international context of the Cold War and its aftermath that help explain weak postcommunist class consciousness, or why the Starachowice unionists say they "should be leftists, but are not."

1) *The ideology of anticommunism.* If the structural legacy of communism

helps explain the weakness of class, so does the ideological legacy of anti-communism. For the fight against communism was organized successfully around an essentially liberal paradigm. Opposition was mobilized around the slogans of freedom and human rights; class was the language of the enemy.[21] Even where the original civil society theorists such as Michnik, Kuron, Havel, Konrad, and Kis embraced left-wing ideas of active citizenship and full participation, theirs was the leftism of the New Left, with its cult of autonomy and individuality, not the old left, with its theory of class struggle. Solidarity, with its focus on autonomy and self-determination, embraced a liberal discourse early on. The union repeatedly emphasized procedural over substantive outcomes. As a result, when the procedural problems were finally resolved with the coming of political democracy in 1989, Solidarity had no working-class program to reach back to. Instead it became increasingly mired in a liberal pro-market ideology, following its former intellectual advisers who, while maintaining their focus on individual rights, revised their theoretical views quite dramatically in ways I have already discussed. The very language that in 1980 both underpinned and promoted an engaged civil society, providing the theoretical foundation for the struggle against communism, was used after 1989 to legitimate policies aimed at creating and empowering a new dominant class. When the new class economy emerged, labor was stuck, as it were, in a discourse embracing the ideology of the wrong class.[22]

2) *The ideology of the Cold War.* For all of their differences, both sides in the Cold War agreed that the working class occupied a subordinate role under capitalism. Communist ideology claimed that capitalism oppressed workers, while capitalist ideology claimed that workers gained enormous benefits in return for allowing business to shape the economy and dominate public life. As it became obvious to all that workers in the West (more precisely, the North-West, not Latin America) had indeed attained standards of living unimaginable in the East, the capitalist claim seemed to be more persuasive. It was, of course, constructed on myths: western labor made its gains not by passively allowing business to shape the economy but by forming strong class organizations and, in western Europe, large socialist parties that challenged the rights of business and insisted on labor's economic inclusion. *That* history, however, was largely unknown in Eastern Europe, since the strong role of labor in shaping modern western capitalism ran counter to the official ideologies of both sides. East Europeans thus tended to read the western experience as confirmation of the myth that it is the domination of capital and the passivity of labor that brings wealth to labor, thus leading many workers to believe that class interests were best served by abjuring class consciousness. This leads into the next reason for the decline of class.

3) *The collapse of socialism.* The trade union movement has always needed

socialist intellectuals, not only to mediate interactions with the elite but to provide the convincing narratives able to win potential members over to class paradigms, and inoculate them against the competing pulls of religious, ethnic, and paternalist communitarian claims.[23] The collapse of socialism, however, and more specifically the abandonment of socialist ideology by intellectuals, turned the language of class into something both distasteful and unfashionable. Opposition activists who had deployed it in the past, when it was both necessary for entry into the public sphere and experientially plausible, came to see the very category as a dangerous relic of state socialism, something that could only damage the transition process. Not even many scholars seem interested in the concept, which is quite paradoxical, since the building of a capitalist class society has been presented as the key goal of transition.[24] (Part of the same phenomenon is the habit of referring to the new dominant classes as simply the "middle class," which prevents one from having to talk about class formation as a process of empowerment and disempowerment.) Even the social democratic successors to the old communist parties rarely speak of class, and almost never of socialism. Their success is due to their defense of, and association with, the old welfare states, not class struggle. In short, the discrediting of socialism and the abandonment of socialist ideology (in favor of liberalism) even by left-wing intellectuals,[25] leaves no inclusive democratic ideology promoting independent working-class organization, and has meant that even trade unions are frequently seen as unnecessary or harmful institutions. Whereas socialism helped consolidate democracy in the West, its absence helps discredit democracy in the East.

4) *Personal experience.* It is wrong to say that East European workers experienced capitalism only after 1989. Hundreds of thousands had already had that experience—as temporary and usually illegal workers in the West. This was particularly true for Poles and Yugoslavs, thanks to minimal travel restrictions and expansive personal and family networks. But what did this experience entail? It meant that one had no possibility of government protection, was part of no trade union, had no say over company practices, and frequently worked in dangerous conditions for far longer than a typical workday. It was a life of no rights and low wages. But not completely. For the wages, while prohibitively low in the country where they were earned, turned into gold back home. As valuable hard currency, the minimal pay was worth far more than anything that could be earned at home. For the millions of East Europeans who either worked illegally in the West or knew of others who had done so, capitalism appeared as a system in which workers have few rights yet get good pay for a hard day's labor. Little surprise that this is what so many workers seem to have expected from the new market economy after 1989.

The *Gastarbeiter* lesson of individual effort rendering class identity unnecessary survived the trip back home.

Postcommunist Rejection of Class

The result was that Polish labor after 1989 experienced the downside of capitalist class formation, but was unable to muster up a conception of itself as a competing class, thus limiting its ability to shape outcomes in a more acceptable, inclusive way.

Polish labor's resistance of class identity is demonstrated in a variety of ways. Guglielmo Meardi, in one of the best studies on this topic, compares the discourse of Fiat union activists in Italy and Poland and finds "an antagonistic and class-based vision of work relations" in the former, and a moralist, historically focused view in the latter.[26] The Italians, who made regular and explicit reference to themselves as workers, were proud of their status as producers and convinced that, as such, they were being exploited. Polish activists, meanwhile, working in Fiat-owned plants in Silesia, identified themselves chiefly in national, political, or religious terms, and always as part of a moral community. They weren't "workers" but "anticommunist Polish Catholic workers," with emphasis on the adjectives (alone or in combination), each of which was embedded in a broad symbolic struggle of its own. As Meardi puts it, "Their identity as union activists is . . . grounded in historical action, rather than on current social relations."[27] And since this historical action consisted chiefly in the struggle against communism, they saw the Fiat capitalists not only as an ally but as a teacher.

Italian unionists believed that labor had a different ethos from capital. They counterposed the "production logic" of workers taking "pride in their work" to "the financial and political logic of the employer," interested not in producing goods people need but in maintaining his or her own privilege and power. Polish unionists, however, had experienced only state employers as being uninterested in producing goods for people, and they imagined private owners as uniquely able to organize efficient and humane production. Meardi describes Polish unionists having "a sense of inferiority towards Fiat."[28] He quotes one Solidarity activist as saying, "The employer has changed, he is very well organized, we have to learn from him, *we have to love the employer;* we have to respect what he does"[29]—all of which sounds like what national Solidarity official Wojciech Arkuszewski urged in 1989 when he called on unionists to accept that wages, jobs, and "the general state of our factories depend on the level of the cadre governing the firm."[30]

Polish unionists did not have a clear sense of who or what they were supposed to represent. (And Meardi's evidence, it should be noted, comes from Silesia, historically the most blue-collar part of the country.) Thus, whereas the Italians focused on upholding the rights and wages of workers in the workplace, among the Poles "any positive reference to defending the interests of workers *as workers* was very weak."[31] The Poles saw their interests as being defended by and through the market, meaning they saw their conditions improving in tandem with the building of a capitalist economy. The comment Meardi heard from one Italian union leader—"We know very well that when a company makes large investments, this is not to increase the number of jobs but to reduce them"[32]—would have been simply unimaginable coming from a Polish trade unionist in the early days of privatization. Indeed, at the same time Meardi was doing his interviews, a Polish unionist at a state-owned firm told me that he "knew very well" something quite different: that "private owners have an interest in providing good pay for workers who work hard."[33] The same self-assuredness as the Italians—but without an assumption of class as a salient cleavage.

All in all, Meardi says that in the Polish interviews he conducted, "it was impossible to find a conception of socio-economic cleavages, even of the most simple kind (such as a division between rich and poor). The few distinctions articulated are moral rather than material." In Italy, in contrast, unionists had "a very clear (and very class-based) conception of society," in which workers, representing their class, were engaged in an ongoing struggle against "bloodsucking" managers, representing the elite.[34] The moral dimension is strong among the Italians too, but it corresponds to class rather than to historic or religious affiliation.

Meardi's evidence comes from conversations with union activists in a newly privatized firm in 1995. My own research at that time, conducted through open-ended interviews in large state-owned firms between 1993 and 1995, as well as through a survey (conducted with Marc Weinstein) of ninety-five state and private manufacturing firms in 1994, confirms these findings of low class consciousness. Polish unionists, we found, did not identify as or with workers, expressed deferential sympathy to owners, and saw labor's interests as best defended through market strategies.[35]

The survey[36] provides strong evidence that Polish unionists did not believe they represented interests contrary to those of management. For example, when asked why they were involved in union activity, over half the Solidarity respondents said they were in the union in order to promote market reform and speed the privatization process, while less than a fifth mentioned fighting the effects of shock therapy. (Comparable figures for OPZZ activists were 36, 42, and 14 percent, respectively.) Their behavior in the firm was quite consistent with these beliefs. Unionists accepted without challenge management's introduction of a rash of new "human resource management" techniques aimed explicitly at promoting internal competition and weakening employees' sense of community, techniques that had entered Eastern Europe through official western aid programs. Wages, for example, which in the communist period had been posted in public areas, now became the subject of personalized and private discussion between employer and employee. Bonuses, which since the 1970s had been treated as an essential part of a worker's salary, guaranteed to all, now came under the direct control of line managers. Unions were increasingly cut out of decision-making roles in enterprises, and the unionists cheered this on.

Unions supported such exclusionary policies particularly in private firms. For example, when asked whether employee councils with an active role in enterprise management were needed in state-owned firms, three-quarters of both Solidarity and OPZZ unionists said they were.[37] When asked whether such councils were needed in private firms, the response dropped to about one-fifth for Solidarity and one-third for OPZZ. Managers and unionists both reported that behavior followed belief: there was substantially less consultation in private than in non-private firms.[38] The chief reason unionists supported councils in state firms, moreover, was not because they saw themselves as having different interests from management. (Under the terms of a 1981 law, which went into effect only in 1989, employees in state firms elected both the director as well as an employee council that had final say on all key firm decisions.) Rather, it was because they saw themselves as having different interests from the state, and they wanted to protect the firm against the state.

Union activists, in other words, agreed that employees *ought* not have much influence—this was the desired state of affairs—but thought they had to retain some influence until firms had made the transition out of socialism. They believed participation in state-owned firms was necessary because they saw such firms as "ownerless," and therefore lacking the efficient and benevolent control they believed ownership confides. They supported such councils not because they saw participation as a positive good, but because they distrusted the state's ability to act like a "real" owner. Councils were seen as caretakers for ownerless property until real owners came and did their job. These "caretakers" were seen as necessary both to make sure that the old *nomenklatura* managers did not pillage state property and to help ensure that such firms enhanced their economic viability for eventual privatization.[39] In the desired economy, where owners would supposedly take care of their property and reward hard work with good wages, employee involvement could be dispensed with. Until then, some employee vigilance was needed.

Union activists thus believed that the goal of workforce involvement was to create conditions in which the workforce would cease to be involved. In this sense we can see how, to the extent that it existed at all, continued union involvement in state-owned firm governance was a way not of asserting labor's rights but of negotiating the terms of labor's demise.

Available evidence shows that the rank and file largely shared such views. Workers came to adopt these beliefs precisely with the coming of capitalism. Asked in 1983 whether they agreed with the view that worker participation is good for the firm, 64.3 percent of a national sample said that they did. In 1991 that figure had dropped to 21 percent.[40] When asked whether they agreed that worker involvement in management affairs is detrimental to the firm, only 5.1 percent of the 1983 workforce said they agreed. In 1991, 29.3 percent agreed.[41] These results are corroborated by other enterprise surveys from 1992, which also show widespread support, among all categories of workers, for the statement that managing is the responsibility of the management alone and that workers should not get involved.[42]

In both groups, therefore—union activists and the rank and file—we see an underlying belief in the sanctity of ownership rights. Governance rights, they believed, derive from ownership, not from employment. Workers should not have many rights in private firms because they are not the owners of private firms. State-owned firms, however, are treated as if they are owned by all, which means that they are owned by workers, too. Being a worker is not enough to warrant influence over firm decisions. Being a part-owner is. Owners have rights; workers do not.

The prevalence of these attitudes helps explain why Solidarity, from about 1995 to 1998, put such emphasis on "universal privatization," or giving citizens vouchers valued at a portion of all privatized property, and so little on reviving union influence in the workplace or on unionizing private firms. For Solidarity believed that only when workers were part-owners could they legitimately stake a claim to participation. Those observers, both inside Poland and out, who saw Solidarity's focus on universal privatization as an example of union militance thus miss the point. Solidarity was pushing for workers to have influence not as workers but as owners.

To those versed in the western experience, all this is quite paradoxical: workers and their representatives opposed workplace participation at just the moment when they would seem to need it most. But that is precisely the point: Polish unionists responded to a different set of experiences than western unionists. Each had an experience with different kinds of enemies, and each tended to see the desired future as entailing elements identified with the purported antithesis of those enemies.

Divisions within Postcommunist Labor

In the West, both trade unions and working-class identities arose out of the milieu of skilled, male, factory labor. Understanding the weakness of Polish unions and class identities requires that we understand the peculiar perspective this particular group brings to postcommunist society. And this requires that we again go back to their experience under communism. There are two crucial points about the relationship of communism to skilled workers and engineers: it did not use their talents fully, and it did not distinguish them adequately from unskilled workers.

Communism may have been good in providing universal basic social welfare, but it was never able to make good use of talented and ambitious craftsmen. Supply bottlenecks and an underemphasis on quality, together with minimal wage bargaining and guaranteed employment for everyone else, meant that artisans had little chance to bond with their work and got little reward even if they did. Party leaders understood that the biggest incentive they could offer was a moral one, which was why "socialist labor competitions" were employed throughout the Soviet bloc. But while such incentives worked quite well in the early days of communism, when workers could be persuaded that they were building a grand new world, they had decidedly much less cachet in "mature" state socialism. During the Brezhnev era the Party leadership famously both reconciled itself to the inevitable outcome and promoted it—it turned the system into one that rewarded not good work and strenuous effort but stable authority and toeing the line. Scholars and others who presented this as part of a "new social contract" usually stressed its positive sides, such as the decline of repression and the slow increase in the standard of living. But such advantages did not change the fact that for skilled workers and engineers, this was a decidedly unheroic time in which it scarcely seemed possible to do good work.[43] This is perfectly captured in the wry refrain that spread throughout the region in the 1970s: "They pretend to pay us and we pretend to work." Far from an homage to proletarian craftiness, the saying was a lament and critique on the part of skilled workers about the poor organization of the labor process that squandered their talents and energy.

Those who didn't mind "pretending to work" wouldn't much mind "pretending to be paid," since it was perfectly possible to live a reasonable life that way. But those for whom this slogan had such resonance were precisely those who *did* want to do good work. And what bothered these people so much was that the system tended to treat them the same as those who didn't care about their work. Here, then, we get to a crucial point about the *postcommunist* experience: skilled workers wanted, finally, to distinguish themselves from the unskilled. They believed that they *should* be better rewarded than these others, and also that they *would* be.

This helps explain why Solidarity activists, who in the large factories were overwhelmingly male, typically combined such apparently irreconcilable positions: of ardently defending their own factories, welcoming market reform, and fearing the creation of strong unions. They defended their own factories because they believed that once these worksites got rid of their excess workers, they could be fully productive firms again. After all, they believed *themselves* to be good, productive workers, and they saw the products these firms were making as good and useful ones. The problem, they believed, was that their firms were not operating rationally. They thus wanted someone to take control and "rationalize" the firm, which meant getting rid of the excess "unskilled" workers, who they usually identified as women and peasant-workers. Far from private property and market reform being the enemy, they looked to these institutions to finally organize the economy "properly." The skilled workers and professionals who tended to run Solidarity's factory locals uniformly believed their own labor would prove both necessary and worthwhile if only it were well-organized. And this was precisely what they were looking to private owners to do: to rationalize the labor process and reward qualified labor instead of all labor. Market reform, they thought, would (or at least should) harm only those workers with whom they emphatically believed they had nothing in common. It would allow them to become the labor aristocracy they felt they should be.

This also helps explain why they feared building up their unions: they feared that those who were to be dispossessed might use those unions to thwart the changes the leaders supported. Many Solidarity local officials, therefore, went along with the right-wing and Christian fundamentalist turn in the national union not because they shared these political beliefs themselves, but because they too did not want to defend all workers in their workplace roles. They shunned "class" appeals because they feared marginalized workers would use such appeals against *them*.

The Mielec Example

For a look at the kind of trade union that emerges from such factors and the feelings of solidarity that bond (or do not bond) its members, I turn to Mielec. As a medium-sized city (population 65,000) based on a single large industrial plant experiencing a sharp post-1989 crisis in demand that translated into a severe depression for the city, Mielec is representative of many cities in Poland, as well as elsewhere in Eastern Europe, struggling to make their way in the new era. Every town has its own unique story, but the pattern of extensive communist-era build-up, large factories employing the majority of the town's residents, owning much of the local infrastructure (housing, hotels, vocational schools, museums, libraries, theaters), and supplying virtually the entirety of the town's political elite is typical of numerous medium-sized cities dotting the landscape not just of Poland but of Slovakia, Hungary, and the Czech Republic. Mielec lies in the heart of the area known in the 1930s as the Central Industrial Region, an area specially selected by the government for large-scale industrial development right before the onset of World War II, but which experienced its enormous growth only in the communist era. Starachowice, discussed at the beginning of this chapter, with a population of just under 60,000, and Stalowa Wola, mentioned below, with just over 70,000 people, are located in this same region. I spoke with unionists at all of these sites, as well as in neighboring Rzeszow and in heavily industrial Silesia, and chose Mielec as the site to study more closely due to both its very representativeness and to its brief national prominence in 1992, when the Polish media presented its exceedingly difficult situation with the desperate strike over nonpayment of wages (discussed in chapter 4) as a harbinger of the future. I traveled there for at least five different stays between 1993 and 2001.

The factory at the heart of Mielec is the WSK aircraft manufacturing plant.[44] The plant began operations in 1939, just before the outbreak of the war, but saw its big build-up in the early 1950s when it became a chief producer of Soviet MIG fighter jets. Over the course of the next decades, the plant added to its product line an array of small airplanes (passenger, military, and crop dusters) as well as other big items such as fire trucks, passenger buses, ambulances, refrigerators, refrigerated cars, television broadcast vans, diesel engines, fuel injection pumps, and full-size retro-style collector cars. It entered less high-tech markets as well, producing a golf cart ("Melex") that won so much of the U.S. market in the 1970s that Washington initiated anti-dumping procedures against it. All this production made for a prosperous town. One mark of its prosperity was that for many years it fielded the best soccer team in the country—athletes being formally employed by the factories—with a stadium big enough to seat nearly everyone in town.

As production grew, so did employment. But as was usual in socialist factory towns with only one dominant firm, employment came to be seen more as a way for the state to meet its social welfare goals than for the factory to meet its production targets. Already by 1960, this one firm alone employed 80 percent of the city's workforce, a figure that stayed constant or even increased over the next twenty years, as the city's population doubled from 22,000 to nearly 44,000.[45] By the early 1990s, however, WSK was on the brink of collapse. The crucial Soviet market had disappeared, its large debts unpaid, and the domestic market could not fill the gap, both because of low demand due to the recession and because NATO, which Poland was trying to join, pressured the military to favor western suppliers over domestic ones. A new fighter jet project in which the firm had invested heavily was thus left hanging. By 1992, the firm had let go nearly half its employees, and most of the rest went months at a time without pay.

Because of the firm's skilled workforce and proud past, as well as the legacy of the 1992 strike for back wages, I expected to find a tough union local angry at the government and fighting for employees' interests when I first visited there in spring 1993. Instead, I found a union leadership that saved most of its displeasure for the workers it represented. When I began by asking him about the recent strike that had garnered national attention, Solidarity president Jan Branek,[46] a skilled worker in his fifties who had been at the plant for over thirty years, responded by complaining not about the nonpayment of wages but about workers too concerned with getting their wages "when the firm wasn't selling anything." When I asked about unemployment, he replied that there wasn't enough of it. "Communism was a fiction, giving all these people jobs. Even when we had 21,000 workers on the books, there were never more than 7,000 actually working." Now the plant was down to 11,000 employees, "but there's still room only for seven or eight thousand; that's what the sales figures make clear."

The Solidarity vice president, a 44-year-old die maker named Artur Olinowicz, said union work in the 1990s had become largely "the defense of losers":

> Most people in the plant don't want to work, they want the state to take care of them. They complain to the union that they're not making enough money, basically they complain about everything, but in the end most of the problem is their own. The ones who are good workers, they are only a handful.

Here we hear the voice of Solidarity's skilled artisans, so prominent in the large manufacturing plants. Olinowicz had personal links to the prewar labor elite. His grandfather was a blacksmith with his own workshop and seven apprentices, and then his father ran the shop until it was squashed, slowly, by the new regime.

> I wanted to follow in their footsteps, but when I was a kid there was no chance to do so in the old way, as an apprentice to a craftsman. So I did so the "new way," entering the WSK vocation school on the plant premises

when I was sixteen. Everyone was doing it, and there were jobs for everyone.

He began work in 1969 satisfied with his pay, an indication of Mielec's clout at the time. But the work process, he says, squandered his talents by treating serious artisans like himself as not very different from the surrounding rabble.

In the West, you have firms that try to produce goods well. Our firms had a different aim: hire people. Any people. All people. We had to give folks jobs. So there were those of us who really knew how to work, and loads of others who didn't and didn't care.

When there were plenty of orders and guaranteed revenues from the state, people like Branek and Olinowicz did not have to worry about supposed slackers. They found their high-profile aviation jobs interesting, and managers, fearful of losing them, offered non-wage rewards such as better housing or coupons allowing the purchase of scarce consumer goods. But things changed after 1989. When the firm lost its clients and the state cut subsidies—in short, when money became meaningful and budgets became "hard"—unskilled workers demanding timely payment of wages seemed to threaten the interests of more skilled workers. I met few union officials who believed their firms to be obsolete. Where western consultants saw "outdated" plants that should be closed, they tended to see old but useful machinery and a sizable number of good workers who knew how to get things done. ("If we could produce all we did despite the chaos of communist conditions," the Solidarity leader in Stalowa Wola told me, "imagine what we could do in well-organized capitalist conditions." The country was lacking so much, said Branek, and "we can produce it back to health.") The combination of seeing themselves as the true producers and the unskilled as loafers made them sympathetic to neoliberal economic claims that layoffs were needed. Get rid of the slackers so the producers can produce! It was to make the firm serve "producers" such as themselves that Branek and Olinowicz got involved in Solidarity in the first place. The problem for them now, however, was that the union they headed increasingly represented "the slackers."

That they could perceive it like this had to do with the way Solidarity ranks had thinned after 1989. The hemorrhaging had been anything but random; it affected professionals and skilled and unskilled workers quite differently. The pattern in Mielec was the same as in Starachowice, Stalowa Wola, and many other factory cities: after 1989 technical professionals stayed away from unionism, skilled workers often found jobs elsewhere, meaning their share of the union also declined, leaving unskilled blue-collar (largely male) and low-level administrative (largely female) workers as the bulk of the Solidarity base.

The engineers and others with higher education who were so important to Solidarity in its first incarnation were the first to leave. More precisely, most simply declined to rejoin after 1989, as membership had ceased to be a political statement.[47] Diverse career paths had opened to them, and unionism seemed both a relic of the past and not proper to their new aspirations. Immediately after 1989, Solidarity *leaders* tended to be professionals, but most of these soon left for higher stations: in the early 1990s a skilled technician with a good Solidarity pedigree at a large firm was a natural candidate for the new positions opening up in state administration, factory management, or new private business. Of Branek's three post-1989 predecessors, all engineers, one became an official at the Ministry of Industry in Warsaw, a second was named director of the Regional Labor Bureau, and the third, after failing to win a seat in parliament, became head of the Mielec Agency for Regional Development, a state-funded and western aid-funded business incubator and chamber of commerce charged with bringing new investment to the area. Other former Solidarity WSK professionals became government restructuring advisers, local politicians, consultants, and businessmen of various sorts. One founded a new newspaper, while another was tapped by the WSK director to become personnel manager responsible for introducing massive layoffs. Waning interest and new opportunities combined to deplete the union of its professionals.

As for skilled workers without higher education—people like Branek and Olinowicz—their union density levels declined too. Some went to work for the few new private manufacturing firms opening in the area. (The largest of these, founded by former WSK managers and Party officials, produced automatic ticket punchers and computerized navigation equipment for city buses, and recruited almost all of its 350-strong, union-free workforce from among the ranks of WSK's skilled workers.) A large number left the union simply because they were hired by the new, debt-free spin-off companies carved out of the WSK "mother" firm. This was a common restructuring strategy in the 1990s, whereby giant firms were formally broken up into several independent companies, with the new ones taking much of the workforce and the mother-firm left saddled with old debts. In Mielec, WSK spun off some of its most profitable units, such as its diesel engine, fuel injection pump, golf cart, and Gepard (retro-automobile) units. When the firm won a contract from Boeing to build doors for 767s, the sixty workers employed on the project formed yet another independent company. These "new" companies, no longer responsible for providing employment to the community, restricted their hiring to skilled workers alone, leaving the mother firm (still ostensibly producing airplanes) with a disproportionate number of the un- skilled old socialist hires. The problem for the union was that the formal change of ownership meant that unionists employed by the new entities had to reaffirm their membership, even though they might be working in the same place and at the same jobs as before. Yet many no longer saw any need for a union. The debt-free status of the new companies meant that wages were typically higher than before, and the mere fact that they were formally privatized (even though typically owned by a combination of the mother company and various state agencies) led many workers to believe unions were no longer needed. Branek and Olinowicz did not encourage them to think otherwise. Indeed, Olinowicz began wishing he himself had joined one of the new companies instead of being "stuck" as union vice president. Union den- sity among the skilled workforce plummeted.

The result, then, was that the Solidarity rank and file, in Mielec and else- where, consisted increasingly of those workers whom the leadership consid- ered dispensable. Wanting to serve "producers," Solidarity leaders less and less wanted to serve the interests of those the union actually represented. Branek viewed those who had left both the firm and the union as the best and most energetic workers. Olinowicz was more blunt: "What's left here is the very worst element: those who can't manage on their own, who are afraid of work."

"[The] mechanic and unskilled laborers have no interests in common, and whatever is gained by unskilled labor is at the expense of skilled labor."[48] These words, written in 1886 by the editor of an American trade union jour- nal, seemed to have been taken to heart by many factory-level Solidarity lead- ers in the 1990s. They wished to represent what used to be called the "labor aristocracy." Instead, as Olinowicz put it, they stood at the head of "a union of losers" (*nieudacznikow*).

Why can't the rank and file be more like us? they lamented—much the same way the liberal leadership mistakenly lamented about *them*. "Most of our members join to be defended against layoffs, or to get some kind of loan," Olinowicz said sadly, as if the desire for economic protection on the job were somehow illegitimate. (One of the regional leaders of Solidarity in Krakow told me the same thing: "They want us to defend every job, to not allow any layoffs," he said angrily of his members. "But we can't do that. We won't do that. We are for reform.")[49] "More lofty matters," Olinowicz continued, "simply don't interest them." Such as what? Branek, the older and more politicized of the two, was somewhat unsure. He spoke of the "reds" still in government and decried the "socialist mentality" still prevalent among the rank and file (as manifest in their hope that the union would ensure them concrete gains such as wages nearer the national average).

Olinowicz had a clearer vision of "loftiness": to create a system in which work would be valued. He wanted to build "a union of professional, qualified workers, able to work with managers as men." Instead, he felt he represented too many unprofessional and unqualified workers, and certainly too many women. Like every union leader I met in the large state-run manufacturing firms of the early and mid-1990s—and the leaders were all men— Branek and Olinowicz thought their firm employed too many women and that women ought to be laid off before men.

The displeasure was evident on Olinowicz's face when he met with three middle-aged female supply workers who had come to him to ask Solidarity to stand up for their interests in the forthcoming wage negotiations. He responded curtly and evasively, and when they left he turned to me and said he had these women in mind when he said there are too many employees here: "They take a piece of equipment off the shelf and hand it over to someone else, and for this they want a pay raise?!" That the women were making barely above minimum wage and, as they later told me, also had the responsibility of maintaining equipment and keeping inventories, did not impress Olinowicz.

Since women were much less likely to have had prior technical training, some unionists framed their recommendations for lopsided layoffs in educational rather than gender terms or spoke of the needs of the firm. For example, when I asked Andrzej Lugosz, head of Solidarity at the big steel plant at Stalowa Wola, whether there had been large-scale layoffs at his plant, he answered equivocally at first: "Yes, sort of, but this was limited to people who had, let's say, a 'light' attitude to work." It turned out that one reason he did not take layoffs seriously was that the majority of those affected were women. "The situation was this: a steel mill, metal plant—this is men's work. But these men had wives, and in the 1960s something had to be done with these wives. Since there were no textile firms here, the factory took them on, just like a good mother. Administrative offices were built up, entirely unnecessarily, without economic justification, and the women were hired. When the crisis came, naturally women were the first to be fired. We didn't object."[50]

Women working on the production floor were equally criticized. "This is a metalworking factory," Branek told me. "It's hard work, a place for men, but unfortunately many women still work here. They should work outside the plant in the service industry. Women in metalworking—that's the Russian way, where women were turned into tractor drivers so they'd be exhausted and would no longer be a woman but some kind of strange creature." He did acknowledge that women earned much less than men and also had much less chance at overtime, due to their high presence in non-production jobs. Even so, he thought there were too many of them.[51]

The problem, though, was not just women, but too many unskilled laborers left in Solidarity. Olinowicz compared the Mielec situation unfavorably with what he remembered from West Germany, when he worked there briefly in the early 1980s. "That, I tell you, is an elegant capitalism! You get paid well when you work hard on a job with lots of responsibility. And when you have less skill and work on a job with less responsibility, you get paid less. Everything is clear, and no one has any gripes." In Mielec, by contrast, "all I hear is gripes."

Why then did they want to be union officials? Branek and Olinowicz were unsure how to answer. They *used to* know why they were active, but not anymore. They were bewildered by the change in their role, and to the extent that they reconciled themselves to remaining union leaders, they did so through a notion of noblesse oblige. As Branek put it, "Not everybody is born a manager, and somebody has to take these others in their care." Or Olinowicz: "An employee who's well-trained and good in his job doesn't need any union, because he can defend himself through his work. But the weaker ones need unions." Thus they did not try to recruit the skilled workers who had gone to the spin-off firms. If neither private firms nor good workers really needed trade unions, there was no point in considering such things.

That attitudes like this were common among Solidarity's factory officials is clear from our 1994 survey, where almost three-quarters of the entire sample said they saw it as *part of their role as unionists* to explain the rigors of market reform to the rank and file. Unionists were at the top of organizations perhaps the majority of whose members they did not respect. They wanted to change those people in order to make their own lives as union leaders meaningful once again. The rank and file tended to respond in kind. Opinion polls taken throughout the 1990s consistently showed that when workers were asked to identify who best defends their interests, the overwhelming winner, even by union members, was "no one."[52]

Did Branek and Olinowicz fight hard for the interests of skilled workers? They did want to improve their lot over that of the unskilled. (When I visited in 1994, they were negotiating with management to ensure that the recent small pay increase would not be distributed equally.) But Olinowicz made it clear that these workers too needed to understand the nature of the modern market economy:

People are pressing me to get them their bonuses. But what, are we supposed to fight with windmills? I won't fight for lost causes. If we're not producing, we shouldn't get bonuses. As a unionist I do not have the moral right to fight for unrealistic matters. I am not a utopian. And I don't want to be seen as an idiot by the management board. We have to tell people the truth. If we're not producing, I have no moral right to shout that we should earn half the national average [which would be a wage increase—d.o.], even if I am the vice president of Solidarity. And OPZZ won't shout either; they're still the union of management and foremen.

As revealing as whom these unionists looked down upon within their organization was to whom they looked up. It was not the national leadership. In no plant that I visited, and certainly not in Mielec, did I find enthusiasm or even much support for Solidarity's national authorities, whose constant political dealings were considered largely irrelevant to the issues facing the local branch. They did not oppose the national leadership, and they certainly agreed with the general push for "reform," but they saw themselves dealing with entirely different problems. Lustration, for example, they saw as a moral issue, not a union one, since most top factory managers in the early 1990s were themselves from Solidarity circles.[53] Local activists could, and did, attack Lech Walesa at the 1992 national Solidarity conference when it appeared that he himself might once have been a collaborator, but when union president Krzaklewski tried to make communist affiliation a union issue, calling for openly political strikes against the DLA government in 1994 and 1995, the local union response was tepid at best. Local officials saw the national authorities in Gdansk as having a separate agenda, and they soon came to realize that they were largely on their own.

The only ones they could look up to in these conditions were those who understood the problems they faced but had somehow escaped from the morass. This meant those former union leaders, almost all professionals, who had left the firm and the union and were now ensconced in local government administration and the jobs of the new civil society. Branek and Olinowicz saw these former Solidarity officials as the successful ones, "the ones with brains" who were doing something good with their lives. I encountered this attitude at all the heavy manufacturing plants I visited in the mid-1990s: firm-level Solidarity officials immensely proud of their predecessors, almost invariably engineers and professionals, who had moved straight from the union to more influential and lucrative positions in government, business, and administration. Few saw them as having used the union as a stepping stone to personal advancement, but rather as having succeeded precisely because of the extraordinary qualifications that had once made them union leaders. They were the models for those they left behind.

Perhaps not surprisingly, however, those feelings were not mutual. Just as Branek and Olinowicz looked down on the unskilled workers still at the plant, so the former leaders maintained a mild disdain toward those who had succeeded them. Former unionists who had gone on to other work tended to look at the union much as the political liberals did: as an outmoded blue-collar bastion whose assertiveness could only be detrimental to reform. The former WSK president who now ran the regional development agency still had Solidarity paraphernalia decorating his office as some sort of revolutionary nostalgia, but he evinced unease whenever talk turned to the union itself. "They're not the most qualified people," he told me. "And they don't seem to understand how deep the crisis is, or that things are going to get worse before they get better." What Branek and Olinowicz say about their members is exactly what their professional predecessors say about them.

In the end, the only ones thinking in terms of class were the professionals who had left the factory and union behind. As government and reform advocates spoke of building a system "in the interests of a class that does not exist," these were the ones who saw themselves as constituting this new class. And unionists, paradoxically, urged them on. Far from wanting to forge "class unity" against the new elite, most union activists were "wannabes" themselves. They looked at their rank and file and saw the "working class"—and wanted nothing more than to escape.

"It is not knowledge of exploitation that the worker needs in order 'to stand tall,'" writes French labor historian Jacques Ranciere. "What he lacks and needs is a knowledge of self that reveals to him a being dedicated to something else besides exploitation."[54] Professionals and intellectuals were so attractive to Polish workers precisely because communism had prevented them, the professionals, from getting too far ahead. That's why workers were able to see them as their own "better side," making possible the alliance that was so powerful in the 1980s. Unfortunately for labor, workers thought that this alliance lasted into the 1990s as well.

6

Labor at Work: Unions in the Workplace

So far, this book has told a story of postcommunist labor weakness and its impact on politics. The aim of this chapter is to explore the changes in union behavior and industrial relations at the level of the workplace. Because institutional patterns tend to be maintained once established, tracking shopfloor developments will tell us much about labor's situation not only at present but in the future. I discuss politics here only in order to look at how political alignments have affected labor's workplace power. In the last section I look at some recent indications of union revival, and I conclude with a theoretical discussion of what this tells us about the conditions for strong unions.

We can divide postcommunist union activity into three periods, correlating to 1989–93, 1994–99, and 2000 to the present. In the first period, when patterns of postcommunist industrial relations were just emerging, Solidarity treated the promotion of market reform, privatization, and the interests of the firm as the mainstays of its workplace activity. (The unions' previous role as provider of diverse goods and services, including housing, vacations, and summer camps, decreased rapidly as such activities were spun off from the firm and commodified.) Rank-and-file workers came to the union with grievances about the effects of these policies. They sought protection against dismissal, complained about low wages (due both to the legal wage tax and the illegal managerial withholding of wages), and asked for assistance in finding short-term financial or legal aid.[1] In other words, they wanted the union to perform the basic services of a trade union in an endangered firm. Although union activists largely supported the policies the workers were protesting, their response was to alternate between explaining the "need" for such painful policies and engaging in symbolic actions (such as "leading" a strike) to show their concern. The union's response often depended on the nature of the management. When old *nomenklatura* management talked about the need for layoffs and other painful cutbacks, Solidarity challenged them. But when new managers elected by union-dominated enterprise councils—managers who were often Solidarity members themselves—said the same thing, Solidarity now agreed that alas, reason demands sacrifice.

This does not mean that all new managers demanded massive and immediate downsizing. Some sought to use a large workforce as leverage to gain restructuring assistance from the government. The funds would be used to help the firm become more competitive and not to maintain employment levels, but managers had a better chance of getting the funds if they claimed that they could not, for reasons of hardship, carry out massive layoffs. Such a strategy fit well with Solidarity's organizational requirements. Management and union could appear to be taking a stand in the interests of the dispossessed, all the while thinking of the good of the *future* privatized firm after the dispossessed had been jettisoned. This explains the large number of rallies, demonstrations, and symbolic "strikes" (ones entailing no work stoppage) that took place in the early years, which some observers mistook for signs of a vital civil society. It also explains the factory delegations that flocked to Warsaw in 1990–92 to meet with ministry officials (all large factories could find a former Solidarity friend now ensconced in a relevant ministry) to plead their special case. The meeting rooms would be filled with angry workers, believing they were fighting for themselves. Managers and union officials, meanwhile, wanted funds to carry out restructuring or a break from the wage tax so the firm could keep professionals from leaving. Jan Litynski, the veteran Solidarity activist who was a frequent participant in such encounters on the ministerial side, points to the dynamic here: "There'd be all these workers up front, talking about the hardships they would face if their firm didn't get special dispensation. And then I'd notice there's always some guy sitting in the back, not saying anything, and it would turn out to be the director."[2]

While workers wanted defense against dismissal, Solidarity satisfied itself with negotiating the terms of dismissal. The unions did not try to stop layoffs, but they did press for downsizing to be carried out chiefly through attrition. Parliament passed special laws allowing men to retire at 60 and women at 55, and it encouraged the practice of conferring invalid status on less skilled workers with the most minor of disabilities. Unions also engaged in formal discussions with management over layoff procedures. At the WSK plant in Mielec, for example, Edward Grosz, a former Solidarity engineer elevated to personnel director in 1990 so he could be responsible for layoffs, told me how he would sit down with the leaders of Solidarity and OPZZ and tell them how many pink slips needed to be issued. Then they would talk about who would get them. "They were always very understanding," Grosz said of his union interlocutors. "We agreed on the kinds of people and jobs that would have to go, and the talks always went very smoothly. But in the end, when we were supposed to sign the protocol of agreement specifying layoff proce-dures, the unions always balked. They accepted everything we proposed, but they knew it didn't look right for a union to acknowledge this openly. So it always looked like we were doing it ourselves. But we weren't."[3] Local Soli-darity leader Jan Branek saw it much the same way:

> Layoff agreements were easy in 1990, when unemployment benefits were not much worse than the plant's wages, and people still believed new jobs were forthcoming. But by 1991 and 1992 there was more fear of unem-ployment. Benefits were lower, and people no longer expected to get other jobs, certainly not in Mielec. So then we negotiated with the directors and drew up a list of who would be laid off. We generally OK'd the dismissal of those who had some other source of income, such as a farm, or a private store, or those who had to travel from far away (transportation costs them-selves ate up a good part of one's salary). But we didn't sign anything, be-cause we didn't want to be seen as "sentencing" these people.[4]

Over time, the unions got less and less involved in the issue and began to let management decide everything. In 1994, I had the opportunity to sit in on a meeting between Grosz and the plant's union leadership to discuss the coming round of layoffs. The Solidarity officials appeared bored with the dis-cussion, willing to accept Grosz's entire list. OPZZ quibbled on behalf of maintaining employment for one woman whose husband had recently left her. Grosz accepted the plea, OPZZ accepted the rest of the list, and the lay-off discussion ended there.

While negotiating the terms of dismissal is certainly not meaningless, it is hardly a great trade union achievement. And indeed, the major accomplish-ments of Solidarity in this first period lie not in defending the interests of its members, but in protecting the integrity of the firms. For while liberals warned of the damage class-conscious employees could do to the enterprise (their justification for the excess wage tax), the biggest threat to firms came not from below but from above—that is, the danger of asset-grabbing by the old elite. Solidarity's focus on protecting the firm more than the rights of its members prevented such thievery from happening on the scale it did in other postcommunist countries. Insofar as its success in getting Poland to avoid the corrupt, insider privatization schemes that tore apart neighboring countries is the strongest example of Polish unions shaping policy in the postcommunist period, it is worth taking a closer look at it in comparative perspective.

In Hungary, enterprise managers were using existing reform measures to begin taking control of firm assets even before 1989.[5] Although enterprise councils existed there too, they were thoroughly dominated by management. The few non-managerial personnel on the councils were beholden to the official trade union, which had not yet broken from its traditional loyalty to management. After the political transition in 1990, the new government, motivated by ideological conviction, a desire to please the West, and the need for revenue to offset budget deficits and a large foreign debt, embraced a program of rapid privatization. When simply putting firms up for sale failed to attract buyers, due to low domestic savings, the state turned again to enterprise managers, who came up with privatization plans, "almost invariably approved by the government,"[6] that transferred large blocks of shares to foreign investors while preserving most of the rest, along with the top new management positions, for themselves. When discontent with these procedures and a rash of new bankruptcies pushed the government to allow the sale of firms to employees, the sales were organized in such a way that management ended up with controlling packets and individual laborers got next to nothing.

In Russia, *nomenklatura* managers of state enterprises had also largely taken control of their firms before the collapse of the Soviet Union in 1991, a result of the general chaos of the times. Afterwards, with the explicit aim of turning de facto control into de jure control, they pushed for a privatization program that formally transferred assets to firm insiders. As Clarke and Kabalina put it, "The privatization program issued in July 1992 marked an almost total capitulation to the demands of the industrial *nomenklatura*."[7] Although each firm's choice of privatization path nominally rested with the labor collective, in the absence of independent labor representation management was able to manipulate the flow of information to get the desired outcome, ensuring its continued control. Employees got shares too, but in years to follow managers got workers to sell them at nominal values, largely through policies of low wages and frequent non-payment of wages that were often imposed with the express purpose of making workers willing to part with their shares for short-term cash. The result was an almost complete expropriation of labor, resulting in the staggering poverty rates of the 1990s.

In Czechoslovakia, the process of elite privatization was somewhat more roundabout. The lack of real economic reform prior to 1989 left the old *nomenklatura* without a head start, and the new government quickly introduced a widely heralded privatization plan that seemed to empower common citizens. The plan hinged upon distributing, for a nominal fee, stock vouchers to all citizens, who were then to invest them in the enterprises of their choice. This, its proponents claimed, would be a program of popular capitalism. But inadequate information and unfamiliarity with stock markets, as well as wages lower than elsewhere in the region, soon led most people to sell their shares to private investment funds. As a series of scandals that emerged in the mid-1990s revealed, however, most of those "private" funds were actually controlled by state banks. Here, then, the result was a situation where most of the so-called private firms—the Czech Republic had boasted of having the highest proportion of private firms in the region—were in fact owned by state institutions and controlled by a small group of individuals with close ties to banks, political parties, and the state. Workers and citizens, it turned out, had been disenfranchised from the outset.

In all these cases, corrupt privatization processes went through due to the lack of an active, self-confident workplace-level trade union, both independent and distrustful of *nomenklatura* management. With its legacy consisting precisely of independence and distrust of the old *nomenklatura*, Solidarity did not allow this to happen in Poland. From the very beginning, it resisted quick attempts at privatization that might transfer control to existing management. Indeed, this was the one policy area where Solidarity unions in the workplace rejected the lead of the former Solidarity leaders in the government. Early in 1990, the latter had called for the transfer of effective control of workplace assets away from the employee councils and into the hands of the state, in order that the latter prepare for quick privatization.[8]

The national union leadership was amenable to the idea, but activists in the firms, who had just come into a position of authority, were unwilling to give up their monitoring power so easily. It was not that these local activists opposed privatization (previous chapters have shown precisely the opposite), but that they were committed to making sure the old *nomenklatura* would not be the ones to benefit. This is why Solidarity, early in 1990, took the lead in organizing elections both for the employee councils and for new firm management. It put forth its own candidates for managerial positions and fought hard against what it considered insufficiently reform-minded managers from the past. And once the new authorities were chosen, Solidarity sought to make sure they would guide the firm into the new market era without stealing and appropriating firm assets for themselves. Solidarity, in other words, saw its chief role as one of *controlling* the workplace, not in the sense of running it but of monitoring it. This constituted the only significant example of Solidarity at the workplace resisting reform requests from the Solidarity-supported government.

As a result, privatization took longer than in neighboring countries, and it occurred without the same degree of *nomenklatura* empowerment. In fact, most Polish firms were privatized only *after* the *nomenklatura* elite was out of the picture, voted out by employee councils when the firm was still state-owned. Privatization then took place most commonly through a process known as liquidation. Essentially a form of leasing, liquidation entailed the formal dissolution of the firm, followed by the state, resorting to its formal capacity as owner, leasing the assets to the firm's employees. In short, they became employee-owned firms. Shares, however, were not distributed equally. Labor sociologist Juliusz Gardawski describes the typical result: "On the average, one quarter of the shares is held by an elite of some dozen or so persons concentrated in the managerial staff and the supervisory board, whereas a group of employees which is ten times more numerous has a total of half the shares. Furthermore, the elite is constantly increasing its share, and the employees' share is declining."[9] Solidarity did not mind the privatization of enterprise assets to a new elite; it minded, and fought hard against, only the privatization of assets to the old elite.

The other major form of privatization in Poland, used particularly in large manufacturing firms ("liquidation" occurred chiefly in small and medium-sized ones), was to turn the firm into a "state treasury" or "corporatized" firm, whereby the state seeks to sell the assets to a single strategic buyer. Of course, this meant dissolving the employee council and having the state take control, precisely what the unions rejected in 1990.[10] By 1992, however, two things had happened to make unions more acquiescent. First, the government agreed to cancel the excess wage tax in privatized firms, and state treasury firms, despite the fact that they were directly under the control of the state, were considered, for ideological reasons, to be private.[11] With the wage tax the most detested (and contested) part of the entire Balcerowicz Plan, as it kept managers from paying market wages even to skilled workers in flourishing firms, the opportunity to get rid of the tax was enough to sway many union-dominated employee councils to accept state supervision. Second, most employee councils by this time had already carried out elections for new managers, meaning that unions no longer saw state-sponsored privatization as favoring the *nomenklatura*. It might enrich new managers and a new elite, but that was fine with the Solidarity folks, who were neither antimarket nor pro-egalitarian but only anticommunist.

In the end, of course, none of this helped workers or unions very much. That is, on the one hand, by blocking *nomenklatura* privatization, Polish unions were thereby the only unions in the entire postcommunist bloc (including the Asian countries that have dropped communism in all but name) to have had an important influence on the privatization process. On the other hand, the country ended up instead with a large number of new managers and new owners, including many who had once been part of the Solidarity opposition, who were often more antilabor than the *nomenklatura* had ever been. A 1998 study of over 200 enterprises from a cross-section of the economy found that 20 percent of the directors had belonged to Solidarity in 1980, with 10 percent active in underground Solidarity.[12] Among directors at least forty years of age—in other words, among directors who *could* have been in the first Solidarity—the percentages double. These managers were in no way more pro-labor than others. Frequently they were worse.

The stories are legion. As we saw in the relationship between Mielec union leaders who stayed in the plant and those who had gone on to bigger careers, workers tended to admire those who had gone on to become businessmen, but the appreciation was not mutual. Take the case of one Solidarity leader from the Radom telephone manufacturer RWT, a communist-era giant which had once made the phones for Kremlin crisis rooms. When the Soviet market collapsed, so did the firm's fortunes. It became a state treasury firm, and then, in a pattern typical of large manufacturing firms privatized in this way, had its units divided and sold off as separate companies. Workers were pleased when Grzegorz Kurbiel, a one-time plant Solidarity leader, became head of the new supply and equipment spinoff. This was an example of the kind of non-*nomenklatura* privatization they championed. But once so ensconced, Kurbiel no longer thought the union necessary. Ignoring the law, he imposed restrictions on the union's use of firm resources for its workplace activities and pressed his employees not to use their annual sick days. He dismissed the union's protests of such behavior as so much defense of laziness.[13]

Or listen to Jaroslaw Mroczek, one of the leaders of the Szczecin Interfactory Strike Committee in 1980, the major center of labor resistance outside of Gdansk at the time. Mroczek formed his own business in 1988 designing navigational systems and computer programs for the ships he once built. His firm had no trade unions, and on the twentieth anniversary of the 1980 strikes he veritably gushed to *Gazeta Wyborcza* about how proud he was of this fact. How to explain the absence of unions in a firm led by one of the heroic fighters for the right to form unions? "Because only sensible people work here," he replied.[14] Was Mroczek perhaps firing union organizers, as had happened elsewhere, or did his largely professional workforce just not believe unions were necessary? *Gazeta* did not probe, which was itself not very surprising: more than a decade after the triumph of Solidarity, even Adam Michnik's *Gazeta Wyborcza* had no trade unions.[15]

Managers in worker-owned firms, or firms privatized to their employees, did not treat workers any better. For in practice, as Gardawski argued on the basis of a 1991–94 study of such firms, employee buyouts only "strengthened the position of the directors,"[16] who usually initiated the process and who emerged from it with control of most of the shares and an apparent democratic mandate to do what they want. Indeed, some reformers argued in favor of employee buyouts precisely *because* managers became so powerful as a result. Selling to employees, argued one of the main DLA neoliberals, meant selling to strong, popular managers who could push privatization forward while undercutting potential employee resistance.[17] As another observer wrote, it is a "myth that employee-owned firms are a more noble and more human form of privatization, or that they give employees a sense of participation."[18] Or, as one employee of such a firm put it, "it's feudalism! If something bothers you, it's whoosh out the gate. They can do anything with us that they want, and they do it."[19]

Polish workers initially preferred domestic bosses over foreign ones, but all the evidence is that foreign managers treated labor with much more dignity, at least in the early postcommunist years. Whereas managers in Polish-controlled firms insisted on micromanaging their employees and using purely financial rewards or penalties to motivate the workforce, management in foreign-owned firms tended to govern more cooperatively, in line with the post-Fordist style popular in elite western factories. Polish managers in foreign firms often took this as a revelation: "I used to think that you needed to treat workers like this," one director commented, and he put his right thumb in his left palm and twisted it back and forth. "Now, I realize that you have to talk to people, explain to them, teach them, and persuade them."[20] A 1998 study showed that unions were six times more likely to exist in new firms owned by foreign capital than by domestic capital.[21]

Paradoxically, labor relations in foreign-owned firms often deteriorated due to excessive self-effacement on the part of Polish unionists. Moderation, in other words, often had a deleterious effect. For the reason western businesses initially had better relations with labor had to do with their expectations of union militance. Multinational corporations had learned through decades of industrial relations conflicts that labor could be managed well only through negotiation and respect. But the point is that they learned this *thanks to conflict*. The premise of cooperative management styles is that workers are ready to defend themselves against capital. The starting point is an assumption of labor strength. Polish workers, however, entered the postcommunist period believing that real owners are good owners, since owners understand that good work must be properly rewarded. In this view, all that workers need to do in order to be well compensated and respected is follow instructions and work hard. They do not need to organize unions, confront management, or any of the other activities that were necessary in the fight against communism. Recall that the unionists in our survey said that unions and employees must be active in state-owned and state treasury firms but not in private ones, where they believed rational market acquisitiveness compelled owners to pay high wages. Or, as a miner told me, "if an owner is looking out for his own interest, he's looking out for the worker's interest."[22] Needless to say, international capital in the age of globalization understands rational market behavior rather differently.

In other words, foreigners expected unions to act like the unions they were familiar with, while workers expected foreign owners to act like the owners they believed in. Even without a game theoretic model mapping such confusion, it is clear why such different expectations and behaviors should lead to a sub-optimal outcome for everyone. A representative of an American chemical company that had taken over a Polish plant put it best, explaining the situation something like this:

> We all knew and respected Solidarity, and expected it would be a tough negotiating partner. But that was OK; this was Solidarity, after all. Instead, we found that they treated us almost as saviors, expecting us to do naturally what would be the right thing for them. Meanwhile, we didn't *know* what the right thing would be, because we didn't know what they wanted. So we just had to make up the rules ourselves and impose them. After a while we did hear some grumbling, but the point is we didn't have anyone to negotiate with at the beginning. There was no one to tell us *not* to do this or that; they expected everything we'd do to be what they liked.[23]

Let two encounters confirm this description of labor self-immobilization. One occurred during our 1994 workplace survey, while questioning a Solidarity unionist in a firm recently sold to foreign capital. When asked whether there had been any strikes in his firm over the past eighteen months, the unionist responded, "Oh yes, many," without being able to say how many. Surprised that the respondent could not be more precise on an activity extraordinary in the life of any workplace, we pressed, "You don't know how many work stoppages there were?" To which the unionist responded, "Work stoppages?! Are you serious? We can't have any work stoppage here anymore. This is a private firm now!"

The anecdote tells us a great deal: first, how seemingly unproblematic concepts have different meanings in western capitalist and postcommunist capitalist settings. For what the unionist had in mind when he said, "Oh yes, many," as he soon clarified, was that his union had put up flags and banners around its office and at the factory gates to show support for political proposals and protest actions called by the national union in Gdansk. "Strike" meant little more than a public display of solidarity.[24] More important, however, is the evidence here of even a militant unionist, ready to bring his work-force out "on strike" many times, who so plainly and unhesitatingly believes that private property cannot be challenged as state property can. Ownership, the unionist believed, conferred on its possessors rights and respect on which even a workforce in a profit-making enterprise could not infringe.

The second encounter took place at Warsaw Solidarity headquarters in 1993. A union official was telling me about the many private firms in the area that were not allowing unions to organize. These tended to be small and medium-sized firms, new ones as opposed to privatized. "Anyone who even talks about a union gets fired," she said in a concerned voice, "even though this is against the law." I asked her to give me the names of these companies or the phone numbers of those who got fired for their union interest, antic-ipating that she would be eager to comply, if only in the hope that I could publicize the injustice. But she balked. "These are new companies," she said, "and I don't want to do anything to hurt them." Even in the face of compa-nies preventing unions from organizing, the Solidarity representative felt loyal first of all to the rights of capital. She did want the latter to allow unions in, but above all she did not want to do anything to harm business, which she felt publicity of its malevolence might do. Private capital was to be supported even it did not support them.

In the end, Solidarity's activism in the workplace in this first period facil-itated the creation of a new elite class less tied to the old *nomenklatura* than elsewhere. But this proved to be a matter of union "strength" deployed not on behalf of unions or workers but on behalf of reformist ideas that did not matter much to workers.

Politicization and the Decline of Union Influence

The period 1994–99 saw the complete politicization of Solidarity on a na-tional level and the erosion of trade unions on the enterprise level. These were two sides of the same coin: as national Solidarity stopped caring about workplace issues, union membership and influence rapidly declined.

As discussed in chapter 3, the intensely political phase of Solidarity began soon after the 1993 parliamentary elections, which resulted in the victory of the ex-communist Democratic Left Alliance and the defeat of the Christian and nationalist conservatives, whose parties all finished under the threshold required for parliamentary representation. With the fragmented right need-ing a new unifying presence, union president Marian Krzaklewski offered Solidarity's services. The election "saved" Solidarity as a political force to the detriment of its evolution as a trade union.

The first major sign of Solidarity's new focus came in the spring of 1994, when national Solidarity tried to stoke a small miners' strike into a broad national strike wave. Miners from the low-quality brown coal sector were protesting against the consolidation of mines into holding companies, which would inevitably bring a rash of layoffs. When a few nearby industrial enterprises expressed their solidarity with the miners, the national union jumped in. Yet Krzaklewski made no effort to hide that his aim had little to do with winning concessions: "This is not just about realizing specific demands, but about the whole political system."[25]

Krzaklewski called for a national strike action in early May but failed to win much support. Even in the state-owned enterprises of industrialized Silesia, the response was poor. Not a single Wroclaw plant participated, while in nearby Walbrzych, whose entire economy, dependent on poor-quality coal, was threatened with ruin, only eight plants struck for a single hour. Outside the region, essentially only economically devastated Lodz joined in.[26] Rank-and-file members were telling Solidarity that they were reluctant to be used for hazy political goals. They were saying that they no longer tied their fate to the old industrial sectors. They had other concerns, most of them to do with economic problems in privatized firms.

The union did not want to listen. On the contrary, at every possible occasion national Solidarity went out of its way to emphasize that its aims were precisely about challenging the political system but *not* the economic one. Take the slogan I saw on the banner prominently displayed at the national demonstration (about twenty thousand participants) that Solidarity organized in Warsaw in late May 1994:

Managers in Europe = Prosperity
Managers in Poland = Exploitation

Once again, the union was asserting that the economic problems of Polish workers stemmed from the identity of the new dominant class. Capitalism is a good and desirable thing provided it is not run by ex-communists.

Despite the lack of enthusiasm from union members, Krzaklewski soon turned his focus exclusively to politics. As noted earlier, this was made possible by the organizational weakness of the right-wing post-Solidarity parties. Without any real organizational base, existing mostly as talking heads on television, their failure to win parliamentary representation left their leaders looking longingly at the union, with its ready-made activist network and panoply of resources (employer-paid officials, factory newsletters, access to the press) easily deployable throughout the country. With his enormous political ambitions, Krzaklewski eagerly obliged, and by 1996 he was doing all he could to transform the union into the organizational arm of Solidarity Electoral Action.

When one of his closest lieutenants, Katowice union leader Marek Kempski, addressed Solidarity's national convention in July, he began with "Ladies and Gentlemen," before interrupting himself: "I feel like saying 'Mr. Speaker, Members of the House,' but we have to wait a bit longer for that."[27] A month later, celebrating the sixteenth anniversary of Solidarity's formation, Krzaklewski spoke almost solely as a political leader: "We meet here today not only as the trade union Solidarity but as part of a national solidarity, a solidarity of spirit." He stated that Poland is, however, confronting a powerful enemy: not the market but the "market-communist system," represented by "an ideologizing state causing confrontations with those who cherish Christian values and Catholic traditions." The people must make sure abortion stays illegal, since "there is no workers' solidarity when there's no solidarity with life." And they must work for swift implementation of "lustration and decommunization" and the prosecution of state officials selling economic assets to foreigners—the identity of the buyer rather than the selling of the assets being the problem. Krzaklewski concluded by calling on people to join SEA, but not everyone: he offered a special welcome to "anti-abortion movements and Radio Maria," but told those who opposed the total ban on abortion or a constitution based on Christianity to stay away.[28]

The emphasis on politics promptly took its toll on union activity. As noted earlier, a national recruitment training project sponsored by the AFL-CIO quickly lost steam, as Janusz Tomaszewski, the Lodz union leader who had coordinated Solidarity's effort, all but dropped the union's involvement in the project in order to focus resources on political mobilization instead.[29] Building the union's labor base now took a back seat to boosting the right's political fortunes. As the 1997 parliamentary elections drew closer, the national leadership asked union locals to undertake political mobilization on behalf of SEA. For a time, national directives were focused almost solely on politics. Local union leaders tended to react with caution. Those geographically closest to Krzaklewski's Silesian base were the most supportive, perhaps expecting political advancement in the event of victory, while those further away saw political engagement as something unlikely to benefit either them or their members and having little to do with the day-to-day issues they faced. The reactions of rank-and-file members ranged from indifference to disdain. Solidarity's old labor base had not followed the union's electoral instructions in 1993 or 1995, when the DLA and then its presidential candidate Aleksander Kwasniewski won the support of those who feared unemployment.[30] With SEA's platform remaining silent on unemployment concerns, it made sense that it could not win them back. As it happened, SEA emerged the winner of the election with nearly 34 percent of the total vote, but it did not win a majority of labor votes, which were split with the DLA.[31]

Like Walesa seven years earlier, Krzaklewski played the role of kingmaker, appointing the prime minister and supervising the formation of the cabinet, and then retreating to the background while holding onto the leadership of the union.[32] While naming Leszek Balcerowicz as finance minister, despite having denounced him in the past—this was a condition of SEA's coalition partner Freedom Union—he appointed key national union leaders to cabinet ministries and provincial bureaucracies. Silesian union head Marek Kempski became governor of his province, while Tomaszewski was rewarded for his efforts by becoming interior minister.

As for unions in the workplace, power only made the situation worse. For how were they to position themselves in response to the unpopular reforms undertaken by the SEA? The simultaneous overhaul of health care, social security, education, and local government left most of the union base feeling alienated at best, betrayed at worst. Health reform, for example, was a disaster on all fronts. Introduced without adequate preparation, its immediate impact was to turn thousands of patients away from treatment and leave millions not knowing how to take care of their basic health needs—except through private care, which excluded the many working poor. Doctors not well positioned to benefit from privatization also objected. (Anesthesiologists, for example, unable simply to rent an office and ply their trade, conducted a bitter six-week strike.) The press, meanwhile, told endless stories of political appointees in the new regional health bureaus enjoying both lavish offices and lavish salaries. In other areas, social security reform entailed the risky privatization of pensions, education reform threatened the tenure of teachers, and while an administrative reform reducing the number of local governments from forty-nine to sixteen may have helped streamline the bureaucracy, it alienated many supporters living in small cities. In short, Solidarity in power seemed to have learned the wrong lesson from Freedom Union: it introduced laws that sounded good and corresponded with the wishes of western financial institutions but did not worry much how they affected people on the ground.

The SEA government did quickly pass a tough lustration law (which, ironically, made Interior Minister Tomaszewski one of its first victims). And it did greatly increase the public prominence of the Church. On economic and workplace matters, however, the new government offered virtually nothing. Despite the fact that many Solidarity leaders got government jobs, relations with organized labor in fact deteriorated. Treating itself as the voice of labor just like the first Solidarity government had done (and like communist governments before them) and ever anxious to reassure the West of its reliability, SEA saw little reason to negotiate seriously with unions. The Tripartite Commission, for example, quickly atrophied, as government representatives showed up ready only to explain decisions they had already made, not to negotiate agreements. By 1999, OPZZ boycotted the meetings altogether, and even Solidarity understood why. "I'm not surprised OPZZ no longer shows up," Ewa Tomaszewska, a Solidarity parliamentarian and commission participant, told me. It's because of "the arrogance of the ministers—'our' ministers—who come into a meeting and say 'here's our offer, take it or leave it, I can't waste any time talking to you.'" While "there has always been some governmental obstruction to tripartism," another participant recalls, "this government has been the worst." Two Polish sociologists doing research on the decline of tripartism report that all the Solidarity activists they interviewed blamed the SEA–Freedom Union government for OPZZ's departure.[33]

Unions in the workplace rapidly lost both members and influence. In a detailed 1998 study of over 200 worksites from seven different economic sectors, four of Poland's leading industrial sociologists concluded that Polish unions in the late 1990s were undergoing both "erosion" and "marginalization."[34] Unions did not even exist in more than half the sites they studied: they tended to hold on in old, large state firms and in the public sector (particularly education), and vanish as one moved toward the small, privatized, and more technological end of the spectrum. Even where unions did exist, however, Gardawski et al. found that their workplace influence had declined, that they were exceedingly moderate in their demands, and that they were perceived by both employees and employers as almost powerless. Unions did not do much about layoffs, and were not even the chief organizers of grievances: employees with a specific workplace problem were far more likely to turn to their immediate supervisor than to a trade union official for help. Most workers, even most union members, said that "no one" represented their interests in the workplace. Three-quarters of enterprise directors said the same thing.[35] Barbara Gaciarz's analysis of collective bargaining suggests that such perceptions were accurate: many contracts did little more than restate legal requirements and branch-level decisions, accomplishing so little for employees that few even knew such contracts existed. Far from using contract negotiations to strengthen their base, union leaders tended to treat bargaining simply as a way of maintaining communication with management.[36]

One key finding concerned the decline in the status of union members. Except for the large state firms, which were in any case rapidly disappearing, unions had become a place chiefly for low-skilled and poorly educated employees. The highly skilled and educated had dropped out for both ideological and careerist reasons. They no longer believed in unions, and they no longer saw them as politically necessary or professionally advantageous. Only in some large state manufacturing firms was there evidence of active involvement by highly educated employees, often in lower-level supervisory positions, but that seemed to be because only there, in firms awaiting privatization, was it still possible to see unions as avenues of mobility.

The study found that wages were generally higher in non-unionized firms, largely because these tended to be the more technologically advanced ones. But it also noted a tendency on the part of workers to *causally associate* the absence of unions with higher pay. Workers simply expected that wages would be lower in firms where unions existed. This does not mean they wanted their own unions to disappear but that they hoped to work in a firm in which unions would not be necessary. The liberal Solidarity narrative linking unionism with economic decline, it seems, had been greatly successful.

Solidarity in power did nothing to try to change labor perceptions on these issues. On the contrary, it promoted rank-and-file reticence toward unions by its own reluctance to even try to organize the new private sector, even in the large foreign start-ups that traditionally worked with unions. One anecdote is instructive here. In November 1998, I went to the opening of GM Opel's new state-of-the-art production facility in the economically depressed Silesian city of Gliwice. Despite the fact that Opel plants in Germany were thoroughly unionized, local Solidarity had stayed away from the workforce, thinking it inappropriate to establish a union presence at the new plant. The young workforce (average age 27) seemed extremely impressed by the glitter and gleam of management's modern "human resource management" practices, replete with teamwork and everyone calling each other by the informal *ty*. When I asked a 25-year-old worker from a long line of miners whether there was a union at the plant, his expression went from quizzical to incredulous to slightly condescending before offering his answer: "Why should there be?" Given the attraction of such a brand-new plant with its brand-new styles for someone who grew up with only dark dangerous mines as his imagined future, this was perhaps not surprising. And perhaps for the same reasons, it was also not surprising to hear local union officials, mostly middle-aged ex-miners, say the same thing. Still, it said a great deal about the state of Polish unionism when I spoke to leading Silesian Solidarity officials after Opel's grand opening and found them more excited to hear about the festivities than to talk about the need for unions.[37] Even unionists saw unions as something rather retrograde, even a bit shameful.

Union membership and influence continued to decline during the four years Krzaklewski's SEA was in power. Recent edited collections by Poland's leading sociologists all describe not just the ongoing crisis of unionism in Polish firms but also the increase in poverty and social dislocation that unions might be expected to have tried to counteract.[38] But unions have not been active on such matters. There was indeed only one economic issue that Solidarity mobilized around during this period: what it called "universal privatization," or the fight for workers to get a greater share of the privatized wealth. This was, to be sure, a real economic issue, implementation of which would entail a one-time influx of cash to those who had been cut out of privatization proceedings. And yet in focusing only on this issue, Solidarity stuck to a familiar and debilitating pattern of its past: fighting for labor as owners, rather than as workers.

As we saw in the campaign to keep the *nomenklatura* out, questions of ownership were the one area where Solidarity asserted itself. The story so far looked like this. The privatization law of 1990 allowed employees to buy up to 20 percent of the shares of their respective privatized firms at half the going value.[39] Two problems cropped up right away, though. First, even at these low prices, many workers could not come up with the requisite cash. Second, workers in very large firms objected to the provision capping the share value any individual could receive at twelve months of the average national wage. The problems were addressed in an ad hoc way. Some firms started allowing the workforce to buy on credit, often with future profits as collateral. In large and profitable firms where the government had found a strategic buyer (such as the Wedel confectionary company bought by Pepsi-Cola), the government simply caved in and allowed the workplace to buy an additional 10 percent at reduced prices.

The haphazard nature of these deals, all done outside the provisions of the original law, led to calls to change the law and develop procedures applicable to all. The issue was a main topic of contention in the 1993 negotiations for the Pact on State Enterprises. The government proposed 10 percent of the shares for free. Solidarity called for 10 percent free and 15 percent at reduced prices, OPZZ for 10 percent free and 10 percent at reduced prices, and they finally settled on 15 percent for free and no reduced-price sales.

The agreement could not be passed into law before the Suchocka government fell, but the DLA government accepted it. In fact, the DLA added on shares for retirees and for farmers and fishermen, and that should have been the end of it.[40] But Solidarity, looking for any issue to use against this government, now demanded more. Instead of workers just getting shares of their own firms, which of course did nothing for those working in non-privatizable workplaces like schools and hospitals, they called for all citizens to be given a share of the *total* national wealth. "Universal privatization," they called it.

In the period right before Solidarity came to power, this became the single economic issue around which the union sought mass mobilization. It gathered hundreds of thousands of signatures to put a referendum on the matter before voters. The national union press highlighted the issue as of critical importance. Front-page articles with titles such as "Proletariat in the hands of the Nomenklatura" and "They're Taking Everything" (in the same issue, no less)[41] sought to revive the specter of "communist" owners. In other words, at a time when unions were rapidly losing influence in firms at large, when private firms were arising without any unions at all, when the whole tendency was toward a unionless economy, Solidarity focused not on protecting the rights of workers as workers but on fighting for their rights as potential owners, despite ample empirical research showing that even in employee-owned firms workers' rights were violated with impunity.

But if Solidarity remained fixated on this approach, workers were not. The 1996 referendum for "universal privatization" failed, as only a minority of voters turned out. The DLA's bill on employee privatization became law in 1997, and many employees found that they benefited quite nicely. And when SEA came to power, it failed to pursue the issue, nor did it pursue any other economic issue important to employees. Confronted with a leadership that talked passionately only about religious ideals, that haphazardly pursued long-term structural reforms, and that continued to see privatization as a panacea rather than as a process producing a new kind of workplace where labor rights were increasingly violated, more and more workers started turning their backs on Solidarity. By the end of the 1990s, with unions saddled with responsibility for unpopular decisions they had no say in promulgating, the dissatisfaction of local unions finally peaked. Finally, something seemed to snap.

A Labor Revival?

The year 2000 saw the first signs of a new union sensibility aimed at tackling the real problems of the real system that had emerged. In other words, unions finally started acting like unions. They started being concerned about membership decline in unionized sectors of the economy and, for the very first time, began a major organizing drive in the new private sector. This third period is marked by a separation from politics, an emerging desire to organize, and a new focus on professionalization.

The changes seem to have come about for two key reasons: the experience of the SEA government and the cumulative years of actually-existing capitalism. The SEA years made unionists painfully aware of the emptiness of their political approach. Taking direct political power, it turned out, did not do anything to reverse the economic misfortunes of union members. On the contrary, it only meant that the union had to bear direct responsibility for specific policies, such as the disastrous health-care reform or the dismissive stance toward the Tripartite Commission, that most of its members found objectionable. When the country soon experienced a new economic downturn, destroying many new firms and sending unemployment soaring to new post-1989 highs of nearly 16 percent in 1999, the union had to take responsibility for that too. The burden began to suck the life out of the union. By 2001, Solidarity membership had dropped to a new low of under one million, a nearly 20 percent drop from the beginning of the SEA administration.[42] New unions started seriously challenging Solidarity in the workplace. "We've paid a very steep price [for our] effort to consolidate the political right," is how one regional vice president summed up the situation.[43]

But if the experience of government put an end to illusions that things would be better if only Solidarity held power,[44] the cumulative experience of over a decade of a capitalist economy, capped by a stinging economic crisis, was having its own impact. Put simply, things weren't going quite like the first generation of unionists had imagined. Instead of a thriving private sector picking up those dismissed from the public sector and "paying good workers good wages," wages had gone flat and unemployment hit unprecedented levels—from 10.6 percent in 1998 to 15.3 percent in 1999, over 18 percent in 2001 and 20 percent by 2003. (See Table 2.) The psychological effect of this crisis was much greater than the one in the early 1990s for one simple reason: this was the first crisis *of* capitalism itself rather than of the transition *to* capitalism. It apparently sufficed to teach increasing numbers of workers that they did need unions in a capitalist society, and to teach unions that they had better help build them.

It was in the retail sector where things broke first, specifically the "hyper-markets," the giant West European-owned multi-purpose retail stores, each one the size of an American mini-mall. Originally greeted as a symbol of the wonderfully garish opulence of capitalism—a single store spread out over several acres of land, shelves stacked high as if in deliberate snub to the shortages of the past—hopeful citizens in the early 1990s had lined up by the thousands to submit work applications. But it soon turned out that here were all the unfair labor practices that workers had once been taught were endemic to capitalist society, and which for that very reason they never believed. Personnel driven at breakneck speeds, constantly changing job criteria, draconian supervision, managerial misuse of the firm's (required) social fund, mandatory overtime with no warning and without the required overtime pay, and immediate dismissal at the first sign of discontent. Managers treated employees first of all as potential thieves, keeping them closely monitored at all times. They tended to hire people only on temporary contracts, thus mak-

Table 2. Official unemployment
figures in Poland

1990—	6.3%
1991—	11.8
1992—	13.7
1993—	14.9
1994—	13.9
1995—	14.1
1996—	11.5
1997—	10.2
1998—	10.6
1999—	15.3
2000—	16.0
2001—	18.5
2002—	19.7
2003—	20.0
2004—	20.5 [March]; 19.5 [June]

Source: Rocznik Statysytczny (GUS: Warsaw), from
years 1994, 1997, 1999, 2001, 2003. Figures for
2004 from the website of Polish Statistical Office:
http://www.stat.gov.pl

ing it easy to fire them. If the first consequence of such labor practices was annual turnover rates as high as 500 percent, the next was that employees themselves began contacting unions, asking for help.

A common complaint of Poland's free-market liberals is that unions are formed by incompetent workers seeking to take advantage of the legal provision that prevents union officials from being fired. While there is some indication that this does indeed account for the plethora of small unions in core industries like steel and mining, where unions are deeply embedded and have traditionally gotten along well with managers, nothing could be further from the truth in the new private sphere. Forming unions there is a very risky proposition. Those who do so are in particular danger of losing their jobs, as legal protection is a formality easily violated. In the hypermarkets, those who form a union and notify management, as the law requires, can expect to have a full-time "observer" watching their every move, pouncing on the slightest irregularity as cause for disciplinary removal. (When one employee reminded the manager of his right to form a union, the manager, referring to the legal provision allowing dismissal for disciplinary reasons, replied "It's not so hard to pull an Article 52 on you.")[45] Activists might be forbidden to move from their posts or use the telephone. They find that even trips to the toilet start to be monitored, so as to block communication with other employees. In one store where a three-person organizing committee went public, the committee's treasurer, a cashier, was fired for a pricing error, and the vice president resigned after having his apartment repeatedly searched for stolen items—nothing was ever found. When management finally forced the president out on another trumped-up charge, it showed its continuing fear of unions by trying to set up its own company union.[46]

Solidarity and OPZZ both got active in organizing this sector, prompted both by employee complaints and by press accounts unusual in their acknowledgment of the employees' plight. For Solidarity, this was brand-new activity, yet the personnel that could organize this activity had been emerging quietly within the union over the previous several years. It began in 1993, at a training seminar organized by American unionists for Polish health-care union officials. The American team came from the Service Employees International Union (SEIU). Led by John Sweeney before he became president of the AFL-CIO, the SEIU championed the organizing of new employees as a way to counteract union decline, and this was the message it brought to the training seminar in Poland. While most of the small groups formed at the seminar kept focusing on how to procure more funds, one group "got it" and produced a plan for recruiting more members. SEIU then recommended that the Solidarity national authorities use this group to help teach recruitment activity to unionists throughout the country, a request that took on more clout in 1995 when Sweeney assumed the AFL-CIO presidency. Because this was the period of its big political push, Solidarity refrained from putting much resources into the effort. It authorized the group to conduct some training programs but made it clear that building SEA instead was its main union priority. Two years after coming to power, however, SEA had clearly become the source of the union's great crisis. With some top union leaders grumbling that Solidarity had to distance itself from the government and refocus on membership, the organizing initiative reemerged as a way to do precisely that. Thus was born, in 1999, the Union Development Office (UDO), a special branch of the National Commission. Just when the hypermarket issue broke, Solidarity finally had a bureau to do something about it. More to the point, for the first time it now had a *desire* to do something about it.

One of the first Solidarity hypermarket actions went as follows: two women went into a store to distribute leaflets to employees, while the (male) chief organizer tried to make contact with the director. The director refused to see him and security guards detained the women. The organizer faxed the director to the effect that the repressive tactics were not going to make them stop. So they set up a large informational picket outside the store. This was such a novel act that it became the media sensation of the moment, finally leading to meetings between the union and the store director. By fall 2001, Solidarity had a presence in thirty hypermarkets (out of about 400 in the country) from six different companies, with a total of just over 3000 members.[47]

Organizing this sphere required considerable psychological changes on the part of Solidarity activists. As one national union organizer told an interviewer, if a trade union is supposed to be an organization that "protects employees and helps make sure that the employer doesn't take advantage of them," then "Solidarity has been against that idea of a union."[48] The crisis triggered by the SEA government, however, seemed to make local and regional union officials grateful for a chance to rethink the "idea of a union." In 2001, I found local activists positively relishing the opportunity to show they were more than just yes-men of Christian neoliberals. My meeting with Waldemar Dubinski, secretary of Warsaw Solidarity and a main organizer of the hypermarket recruiting drive, was my first encounter with a Solidarity official who seemed excited at and not just resigned to the prospect of organizing new members.

If an organizing drive in the private sector was big news for Solidarity, it was an even bigger development for OPZZ. Until 1999, OPZZ had been almost completely absent from the new private sector—as opposed to the *privatized* sector. Solidarity had hardly been there either—only about 5 percent of new private firms had unions—but if there was any union in such a firm, it was very likely to be either Solidarity or Solidarity '80, and almost never OPZZ. In part, this stemmed from the organizational structure of OPZZ. Unlike Solidarity, a single national union with a single charter, OPZZ was a federation of totally independent factory-based unions. This was the structure forced on OPZZ by the ruling party back in 1983, which, still fearful of Solidarity, wanted to make sure that the new unions it was going to allow, after having outlawed them in December 1981, would not band together into a national force. Independent workplace unions fit in well with the old state socialist system, which wanted unions to work closely with firm management. But such unions are difficult to form in capitalist conditions when owners don't want them. For a group of ten to fifteen employees to get together on their own, draft a charter, submit it to the court, and get formally registered is no easy thing to do under the watchful eye of employers. It can be done if there are others to help, but precisely because other OPZZ unions were themselves independent, none had an interest in organizing elsewhere, since members in other plants would by definition be members of other unions. (OPZZ did have loose-knit branch federations, but these were active only in the state and privatized sectors.) Moreover, OPZZ officials always tended to be cautious and moderate, mostly made up of older, low-level supervisory staff—just the demographic preferred by unions of the old regime, but not one to cause much of a stir in the new system.[49] All of this meant that OPZZ was not very involved in whatever unionism existed in the new private sector.

If the UDO changed Solidarity's organizing profile, within OPZZ the turning point was the creation of the Confederation of Labor (CL). It was founded in 1999 by Cezary Mizejewski, a veteran Solidarity activist who had quit the union over dissatisfaction with its right-wing political turn. Mizejewski objected both to the union's politicized Christianity and its ardent pro-capitalism. Resolutions such as the one passed at an earlier convention holding that workers and owners did not necessarily have different interests made him feel he could no longer continue in Solidarity. He was, in other words, the kind of socialist so typical to trade union movements in the West and so atypical in the East. With his former Solidarity activism, his workerist ideology, and his membership in the Polish Socialist Party (not the ex-communist party but the prewar socialist party, revived in 1987), he was quite unlike those in OPZZ too. But he moved there because OPZZ was at least formally aligned with the left, so he could count on more acceptance there than in Solidarity. Following a period of activism with health-care workers, including an eighteen-day ministry occupation by nurses in 1998, he got the idea of forming a new union for the private sector after learning that "even Solidarity" had just created the UDO.[50]

The Confederation of Labor circumvented the traditional problems that kept private sector employees from joining OPZZ by its radically new organizational structure. Instead of being an independent workplace union, CL was created as a single national union, with the mission of organizing employees in the huge and largely untapped new private sector. It required only three individuals in a given firm to become a legal union cell, with one of the three getting full legal protection. All this represented a considerable departure for OPZZ, which had always focused on protecting the members it already had, not attracting new ones. The new structure also meant potential conflicts with the loose-knit OPZZ federations, particularly as the latter, often under CL's influence, began getting interested in organizing as well. But just as things had changed within Solidarity, they had changed for OPZZ too, and there was more willingness to try, finally, to be unionists in a new way.

By 2000, CL was both going out to recruit those in the private sector, such as the hypermarkets and in banking, and waiting for interested workers to come to them. Indicative of the general decline of unionism in previous years, most of those who came to CL for assistance did so because they feared imminent layoffs and wanted CL to protect them through the legal immunity granted union leaders, or at least help win them a decent severance package. In other words, unions are still looked on as a last resort and as a mechanism for individual protection, rather than as an institution that can help secure good ongoing working conditions.

But CL has recognized that organizing today must be different than in the past, and that it must appeal to non-traditional groups of workers too. One of its most important innovations has been its activity in organizing the self-employed. "Self-employed" has for some years been the fastest growing job category in Poland. In 1992, some 1.5 million people were registered as having their own businesses. Five years later the figure reached 2 million, and three years after that, by the end of 2000, there were 2.5 million "individual firms" in Poland. But as one journalist put it, "what in the statistics looks like an eruption of entrepreneurship is often just a violation of work rules."[51] Among the "self-employed" who have been forced to set up their own "firms" are construction workers, streetcar drivers, X-ray technicians, cashiers, sometimes even primary school teachers. For employers, this is a way to save on employee taxes, avoid long-term contracts, or, as with the X-ray technicians, get around costly safety rules requiring limited work hours (since the hospital is technically dealing with "independent contractors" who can do with their own bodies as they please—and who won't be "contracted" again the next day if they balk at management orders). Just like in the West, this new policy of outsourcing was also a way for employers to avoid dealing with unions. But CL has taken on this challenge as well. In 2000, it organized a group of "self-employed" streetcar drivers for one of the municipal transit companies and became the effective intermediary for arranging pay scales and mutual obligations. It organized salespeople in outdoor markets, becoming their voice in contacts with local authorities to make sure, for example, that they don't allow construction of a fancy new mini-mall on the site. CL even became the voice of a group of traders who bring in junk cars from Western Europe for refurbishing and resale in Poland, putting the union into conflict with autoworkers trying to keep the competition out.[52]

With economic pressure mounting and political ties providing lower and lower dividends, other OPZZ unions began contemplating innovations as well. Finding that private employers were increasingly committed to bypassing unions, for example, the Construction Federation (*Budowlani*) started talking about a German-type arrangement (also the prewar Polish arrangement) whereby the union is moved outside the plant. This, they felt, would deal with a problem that had plagued unions at construction sites: weak local leaders whose very weakness triggered a backlash that weakened unions even more. Plant-level OPZZ activists had been trained to be conciliators, not militants. Unlike Solidarity activists, they were unaccustomed to situations of conflict, and so they were not at all prepared for managerial behavior at the newly privatized and fragmented construction firms. "When the employer yells, our unionist bends," a national leader complained.[53] So local unions became weaker, but local union officials maintained legal immunity from dismissal, leading to strong feelings among the ranks that union officials did not represent workers but only themselves. Basing the union outside the workplace, national leaders now felt, might help both the effectiveness of union representation, since officials would no longer be paid by management, and rank-and-file perception of union officials, since the latter would not have any privileged employment guarantee. (Of course, such an arrangement also fit in with the traditional top-down style of the OPZZ unions.) Professionalizing the union, they felt, would make it better equipped for the challenges ahead.

When I returned to Mielec in 2001, professionalization was the new theme there as well. Branek and Olinowicz had gone, the former to retirement and the latter to Germany. (As soon as his term as Solidarity vice president had ended, Olinowicz revived his old contacts and left to become a "real" skilled worker again.) What really changed, however, was not so much that the new leaders had such different views but that they faced such different conditions. For after having warded off bankruptcy year after year through increasingly creative spinoff and restructuring schemes, the main aircraft plant finally collapsed in 1999, the victim of massive internal fraud. The carefully choreographed layoffs of the past, which at least provided some special benefits for the injured parties, had given way to mass layoffs with no benefits, blighting the futures of those who had managed to survive on the job until then. Only after some months were the firm's remaining assets brought together and a much smaller, streamlined company reconstituted in its place.

Although for the once-proud firm it was an ignominious demise, for the new union authorities it turned out to be an enormous relief. No longer would local officials have to intercede on behalf of workers they didn't think belonged there—after all, such workers were no longer there. With its streamlined workforce, more male and more skilled, the new firm brought together just the kind of employees Solidarity leaders always wished they could represent. The new leadership I met in 2001 was the first that seemed both challenged and engaged by their work, the first that treated a trade union per se as something truly worth having. It no longer had to think of the good of the whole firm because the firm had already collapsed. The worst was over. Now the union, with officials who had not been big players in Solidarity's glory days, had to think about how to get members, both because their own jobs depended on it and because no longer having to think only about the firm seemed to force them to think about the rank and file. They now spoke of providing legal services, of checking arbitrary management decisions, of being watchful defenders of those who were still working.

As for themselves, they saw "knowledge" as their greatest asset. The new seriousness given to legal rules, which I have observed among many activists in this latest period, seems to reflect the awareness that political leaders would no longer represent them, and that private employers were becoming a formidable foe. "When they cite chapter and paragraph of the Labor Code or some other law to justify some new policy they're imposing, we need to know those laws too," one Solidarity steelworker told me. In Mielec, interestingly, both Solidarity and OPZZ officials said the same thing, though in ways that revealed their different pasts. "You can't just go in there and declare a strike, like we may have done in the past," said the Solidarity official. "Now you've got to come in armed with the precise legal codes, telling them what they've done wrong." The OPZZ official explained it slightly differently: "A union is not just for handing out potatoes any more—now it's got to know the rules and laws in order to get things done." And the point that both unions now recognized was to get things done for their members, not for the firm.

Dissatisfaction with Solidarity's political commitments reached a peak in 2001. In May, Solidarity the trade union formally severed its ties to Solidarity Electoral Action. The government that had been in power since 1997 had become so unpopular that most of SEA's other constituent organizations also broke ranks. By fall, SEA ceased to exist. In the parliamentary elections of September the DLA returned to power, winning nearly 45 percent of the seats. SEA's coalition partner, the liberal Freedom Union, failed to pass the threshold for parliamentary representation. However two extremist illiberal parties, Self-Defense and the League of Polish Families, easily passed the threshold, together winning some 20 percent of the seats in the new parliament.

How did the union respond to this new situation? We see a mixed picture. While interest in organizing the private sphere continued to grow at unprecedented levels, the legacies of post-1989 political unionism were proving hard to eradicate.

I have visited countless union headquarters throughout Poland since 1989, but never came across anything like the three young organizers I met in Warsaw in 2002. Unabashedly pro-union, the two 25-year-old men and one 31-year-old woman from Solidarity's Union Development Office regaled me with stories of approaching employees in hypermarkets and elsewhere and talking with them with pride about how unions might be able to help them.

Employees over 40, it seems, tended to be suspicious. Maciej, a 25-year-old who got involved with the UDO after being fired for trying to form a union at the pub in Szczecin where he had worked, told me how one older worker, upon hearing he was from Solidarity, just walked away, saying, "You've had your five minutes in the limelight, so what do you want now?" "Nothing," Maciej said, "but let's just talk about working conditions. Do you have any problems here that you haven't been able to solve? Are you getting paid enough for the work you're doing? Does management listen to your complaints?" When workers complained about Solidarity's political engagement, UDO organizers would now respond that they were not interested in politics. It is hard to convey how new this was in the context of Polish trade unionism. This willingness, even eagerness, to organize employees not sympathetic to them is a long step from Solidarity's initial post-1989 practice of *discouraging* such people from joining, particularly those who had been in the Party or OPZZ. Employees under 30, meanwhile, were not so much suspicious of Solidarity as simply unacquainted with the concept of a trade union not involved in politics. "We explained," says Maciej, using the distinction between the "organizing" versus "servicing" models of unionism that UDO learned in large part from SEIU,[54] "that unions were about employees getting together to act on what was important for them, not for officials to tell them what was important." While it is not at all clear that the "servicing" model is obsolete in Poland, given how little Polish unions have been interested in taking care of their members,[55] this commitment to building unions that work for the members, and not ones that follow political instructions from the top, is something quite new for Solidarity.

Workers in Gliwice's Opel factory had also formed a union, thanks to some international collaboration that might be a harbinger for the future. It began in 1999 when Stanislaw Ciepiera, a 37-year-old who had previously been a mine worker, became dissatisfied with Opel's informal communication system: "We could talk about things, but we couldn't *demand* anything."[56] Without guidance from any established unions, which were still uninterested in such activities, Ciepiera bided his time until he heard about a Jesuit monk in a monastery nearby who had once worked for Opel in Germany and who personally knew the head of the European Works Council there. The monk arranged for his visit to Germany, where Ciepiera met with IG Metall unionists from Opel—"and we then felt we had someone behind us." They then went public to the plant management as a Solidarity local, and when management did not resist (Opel was too unionized a company in the West to do so), employees began signing on. Others benefited too. When management from a supply firm operating on the same grounds as Opel summarily fired a union organizer, Ciepiera got him reinstated by getting the German unionist sitting on the company's advisory board to threaten to have the director fired. When I visited him in the summer of 2002, Ciepiera was involved in the kind of day-to-day union work that had never occurred in the mines. "I was in the miners' union for years," he said, "but it's like I never knew what a trade union was for." He was also working closely with the Union Development Office and had contacts throughout Europe. And even though he maintained his conservative Catholic beliefs and considered himself anti-socialist, he sounded like a class-conscious social democrat when he said, "To have a united Europe, with a single, centralized united union—this is my dream. When there's globalized capital, labor has no other way forward."

Despite these budding signs of class sensibility, however, it would be a mistake to think that union revitalization is now at hand. New private-sector employees still make up only a tiny portion of Solidarity's membership. Moreover, skilled employees at large multinational manufacturing plants like Opel obviously find it easier to form unions than those in small domestic production firms, not to mention unskilled retail staff. There are still only a small number of activists doing such organizing and a small number of employees who believe it's worthwhile. Even in the hypermarkets, unions failed to maintain their progress. The organizing pace dropped off after 2002, partly due to lack of funds for UDO organizers, which in turn reflects the continued low priority assigned by Solidarity to this task. Recruitment by the Confederation of Labor also declined, to some extent because of the decision by some CL leaders to accept positions in the Ministry of Labor after the DLA came back to power. In other words, the damage has already been done. It may take quite a while to change the beliefs of national union officials and rank-and-file workers alike that trade unions are not needed in private firms.

In 2003, Solidarity membership stood at 780,000, a 61 percent decline since 1995. Total union membership in the country was 1.9 million, representing a 71 percent decline since 1995. Union density stood at a near European low of 14 percent in 2001, and has declined since.[57] Yet, despite all the damage politicization had caused, Solidarity still had a hard time renouncing it. My conversation with Wojciech Grzeszek, the leader of the Malopolska region of Solidarity that includes Krakow and several cities to the west and south, made clear why. Grzeszek understood quite well that the union had suffered greatly for its prominent role in government. He had witnessed firsthand the problems political involvement had posed for his union locals—most prominently, the humbling of the Solidarity powerhouse in the Nowa Huta steel mill. (The excessive pro-market attitude of its union leaders and the pride they took in having governmental responsibility led in 2001 to a series of stinging defeats in workplace elections.)[58] Rank-and-file unionists now decisively wanted the union to stay out of politics, with local activists among the chief proponents of this view. Grzeszek knew all the reasons why close political connections were hurting the union. Yet he couldn't stay away completely, and the reasons have to do with the weakness of what in Europe is called the "political class." The "problem" was that as a prominent Solidarity official he had more political knowledge and policy experience than almost anyone else in Krakow. He certainly had more experience than most of the candidates running for office. Not only had he been a key player in local politics during the previous years, but he had been regularly invited abroad to meet with business, union, and EU officials. He could speak with ease about policy experiments in Belgium or Germany, union practices in Italy or Spain, or new ideas they've come up with in Japan. In a context where so few people had such experience, Grzeszek felt an *obligation* to share it with others. Staying away from politics, which Solidarity in 2001 finally decided to do, now seemed to him a waste. And so, when I met him in 2002, he was already negotiating with local right-wing party organizations to have seats on their electoral lists reserved for whoever the union might appoint.

As Grzeszek said, "How can we expect to have influence without this?" By exerting pressure on the parties that do govern, I wanted to respond. Labor in the West, after all, has had its strongest influence not when governing directly but when in close alliance with a governing party separate from the union. But this connects to the problem of Poland's undeveloped party system. Solidarity had intervened so directly in electoral politics that now, when it had finally withdrawn, there was no established party on which it could exert its influence. Theoretically it could have tried to pressure the DLA, now back in power, but Solidarity still treated the DLA as an enemy. (The DLA, for its part, was now more hostile to Solidarity than it had been in 1993.) So Solidarity leaders kept finding themselves drawn back in to politics, even at the cost of alienating the union's own members. The legacy of communist-era unionism also plays a role here. When Grzeszek thought of a union limited to union matters, as so many of his members wanted, he could only imagine a union that "takes care of petty services in the factories, gets things for their members to buy." This was quite different from the new way of thinking evinced by those in the Union Development Office.

Grzeszek's reasoning was easy to understand, but it was still the reasoning of a politician, not a unionist. It might well win him and his comrades some seats on local councils, but it had little chance of doing anything for workers as workers—indeed, was not intended to do so. For what this chapter shows us is that it is only when Polish unionists stopped thinking like the old social movement activists they were and started thinking like "narrow" trade unionists that they had a chance of bringing about some beneficial changes for their members.

In light of recent western industrial relations theory, this is a rather startling conclusion. For much of this work has stressed the role of social movements in *stimulating* unionization. A variety of scholars and activists look to "social movement unionism" as the only way to rescue unionism from the declines in both influence and membership. Defenders of this model distinguish it from traditional unionism by its high level of mobilization and its ambitions to transform not just the workplace but the larger society as well. Seidman defines social movement unionism as a strategy that entails going "beyond the factory gates" with demands that "include broad social and economic change."[59] According to another advocate, it means "making the union into a vehicle through which its members not only address their bargaining demands but actively lead the fight for everything that affects working people in their communities and the country."[60] This approach has made sense for unions in capitalist countries, where it is a matter of getting the broader community to support struggles for labor rights. In Poland, however, it is precisely labor's focus on "broad social and economic change," its commitment to "lead the fight" for political change, that has been its most serious problem. For this social movement has been about building a market economy, not defending labor within it. Thus the focus on broad civic transformation has led unions to neglect their responsibility to their members' economic needs. We can certainly understand why they made this choice, given the nature of the communist system and the way this system structured their sense of interests, as discussed in the previous chapter. But it has been disastrous policy when it comes to defending workers in the postcommunist system.

If we look at the more recent efforts of unionists that have had some success, they have all been based on a move *away* from broad civic and political concerns and toward narrow economic ones instead. The Mielec unionists I met in 2001 were relieved to put politics and movement activism behind them, because they knew how much it had cost them: "For the past four years, we got blamed for everything."[61] With their more modest emphasis on knowing the law in order to deal with specific employee grievances, they were able to appeal to laborers who for years had written them off as de facto managers. Opel got organized by an activist who shunned politics in favor of local workplace issues, and the hypermarket organizing drive has focused solely on narrow economic issues, such as work load, overtime, and compensation. In other words, it was only to the extent that Solidarity broke from its social movement foundations that it was able to gain members.

What the Polish experience suggests, in other words, is the continuing importance of old-fashioned economic unionism, often pejoratively called "business unionism." Unions must act like narrow trade unions, in terms of defending the short-term economic interests of their members, before they do anything else. Far from shunning class concerns, economic unionism in fact *embraces* class cleavages, insofar as it explicitly promotes the interests of one side in the workplace against the interests of others.[62] In this way, it can lead to the economic inclusion of labor and thus a deeper consolidation of democracy. Theorists of social movement unionism no doubt assumed that unions would work first of all on behalf of their own members, but as we've seen, that is not necessarily the case. Whether social movement unionism will be beneficial to labor thus depends on the kind of social movement unions belong to.[63] The Solidarity social movement model has been disastrous for workers, and the union is beginning to get back on its feet to the extent that it is discarding that model.

As we have seen, however, Solidarity has begun to recognize this itself, as manifested in its May 2001 decision to formally sever its ties to Solidarity Electoral Action. In September 2002, the national conference took the more important step of voting union president Marian Krzaklewski out of office, precisely on the grounds of having overpoliticized the union. The delegates stopped short of electing mining leader Kazimierz Grajcarek, the candidate who had promised to revitalize Solidarity's union activity and even work together with OPZZ. In a fiercely contested battle, they settled instead on Krzaklewski's vice president, Janusz Sniadek, who has presided over a much-humbled union. The 2002 conference did make clear that the union had rejected the politicization of the past. A battle over the nature of the union has now been engaged at the national level.

In the first years of the new century, then, Polish unions finally began the process of becoming the kind of trade unions needed in a democratic market economy: organizations for the articulation of labor interests in the workplace. While numbers continued to shrink, due both to skyrocketing unemployment and the legacy of union political involvement, unions started organizing in the important new private sector, and they started to act differently in the old manufacturing firms, now mostly privatized. Unions, in other words, began to direct economic anger against economic others, and to even revive a class discourse. The process, however, has been slow and hesitant, and it is still far from able to make up for the self-inflicted losses of the previous decade. Moreover, as the strong showing for demagogic populist parties has made clear, these changes have not been able to break the tendency for economic anger to be politically expressed in illiberal ways. Labor anger, in other words, continues to produce right-wing political outcomes. In the conclusion, we look at the likelihood of this changing any time soon and explore more broadly the lessons of the Polish experience for the building of democracy.

7

Conclusion: Class, Civil Society, and the Future of Postcommunist Democracy

The argument of this book is that postcommunism set in motion the articulation of class differences that the political world was unable to process as such, due to both structural legacies and current ideological fashions. As a result, emerging class conflicts became articulated not as conflicts over interests but as conflicts about identity, thus promoting an illiberal political culture that has haunted Poland's democratization process ever since.

If I am right that it is the failure for social conflicts to be organized around economic cleavages that leads to illiberalism, then it follows that it is irrational and counterproductive for supporters of liberal democracy to oppose class conflict. I posit this lesson as a universal one. That democratically minded capitalists and pro-market reformers ought to support the mobilization of anger around class conflicts is one of the key lessons of the Polish experience. They should do so in order to avoid anger being mobilized around ascriptive or other non-negotiable cleavages that inexorably push society toward dangerous and irresolvable internal divisions.

My aims in this final chapter are to highlight and argue the importance of the theoretical claims of the book and to look at the political prospects for the future. In doing so, I re-examine some of the broader themes and theoretical constructs of the book. I also take a comparative approach by setting the Polish experience alongside that of some comparable East European countries and examine political prospects in light of Poland's recent entry into the EU.

179

Organizing Anger in Postcommunist Eastern Europe

I begin by summarizing here the Polish experience and then looking briefly at labor and politics in other East European postcommunist contexts.

The Polish elite after 1989, including many Solidarity leaders, entered the new era convinced that labor was the new enemy. Expecting to deal with a powerful class opponent fighting against the new capitalism it was promoting, this emerging elite tried to nip class opposition in the bud. It did so in a variety of ways. First, there were the policies minimizing labor input in the workplace, such as a privatization law requiring abolition of employee councils, restrictions on issues open to union-management discussion, and a long delay before permitting collective bargaining. Second, there was the constant media barrage prescribing support, patience, and acquiescence as the correct emotional response to the calamitous post-1989 economic depression. News coverage of labor protests presented activists as irrational hotheads,[1] while popular grievances directed at government policies were interpreted as grievances "really" aimed at the old regime, which the present policies were finally dismantling. Finally, the elite tried to nip class opposition by channeling it along other lines. Solidarity played the key role here. Unable to eliminate economic discontent, it turned itself into an organizer of that discontent, and from Lech Walesa through Marian Krzaklewski systematically sought to direct it against communists, crypto-communists, liberals, non-believers, "foreigners" (often defined simply as Poles who did not fit "Polish Catholic" norms), criminals, and other assorted "aliens." Solidarity still hoped to maintain class unity—it did, after all, claim to speak for labor—but it sought to organize workers along other than class lines.

The paradox, of course, was that as much as workers opposed the effects of the market economy (thus generating anger), they did not see themselves as anticapitalist at all. In line with what their former leaders had taught them, they largely believed, at least for the first postcommunist decade, that capitalism was in their own economic interests. In survey after survey, not to mention inaction after inaction, rank-and-file workers as well as local union officials demonstrated their acceptance of market reform. All they wanted was to have some say in that reform, to be treated as rational actors who could legitimately have a different opinion (such as about the wage-tax or infant-industry protection) and be talked with rather than lectured to. But since any criticism of the government's specific marketization policies was perceived as a sign of incipient class opposition, which itself was perceived as ruinous to reform, it was not permissible for workers to be heard. As liberals ignored them, an emergent political right was able to capitalize. For with discontent treated as irrational and illiberal, it made sense to embrace the opportunity the right wing offered, for only then could workers escape condescension. The political liberals thus pushed labor to the right. So egregiously did liberals flub the test of representing an increasingly disenfranchised working class that it fell to the former communists in the Democratic Left Alliance to act as chief defenders of liberal principles of tolerance. But while DLA victories helped stem the advance of illiberalism, the communist-era legacy and the resurgent economic crisis prevented it from becoming a hegemonic party. Indeed, after unemployment hit all-time highs of over 20 percent[2] and a series of DLA scandals made headlines, the party imploded in 2004, falling to single-digit support and forcing second-tier leaders to form a breakaway party in order to salvage something from the sinking ship. As a result, voters remain politically available for incorporation by illiberal parties, as demonstrated by unprecedentedly strong 2004 polling numbers for the extremist parties Self-Defense and League of Polish Families. (After combining for 18.1 percent of the vote in the 2001 parliamentary elections, the two parties won 26 percent in the 2004 European Parliament elections.)

The stifling of class politics, in other words, ended up having profoundly illiberal and antidemocratic consequences. It did not lead to the absence of economic anger but to the organization of that anger in illiberal ways. Economic anger not organized around class lines must find other axes around which to revolve.

Experiences of other countries in Eastern Europe confirm this conclusion. For they too have been struggling with the issue of how new class anger is politically expressed. Everywhere we look, we have had labor crippled by neoliberal reforms and new elites anxious to stifle labor discontent, leading to weak trade unions, low class sensibilities, and burgeoning class anger looking for ways to express itself.

In Czechoslovakia, economic discontent became fuel for the break-up of the country, particularly in poorer Slovakia, where the nationalist Vladimir Meciar succeeded in the early 1990s by blaming Slovak economic troubles on Czech domination. When independence rendered the nationalist narrative moot, Meciar sought to deploy the base he had built to consolidate his own illiberal rule, and had a great deal of success, his party overwhelming its competitors in the 1994 election. Throughout the 1990s, as Jonathan Stein writes, Meciar

> attracted significant working-class support by channeling economic fear and frustration into nationalist resentment directed against "anti-Slovak" influences: pro-federalists, the country's ethnic Hungarian minority, and liberal reformers portrayed as "selling out" the nation's interests and assets to foreigners.[3]

An authoritarian rule sufficient to make it a virtual pariah to the West was the result.

Czech labor woes also needed outlets. Things were not so bad in the early 1990s, when a combination of relative union strength and shrewd government policy kept unemployment rates lower than anywhere else in Eastern Europe.[4] By the end of the decade, however, labor's advantages had dissolved. The unions never sought to capitalize on their initial strength, instead relying on economic growth alone to help their members. It soon turned out, however, that that growth had been a mirage, sustained by a combination of foreign investment, cooked books, and widespread corruption in the privatization process that had enticed the foreign investment in the first place. When the bubble burst around 1997, unions were as weak as they were elsewhere in the region. In fact, they had lost their clout as early as 1994, when the government stopped signing even the weak annual agreements it had earlier negotiated with labor, effectively governing as if the unions did not exist.[5] (It should be noted that throughout Eastern Europe, attempts to incorporate labor through tripartite councils proved to be mere window-dressing, a kind of "illusory corporatism" that only revealed the extent of labor's weakness.)[6]

With unions an increasingly inappropriate vehicle for the articulation of economic discontent, vulnerable workers, mobilized by right-wing politicians, resorted to a familiar practice of the weak: they began deploying their anger not against the wealthy and corrupt but against the poor and defenseless. Right-wing extremism peaked in 1996, when a radical nationalist party won 8 percent of the votes; even though the party soon declined, the continuing lure of its appeal was made clear by a rise in anti-immigrant violence and one dramatic event in 1999: in the depressed mining city of Usti nad Labem, suffering from high unemployment and terrible environmental degradation, local officials responded to growing complaints about hard times by erecting a wall in the city to separate the Roma from the rest of the population.

According to most analysts, Hungarian unions are almost powerless. On the one hand, this is an inheritance from the late communist period, when extensive market reforms empowered managers and gave workers the ability to make extra money in quasi-private firms where neither government nor official labor relations intervened at all. As Laszlo Bruszt wrote, "Hungarian workers 'arrived' [at 1989] with the highest number of market institutions and the weakest and most divided trade unions."[7] Unions continued to be marginalized after 1989 as well. First of all, the country adopted the German system of works councils, which only undercut the influence of unions in the firms. The councils, however, are much weaker than in Germany, with managers not required even to discuss layoffs with them, or with the unions. Moreover, while the councils are supposed to guarantee employee representation even in non-unionized firms, in reality they often do not arise without unions being there to press for them. This combination of weak legacy and marginalizing policy has contributed to the dramatic weakness of labor in the workplace, as manifested in widespread and flagrant disregard of work rules. Unions usually do not contest these violations, but even when they do, protest is ineffective because of government commitments not to alienate employers.[8]

While labor did move toward the Socialists (former communists) in the early 1990s as a response to the deterioration of conditions after 1989, the Socialists' decidedly neoliberal administration created new political problems: in what ways would economic anger be articulated now? The answer came in the form of a party that reinvented itself precisely for the purpose. Fidesz, or the Alliance of Young Democrats, had been a liberal party in the early 1990s, but its weak initial showing, together with astute observation of the collapse of other liberal parties in the region (Hungary's Free Democrats, the Czech Republic's Civic Democrats, and Poland's Democratic Union/ Freedom Union) led it to remake itself explicitly as a party of anger during the Socialist administration. It replaced its benign, fuzzy image as a party of "not quite ready for prime time" young activists[9] with a stern new look emphasizing the defense of diaspora nationals, a radical purging of "communists," the implementation of Christian morality, and the protection of the rural dispossessed against the new elite. Fidesz opposed the trade unions because of their institutional ties to the Socialist Party, but since, as in Poland, such ties did little for labor except provide administrative jobs to some union officials, Fidesz managed to pick up some labor votes, too. Fidesz had drawn the correct political lesson from the collapse of Eastern Europe's liberal parties: parties had to organize anger, not shun it. With this line it swept to power in 1998. After four years of Fidesz's politically illiberal rule, voters swung back to the Socialists in 2002. Fidesz then transformed itself into an even more nationalist, anti-European Union party, despite having negotiated most of the terms for Hungary's entry.

The most egregious example of economic anger finding dangerous, non-economic, non-class modes of articulation remains, of course, the former Yugoslavia. This country that exploded in paroxysms of blood fury was one of the first to tread the path of market reform, and the consequences were among the deepest. Indeed, the key story for most of the 1980s was precisely the country's escalating economic crisis. In response to a rapidly increasing foreign debt, triggered by the system's underlying inefficiency as well as by the western recession (which led to a dramatic decline in hard currency repatriation by immigrant laborers), the government began harsh austerity measures already in 1982, when food subsidies were abandoned. Prices on essentials rose by one-third the following year, and imports were drastically curtailed as the currency lost 90 percent of its value. By the mid-1980s, inflation was rising by more than 50 percent each year, unemployment soared, and the entire economy was plagued by shortages.[10] Successive deals with the IMF only made the situation worse for many. And with democratic changes now taking hold, this became a political problem as much as an economic one. For with discontent mushrooming and elections imminent, the political issue concerned how that discontent would be expressed.

That the emerging economic anger did not get mobilized around class cleavages but only around ethnic ones was due both to structural and voluntarist-political factors. "Class" was a particularly weak unifier in Yugoslavia due not only to factors typical of East European communism, as discussed in chapter 5, but also to specific institutional arrangements that encouraged ethnic mobilization instead.[11] In 1971, in response to recent protests, Marshal Josip Tito amended the constitution to move formal power from the federal to the republican level. This not only ensured the creation of strong ethnically based political organizations, but also virtually guaranteed that future opposition to the government would be directed along divisive national lines rather than unifying civic ones.

Economic anger grew rapidly in the late 1980s when the federal government sought to reassert itself with a sweeping economic reform program. At this point, the powerful republic-based ethnic politicians found themselves threatened not just by economic discontent from below but by a reform project challenging their authority from above. They reacted by assiduously stoking the economic anger of the populace and, in order to save their own skins, inventing a new narrative that blamed the economic problems on *national* others, and thus not on an "other" that federal reform could ameliorate. As V.P. Gagnon writes, in a rich empirical and theoretical argument, rival Yugoslav national elites consistently sought to "provoke and create" threats from outside in order to protect their own power bases threatened by the proposed reforms. "By defining the collective interest in non-economic (cultural or ethnic) terms," elites substituted a political fight that they could win for an economic conflict that put them in jeopardy.[12]

In this way, local actors converted economic anger into nationalist rage, leading to a vicious war and sabotaging chances for liberal democracy for years to come.

Class and Democracy

And so, we return to the importance of class. One of the key arguments in this book has been the claim that class cleavages are crucial for the long-term consolidation of inclusive liberal democratic politics. Class as a cleavage is precisely the recognition of the centrality of interests rather than of identities. Organizing anger along class lines allows groups within capitalist civil society to resist and oppose capitalist logic without the need to posit an alternative socioeconomic universe.

As discussed in chapter 5, I am using class conflict here in Hattam's sense of a cleavage that recognizes the domination of capitalism and seeks to win labor a better deal within that system.[13] It is a militant challenge to private property, but not necessarily a rejection. It is premised on the claim that those who dominate the market economy do not represent universal interests, and that civil society is made up of discrete groups whose crucial difference centers on the distribution of wealth and power. Insofar as it is important for democracy, then, class needs to be understood not as a social location, not as a measurement, not as a thing, and not as a process, but as a cleavage around which social conflicts can be organized and economic anger mobilized. Class conflicts organize social antagonisms in an inclusive way because the competing sides are recognized as part of the same overarching community. The class other has different interests, not a different national identity.[14] And so the other is to be outmaneuvered, not expelled; asked to sacrifice wealth and power, not to convert.

It should be noted that this understanding of class conflict does not entail embracing a Marxist concept of class, which focuses on power differences stemming from the production process. Weberian concepts defining class according to different life-chances based on income work just fine.[15] In either formulation, the notion of economic interest is at the forefront. And as Adam Seligman puts it, it is "interest-motivated action" that is crucial to democratic civil society.[16]

As we have seen in this book, however, class is not a natural category. While capitalist societies necessarily generate economic classes, and thus economic anger, they do not necessarily lead to the political organization of that anger along class lines. "Class" can emerge as a cleavage only as the product of a long discursive struggle. "In any conflict between workers and capitalists," write Przeworski and Sprague, "the principal visions of society are one of class and one of universalism, and both of these ideologies rationalize class interests."[17]

Market elites always expound universalism, or the view that the interests of business are the interests of all. In a system in which private investment is the chief source of jobs, this view has the advantage of seeming like simple common sense. If workers depend for their livelihood on the wealthy deciding to start businesses that will employ them, then their interests really are bound up with the wealthy. The prevalence of this logic is evident in the regular calls, in both underdeveloped and advanced capitalist societies, for tax cuts for the rich—calls which could not be made in a democratic polity without the prevalence of an underlying assumption that the interests of private capital dovetail with the interests of all.

Labor, on the other hand, has an interest in class narratives precisely in order to counter the claims of the elite that pursuing its interests benefit everyone. Showing that capitalists constitute a particular class rather than a universal one is the basis for labor to constitute *itself* as a class, one that is larger and more productive than capital and thus deserving of a larger share of the collective wealth.

As we have seen in this book, however, to say that labor has an interest in pushing a class narrative does not mean that it will always do so. Classes can exist without workers thinking they constitute one. As James Scott puts it, the "objective, structural determinations [of class may] find little echo in the consciousness and meaningful activity of those who are thus identified."[18] Whether class narratives acquire relevance in a given society depends on the presence of savvy labor leaders and intellectuals pushing such a narrative, and on a social base able to think past the encumbrance of myriad non-class identities.

That, as we have seen, did not happen in Poland's first postcommunist decade. Class identities did not take shape because former labor leaders strongly opposed the emergence of class politics, because new labor leaders rejected class as a desirable identity for their members, and because the labor base itself, already poorly disposed to the notion because of the communist past, put no pressure on them to change their minds.

What have been the consequences of this? First, and most apparently, it has led to a weak labor movement, unable to defend its interests against neoliberal reformers and a new elite. But, as I've argued throughout the book, labor issues are intrinsically intertwined with democratic ones. And the consequences for democracy have been even more profound. For the weakness of class cleavages has pushed political life in a decidedly illiberal direction, yielding a democracy in which socioeconomic conflicts have been mobilized around identities rather than interests, with others defined as aliens rather than opponents. Economic conflicts in postcommunist Poland have consistently been turned into battles over who is a true member of the community. Every time Solidarity leaders sought to mobilize economic discontent, which they were regularly forced to do by the anger and discontent elicited by marketization, they did so by blaming—well, anyone but economic others. "Communists," "atheists," and "liberals" were the preferred targets.

These were campaigns of retribution, not empowerment. And by failing to empower labor, they only further damaged the project of Polish democracy. For while such campaigns could be successful at securing political victories for the instigators, they did little for those in whose name they were ostensibly fought. Labor remained weak and became politically incorporated in a decidedly illiberal style. No wonder, then, that subsequent political entrepreneurs, seeking to sop up the anger that remained unsaturated, stuck to the same line. Organizations like the Self-Defense party and the League of Polish Families ran with the aggressive posturing and exclusionary rhetoric that Solidarity had initiated, and even more mainstream parties like Law and Justice, led by former Solidarity vice president Lech Kaczynski, have made retribution against criminals both real and imaginary the cornerstone of its push for power.[19] By doing their best to avoid class politics, which they wrongly believed to be dangerous for capitalism and anathema to democracy, postcommunist reformers and Solidarity leaders contributed to the emergence of a "paranoid" political style that is far more inimical to democratic capitalism than class struggle ever was.[20] Instead of social groups fighting over distribution, with each group recognized as a legitimate representative of particular interests, Poland's dominant political tendencies push identity claims, with others attacked not as selfish but as alien to the community.

With its elections and free press, we may still call it a democracy. And for too many observers operating with a minimalist definition of democracy, that's all there is to say. But if we understand democracy as more than mere procedural rules but rather as an "inclusive" system such as outlined in chapter 1—a system that treats all citizens as legitimate members of the community and provides economic inclusion for its workforce—then this is not much of a democratic system at all. With its recurring tendency of defining opponents as illegitimate to the community and its systematic erosion of social rights for labor, postcommunist Poland has neither been very liberal nor very inclusive.

Has the "transition to democracy" thus been a failure? The question, I think, is the wrong one. Formal democracy has indeed been a success. But then it has never really been in danger.[21] Indeed, once the old ruling elite threw in its lot with a new system, which it did in 1989, there was no group with an interest in restoring dictatorship, much less the capacity to do it.[22] So rather than offering a thumbs-up or thumbs-down on "democratic" success, what we need, I think, is a thick, more detailed characterization of the kinds of democracies that have been established in Eastern Europe. Most studies of postcommunist "consolidation of democracy" have been mired in the minimalist approach that sees democracy as little more than governmental respect for a basic package of civic rights. But in conditions where such basic rights were guaranteed early on—and, indeed, were a condition of West European acceptance—this approach has not been very intellectually stimulating. And insofar as it has meant bracketing questions of social justice and economic distribution, it has been morally deficient as well. While key choices were being made in these crucial areas, too many observers and scholars focused on formal democracy instead, thus allowing social exclusion to proceed unexamined and unimpeded.

Where would we be, after all, if the consolidation of minimal democracy was the basis of social science interest in other parts of the world? There would be little to write about America since the Voting Rights Act of 1964, little to write about Western Europe. Democracy is much more than the right to cast a free ballot—if that wasn't so, there wouldn't have been so much pro-democratic social protest after universal suffrage. To understand democratization in Eastern Europe, we need a keen awareness of the variations within democratic capitalism. Rather than offering a scorecard on the existence of basic individual rights, it's time to treat East Europeans like citizens in other democratic countries and examine the nature and quality of the democracy they have. We need more ethnography, less transitology. And more debate about how to achieve a richer democratic life, rather than condescending satisfaction about the minimal forms already obtained.

By saying that the non-economic organization of anger has illiberal consequences, I do not mean to imply that class cleavages are easy to mobilize. As noted above, class is never a natural or inevitable political cleavage. Even in societies with enormous inequalities based on private ownership, class often fails to grab imaginations, being defeated by elite rhetorics of universalism or trumped by ethnicity, religion, or race. Whether "class" emerges as an organizing cleavage depends on political organizers successfully promulgating the idea that class is central. It depends on people and political parties *arguing* that workers *ought* to think of themselves as members of a class and constructing a narrative plausible enough to make the exhortation convincing.

In the early and middle twentieth century in the advanced capitalist states, class often seemed natural, or at least inescapable, precisely because political organizers *had* made it so prominent and had won enough political power to institutionalize class politics. The Keynesian "postwar settlement," after all, was framed and understood precisely as a settlement to the *class* conflicts that had torn industrialized societies apart. Indeed, one of the key reasons why that "settlement" has broken down in recent years is that a new dominant frame has taken over: globalization. Globalization is a frame, or myth, argu-ing something contrary to class conflict. Its proponents claim that states *are* weak, and then use that claim to justify recommendations that states reduce regulatory controls and labor guarantees in order to *become* weak, which is presented as the only way for societies to become prosperous.[23] The bottom line is that whether class becomes a dominant political cleavage depends on political mobilizers and political intellectuals making it so. In this sense, class is but an organizing frame of social activists. It is a myth, implying a certain narrative, proffered by labor supporters who seek a distribution of wealth and power different from that offered by the elite.

But if it has historically been difficult to cultivate class as an operative cleavage in societies marked by private property, it is certainly even more dif-ficult to cultivate it in societies *without* such divisions, such as postcommu-nist Eastern Europe. Here we get to a serious challenge to my thesis. For perhaps I am right that the economic anger caused by postcommunist mar-ketization *ought* to have been mobilized along economic lines. Perhaps that *would* have been better for democratic liberal politics. But was it at all possi-ble? Could it have been done in societies without much private ownership, where class language was associated with the outgoing dictatorship, and where workers, like everyone else, fervently wanted to believe that they'd be better off in the new system? The range of obstacles was formidable indeed. Workers themselves were allergic to the concept. The very term "working class" conjured up images not of employees in factories but of old men in badly tailored suits haranguing those employees. Class did not have much resonance sociologically either. As discussed in chapter 5, communist soci-ety turned everyone into employees of the state, thus reducing conflicts be-tween social groups and eventually allowing for the phenomenal unity of all social groups against the party-state itself. Even after 1989, class did not be-come objectively prominent very quickly. Marketization, after all, was car-ried out not by capitalists but by reformers who *believed* in capitalism, often disinterestedly. They *wanted* to create a dominant class and a system of class inequalities, but they were themselves not—or at least not yet—the "other" from a class perspective. In such conditions, then, what does it mean to say that anger ought to have been organized along class lines?

My answer can only be that ought means ought. *If* the aim is to firmly in-culcate liberal democratic norms, to establish a system where quarrels over economic distribution do not challenge the political rights of others, then political actors in parties, unions, and popular and intellectual journals ought to promote narratives that conceptualize anger as resulting from class in-equalities. This is what social democratic parties were able so successfully to do in Western Europe, thus providing for an inclusive incorporation of labor and long-term stable democratic systems. Saying it ought to happen is not to say it is easy to bring about. Indeed, that it is difficult has been precisely the problem in Eastern Europe. But this only means that the onus is on would-be democratizers to try to instill meaningful notions of class by doing their best to channel social conflicts along economic lines. The democratic goal is for people to see the economy as the domain in which the conflicts most meaningful to them should be resolved. The economic arena is not the only source of frustration for people, but it is probably the dominant one, and it is certainly the most negotiable one—which is why it *ought* to be promoted as the dominant one. Since religious and nationalist conflicts are often little more than substitute satisfactions for economic woes and thus easy fodder in the rise of illiberal demagogues, the task for democrats is to try to frame these conflicts as the economic ones they are.

If old class concepts no longer work, or no longer appeal, democrats need to come up with new concepts that do work, that resonate better with lived reality.[24] To some extent this has been done lately in the United States. Think of the way American trade unions have rethought classes in recent times: by removing male industrial labor from the center point and recognizing feminized, service, and migrant labor as equally legitimate, they have helped revitalize their organizations and build new coalitions.[25] The recent revival of trade unionism in Poland shows the same thing happening there, with service and retail industries finally being recognized by unions as a place where workers work. The point is that the aim of democratizers should be not to repress the political articulation of economic inequalities but to encourage it—not to fear strong trade unions but to encourage them.

Eastern Europe has faced considerable difficulties in this regard, and the problem is far from over. Whether inclusive democracy succeeds depends not so much on constitution-building or specific market mechanisms or the proper sequence of reform or proximity to the West, to name variables others have promoted. It depends on how politicians mobilize discontent, on how they organize anger. It depends on the narratives and paradigms they present to the populace, and the ones they get the populace to accept.

Civil Society, Bourgeois Society, and Political Responsibility

One of the aims of this book has been to defend East European workers and the dispossessed in general against the charge that they are a dangerous antidemocratic force with instinctive illiberal predilections that must be guarded against by intellectuals. It is an old conceit of intellectuals to see themselves as guardians of reason against the "populism" of the masses.[26] In Eastern Europe, the charge of "populism" emerged as soon as people started voting for parties that spoke out against painful economic reforms, for candidates who argued that there were indeed alternatives. There's no question that some candidates who attracted considerable support at the time *were* shady characters offering obviously unrealistic promises, such as Stan Tyminski in Poland. Demagogic, extremist right-wing parties *were* able to capitalize on economic discontent. In large part, however, this has been due to liberal intellectuals not giving the frightened and frustrated an alternative.

It is easy to attack poor people's illiberal manifestations as a product of dangerous innate characteristics and invoke that old canard of "working class authoritarianism."[27] A gathering of Eastern Europe's new liberal elites at Rutgers University in 1991 did just this, complaining about how their populations had turned out to be not so liberal after all and blaming the people rather than neoliberal shock therapy policies for such an unfortunate outcome.[28] The problem with this argument is that it ignores the role of intellectuals in *shaping* politics. For if political organization is largely about actors capturing anger by offering narratives of what is good and bad, friend and foe, then intellectuals necessarily play a major role.

They certainly did play a crucial role in Poland. Solidarity as an organization may have been built by workers in 1980, but its politics followed fully from the narratives spun by democratic intellectual oppositionists of the 1970s. The "anti-political" strategy of social openness and political self-restraint, the commitment to dialogue, the eschewal of force—all of this followed from KOR narratives that identified political dictatorship (not just communism) as the prescribed object of anger.[29] Their great democratic achievement was to successfully organize anger at the communist system behind the emancipatory narrative of civil society. Wherever this narative took hold in Eastern Europe, events unfolded peacefully.

But these same intellectuals have to take responsibility for the collapse of liberal politics, too. On the one hand, having so successfully organized politics up to 1989, they basically gave up as soon as they had won. By refusing even to countenance, much less organize, the discontent of the postcommunist period, they let others organize that anger instead. This refusal to recognize dissatisfaction and anger as inescapable features of capitalism, as attributes not dangerous to democracy (provided they are organized toward inclusive ends) was a major political blunder. Even worse, however—because it was deceptive too—was their reframing of the meaning of civil society. Liberal intellectuals abandoned their earlier use of the concept as a project of complete democratic openness and gave it an entirely new meaning entailing little more than the building of a market economy. Previous chapters of this book have shown again and again how the Solidarity intellectuals who came to power in 1989 continually defended all their neoliberal economic policies on the grounds that this was what building civil society was all about. There was no alternative, they said. If you want democracy, if you want civil society, then you want precisely these specific policies we say are necessary.

This was a monumental shift. By conflating civil society with bourgeois society,[30] they were backtracking on their profound theoretical innovation separating the two. Indeed, it was just this separation that was at the heart of the East European contribution to democratic theory. It was the East Europeans who, in the 1970s, brought the concept of civil society back into western political theory. They did so by detaching it from both state and market and making it into a terrain all its own, based on openness, communication, and rational discourse.[31] By defining civil society in this way and positing it as the heart of democracy, they were able to defend democracy equally well against orthodox Marxist charges that it was merely "bourgeois democracy" and against free-market capitalist claims that private ownership is a sufficient guarantor of democracy.[32] This was something quite new in the context of the Cold War dichotomies of the time, which is why it has been so important to western theorists of civil society, all the more so because the original Solidarity movement put the theory so brilliantly into practice.[33]

However unfortunate this theoretical about-face may have been for the contemporary understanding of civil society in the West,[34] the real damage it did was to democratic consolidation in the East. For by conflating bourgeois society with civil society—that is, by insisting that radical economic liberalism (in the European sense of free-market economics) was the foundation for political liberalism—the new elite allowed those who disagreed with the former to reject the latter as well. With opposition to shock therapy officially construed as opposition to political liberalism, the liberal elite *created* opponents of the latter. (Postcommunist Russia is of course the worst example of this, as the very term "democrat" came to be a pejorative implying the worst of capitalist abuses.) If democratic outcomes in capitalist societies are made possible by intellectual elites providing inclusive frameworks for capturing the anger and discontent market societies produce, then it is not surprising that non-elites began to embrace irrational parties.

For these reasons, I think it is better to understand labor's right-wing turn as the betrayal of the intellectuals than the irrationalism of the masses. Over the course of the 1980s and early 1990s, the intellectuals who had won the workers' trust moved from being champions of political liberalism to champions of economic liberalism. They squandered that trust when they pushed Solidarity into supporting a radical marketization program whose true social costs they disguised in order to secure that support. Solidarity the union invested considerable social capital to support shock therapy. But liberals assigned workers little role in the transition but to sacrifice on behalf of a "greater good" that conspicuously left them behind.[35] So insistent were the liberal intellectuals (former Solidarity ideologues) that shock therapy was mandated by "freedom," "democracy," "reason" and other good things that the only way many unionists could think their way out of liberal economics was to think their way out of liberal politics too.

Liberals throughout the region seem unable to recognize their own role in these developments. Listen, for example, to Professor Zoran Pajic from Sarajevo: "After the Communist system collapsed, all that liberals like me could offer was the free market and free institutions. People were terrified. They were not ready for these insecurities. And this was a gap that had to be filled by nature. So the nationalists arose. . . ."[36] What is revealing here is precisely what has been so common among postcommunist liberals: the resignation in the voice, the sense that liberalism is doomed if and when people are "terrified." We see here, as in Poland, the inability to recognize that liberalism must try to address insecurities too, by trying to structure antagonisms the way they are successfully structured in already existing liberal democracies, along economic lines. Contrary to Pajic, these matters are not determined by "nature." Those who seek inclusive democratic outcomes need to deploy their own will, and try to organize social anger differently than illiberals will.

Theoretical Explanations of Labor Weakness

I have presented in this book an account of Polish labor weakness that stresses the role of ideas. Mine, to use an awkward term, is an *ideational* account of labor weakness in postcommunist Poland. It was the strong pro-market ideas held by union leaders and the rank and file and their low self-esteem, I argue, that left labor unable to defend its interests or pursue its agenda in the postcommunist era. The consequences of this weakness I locate chiefly in the political realm, in the damage it does to democracy by forcing class anger to be expressed in illiberal ways. But the causes of the weakness (including the inability to think in class terms, which is an expression of that weakness) follows from ideas.

Of course, as discussed in the previous chapter, these ideas and attitudes themselves stemmed from the structural legacy of communism. Party control of the economy was the key factor here. Since the Party ran the entire economy, social conflicts were necessarily waged against the state, rather than between social groups fighting each other. This had two effects: it made communism labor's enemy, and it allowed other social groups to act in the name of labor (in whose name all protests against the Party had to be waged). The first effect left labor unusually favorably disposed to capitalism as the enemy's official enemy, while the second left unionists willing and able to recognize intellectuals as their leaders. And both of these factors, meanwhile, left workers after 1989 believing that radical marketization might be in their interests, and that those pushing for such marketization might be their allies. The structural legacy of communism left labor unable to carve out a sense of its *own* interests, and thus unwilling and unable to forcefully defend its interests afterwards.[37] But although communist structures shaped a labor movement unable to defend its own interests, it was labor's *holding on* to these ideas that kept it weak in the postcommunist period. It is in this sense that I am arguing that ideas played the key role.

Since idea-based explanations are still unpopular in the social sciences, and particularly political science,[38] which prefers to look at the interests or institutions behind actions, it is worth exploring whether more popular rational choice or institutionalist accounts would help to explain post-1989 labor outcomes. A rational choice approach would seem the easiest to dispense with, since it assumes that groups fight to realize their interests while what I've shown so far is workers doing exactly the opposite. Union leaders pushing for policies certain to decrease the influence of unions, employee council members pushing for privatization strategies in which employee councils would not exist, unionists advocating weak unions (particularly in private firms), vulnerable workers embracing programs calling for the "acceleration" of market relations: obviously something other than rational self-interest has been at work here. The hypotheses generated from within a rational choice perspective at the outset of the transition, predicting that labor would follow the familiar working-class agenda of struggle against market logic, have not come true.[39] Labor has not waged strong campaigns in its own interests anywhere in the former Soviet bloc.[40] More typical has been the attitude of Aleksandr Sergeev, a leader of the Russian Independent Miners Union who, in 1991, just before the onset of perhaps the worst peacetime depression in history, said, "We naturally support the new bourgeoisie."[41]

Of course, rationality can partly explain the behavior of some former labor officials who were beginning to become aware of their own *individual* interests and used their positions to advance those interests. Intellectuals who now had an opportunity to move ahead in business and government, engineers who were positioned to enter into management, local union leaders who had their eyes set on the new local government positions now opening up—all of them could feel that disciplining the workforce was in their own best interest. The point, however, is that all this was possible only to the extent that the majority of workers were unclear about *their* interests, about which policies would benefit them. In this case, then, we don't have a rational choice explanation of an outcome brought about by masses of actors acting rationally,[42] but simply a story of elites advancing their own interests on the backs of unknowing citizens. So whereas rational choice theory is often criticized for its narrow view of what constitutes interests, my criticism is different: rational choice theory fails to explain postcommunism insofar as it assumes people know their interests.[43] In early postcommunism, that is an implausible assumption.

Institutionalist explanations don't seem to get us very far either. In traditional institutionalist accounts, actors deeply embedded in networks providing extensive contacts with a host of relevant institutions enjoy a decisive negotiating advantage.[44] The problem here, however, is that no organization was more deeply embedded in the post-1989 political structure than Solidarity. Its leaders quickly occupied most important governmental posts, and even institutions outside its control had to take its views into account. This deep embeddedness and broad range of contacts did not make labor strong, however, because labor's priorities were not to help itself, either as unions or as workers.

Historical institutionalist accounts that assume the durability and lasting influence of previous arrangements, meanwhile, also fail to explain Polish outcomes. For as we have seen, Solidarity after 1989 put considerable effort into *undermining* its own organization, along with the influence that labor had secured. The union largely refrained from recruiting new members, admonished current members to take their lead from management, supported the consolidation of hierarchical and non-participatory industrial relations institutions, and exercised no discipline over its parliamentarians. It even let its powerful newspaper dissipate into irrelevance. (Poised to regain its 1981 status as a premier voice in the political public sphere, *Solidarity Weekly* was never taken seriously by the union's leadership, and soon became little more than a shrill mouthpiece of the political right.) Labor developments after 1989 did not evolve in accordance with existing institutions, nor did organizational actors work to further the interests of their organizations. A historical institutionalist approach has little to contribute.

For my ideational thesis, there is always the objection that it was simple objective economic reality that led to this dramatic labor decline, and that ideas merely reflected this gloomy reality. What we are trying to explain, however, is not a labor movement being defeated by economic reality but one that helped bring about the reality that defeated it. Of course there were economic restraints that thwarted possibilities of labor advancement, but the record before us clearly shows that labor was an active participant in its own marginalization. Economic difficulties, interests, institutions—none of these can adequately explain such developments. Ideas and attitudes can.

In the same way, we can understand why things began to change at the end of the 1990s. For as experiences changed, ideas that seemed risible a decade earlier—such as organizing opposition to market-based elites—suddenly seemed to make sense. As time passed, the ideational factors that hindered the emergence of a sense of independent labor interests began to disappear. Most important was the change in the relevant past. In place of communist-era social structures now stood those of a market society. Instead of a single state-owner fighting to maintain political power came diverse social interests competing for money. The unity of social groups (against the Communist Party) turned into clashes among differing social groups. Government policy acting in the interests of a class that did not exist gradually called that class into existence, and when that class acted as policy-makers hoped it would act—in an aggressively acquisitive manner—it both created a non-governmental target of anger and demonstrated to labor that no longer did all anticommunists share common interests. Communism as a common enemy, capitalism as a common project—this picture of the world began to recede into the past.

As I argued in the first chapter, different socioeconomic and political structures yield different anger regimes, or rules governing how and against whom people express their anger. After a decade of a market economy, then, structures had changed sufficiently to elicit new patterns of anger. The old unity of all against the Party, an attitude that lingered long enough to become the basis for "anticommunist" narratives even when communists no longer ruled, finally began to crack under the strains of "really-existing" capitalism. (I use this term as an analogue to "really-existing socialism," the phrase coined by communist-era dissidents to denote the lived reality of the system, not its grand theory.) As people came to learn which marketization policies were in their interests and which were not, as they learned through hard experience that privately owned capital does not necessarily reward hard work, and as a new generation emerged that took Poland's young capitalism as a baseline rather than a grand historical accomplishment, people felt increasingly free to direct anger at targets from the present rather than the past. New structures allowed the emergence of new ideas and generated the people who could propose them.

And so another important development was the emergence of a new labor cohort. The first Solidarity activists, who began their union work in 1980 and renewed it after 1989, were able to use their positions to do rather well for themselves. Self-gain was not the reason they got involved, but when the old order broke apart, a new one emerged requiring new people with correct pedigrees, so the former Solidarity elite naturally found themselves in prime position. Upward mobility, in other words, came with the turf. Intellectual activists became ministers and politicians, engineers became managers and local governmental officials, and the skilled workers who took over the union in the early 1990s held on until the election of the SEA government in 1997 gave *them* a chance to move up and out. It was only with the outflow of this last group of unionists—only with the departure of the Braneks and Oli-nowiczes—that a brand-new cohort came to union work. This was a young group, with little memory of 1980. Stanislaw Ciepiera, the union activist at Opel-Gliwice, was eighteen at the time and not yet in the mines; those I met at Solidarity's Union Development Office or OPZZ's Confederation of Labor were kids. For them, union activism brought no outside benefits at all. If they were going to be involved in unions, it was *only* to be involved in unions. Labor politics had become so marginalized at the time of their involvement, and Solidarity as a political organization so discredited, that it was far more likely that they would pay a penalty for their involvement, in terms of further career advancement, than reap any gains.

As a new generation started realizing that capitalism was not the system they were fighting for but the one they were living in, and that it was not the panacea so many had earlier believed, critical ideas started gaining a new currency. And suddenly this did not just mean the ideas of the right. After years of being marginalized, former Solidarity intellectuals who had stayed loyal to social democratic ideas started attracting a new audience. When former union adviser Taduesz Kowalik published a piece titled "My 1989," recalling various criticisms of shock therapy that now sounded prescient, he was besieged by more requests to give public speeches and media interviews than he had gotten in over a decade.[45] Jacek Kuron, calling his role as a key promoter of shock therapy the biggest mistake of his life, now devoted himself to promoting labor participation and social movement activism—and found himself, in his late 60s, largely ignored by mainstream media and politicians but urgently contacted by young people seeking alternatives. In these last years of his life he became a kind of patron-saint to Poland's budding "alter-globalization" movement.[46] This movement, meanwhile, started attracting real support for the first time at the beginning of the new century, finding one of its most perceptive critics, and promoters, in the work of the young journalist Artur Domoslawski.[47] And in 2002 a group of independent left-leaning graduate students started *Krytyka Polityczna*, a forum for critical ideas that is already one of the most vibrant intellectual journals in Eastern Europe. New ideas were definitely in the air.[48]

There were also changes in the relations of the outside world to Eastern

Europe. Up until 1989, the West related to the people of the region solely through the prism of communism. Even western trade unions did so, aiding Solidarity in its efforts to survive but not dealing much with trade union issues. Of course, doing otherwise would not have made much sense at the time, but the point is that East Europeans entered the postcommunist period without having had much input from western trade unions about how to resist the transgressions of a market economy. Then, after 1989, it was western governments and businesses that most prominently got involved, providing aid chiefly for privatization, currency stabilization, and other aspects of market conversion.[49] Where western unions got involved, their initial emphasis was on teaching good citizenship, not good unionism, as in the 1990 EU-sponsored "Project 'Social Dialogue,'" intended to instruct workers in postcommunist states on the details of West European tripartite and neo-corporatist arrangements.[50] All in all, there were few ways Polish unionists could even hear strong labor ideas in the early 1990s, and in any case, as we have seen, they did not particularly want to.

By the middle of the decade, however, as western labor took stock of the changes in the international political economy, as they saw western businesses and banks moving into the region, buying out state-owned firms and using the region as a source of cheap labor, unions began to realize that they had to get more involved, if only for reasons of self-interest. In Europe, this coincided with the deepening of European integration and the commitment to eastward expansion, making union cooperation more vital than ever. In the United States, it coincided with a change in the leadership of the AFL-CIO, a move away from the old guard closely associated with the Cold War to a new leadership focused on union revitalization. By the end of the decade, interest in global unionism became even stronger, as western trade unions got increasingly involved in the alter-globalization movement. The result was a significant increase in international union activity with and directed at Eastern Europe.

Where unions already existed, this meant visits by unionists to the worksites and headquarters of same-sector union colleagues, and a policy of sharing information about the tactics of common employers. By 1996, most of the mid-level union officials I met in the steel or machine sectors had already been to Western Europe on trips sponsored by western trade unions, often on EU funds. Where unions did not exist, western union activists became interested in organizing them. It was to conduct just such an organizing workshop that the American SEIU came to Poland, as discussed in the previous chapter, leading to the creation of Solidarity's Union Development Office. In 2001, the British retail trade union USDAW launched an initiative to organize Tesco hypermarket employees in Eastern Europe. Sometimes, as we saw at Opel, Polish unionists independently sought out western unionists to support an organizing drive of their own.

Aside from direct union-to-union cooperation, dissemination of knowledge on labor affairs came thanks to imminent EU integration. For this brought workshops, training seminars in Brussels, and other efforts to familiarize new members on the many labor provisions of EU law. If East European workers did not hear many social democratic ideas up to the mid-1990s, they were exposed to plenty of them afterwards, both those already embedded in EU provisions and those western social democrats hoped to add in the future. The latter, after all, understood that they were now fighting for their own future as well.

Last but not least, new ideas entered via increased academic cooperation with the West. Some of this, again, came thanks to the EU. Solidarity became a member of the European Trade Union Confederation, and in 1997 the ETUC's research arm, the European Trade Union Institute, started *Transfer*, a journal heavily devoted to labor issues in transition economies. (*Transfer* provides more mainstream academic analysis than that old indispensable workhorse, *Labour Focus on Eastern Europe*, the British left-wing journal that has played a vital role in facilitating the exchange of activist and academic pro-labor ideas from the 1970s up to today.) Another EU-funded initiative, the European Industrial Relations Observatory (http://www.eiro. eurofound.ie), offers short, current pieces on industrial relations issues all across Europe. Inside Poland, the Friedrich Ebert Foundation, a German social democratic NGO that first set up a regional office in Warsaw in 1990, has played a particularly important role. Ebert finances labor research projects in the country, sponsors conferences, and publishes numerous books and pamphlets (in both Polish and English) that it gives away for free. Many of the Polish books I consulted in writing this manuscript were either published or co-published by Ebert, which funded much of the research contained therein as well.[51]

Aside from research and publications, it is also important to note the creation of Poland's first academic degree program in industrial relations and human resources management, established by sociology professor Wieslawa Kozek at the University of Warsaw in the mid-1990s. By 2002 the program was graduating twenty students a year.[52] This too arrived thanks to international cooperation, including help from Professor Adrienne Eaton of the Industrial Relations Department of Rutgers University, a grant from the U.S. Department of Labor, and strong support by Andrzej Tymowski from the East European section of the American Council of Learned Societies.

In all these ways, then, the idea of labor having legitimate particular interests of its own began entering the public sphere, contributing to the belated emergence of working class activism in the late 1990s.

This belated emergence, however, does not mean that an entirely new era is at hand, either in industrial relations or in politics. Once established, institutional patterns are difficult to change, and the formal and informal transformation of labor relations after 1989 established patterns not just of strong management and weak labor but also of labor that simply did not believe in itself. Some things have begun to change, but there is still little unionism in the country, few collective bargaining agreements, and, for most people in the country, little sense of being involved in the decisions that affect them. (According to Polish industrial sociologists whom I spoke with in summer 2004, the mini-labor mobilization of 2001-2002 had already died down. Even in the hypermarkets organizing had declined, and even under new leadership national Solidarity was still hesitant in embracing a new activist style.) Moreover, as recent research has shown, the bulk of new investment capital coming to Eastern Europe goes to economic sectors not very conducive to strong unionism.[53] It will take a great deal of effort before the damage can be undone—particularly the political damage.

What the Future May Bring

On May 1, 2004, Poland, along with nine other countries, most from Eastern Europe, joined the European Union. Ever since the accession process was finalized a year earlier, many treated the development as proof that the transition was over, that democracy was stable and secure. Grant aid began leaving these countries amid the growing sense that there was little left to worry about. My concern about continuing threats from the right due to weak and unincorporated labor might thus seem too alarmist. Why spoil the fun? As we reach the middle of this decade, certainly the Middle East is more worrisome than the eastern part of Europe.

Let's then take a look at likely future prospects through the prism of the special issue of the flagship journal *East European Politics and Society* (*EEPS*) devoted to EU enlargement.[54] For hidden in the surface narrative of unparalleled success is an important cautionary tale suggesting large potholes in the road ahead.

All the essays agree that enlargement has in no sense been a contract of equals. Rather, it's been a process of the EU setting the terms and agenda, with the petitioning states following along. It was Eastern Europe, of course, that raised the matter in the first place, telling the West, already in 1990, that it was looking forward to realizing the dream of a united Europe as soon as possible. The EU found itself as unprepared to accept—and as unable not to accept—as was West Germany to the reunion pleas of East Germans. But although the EU may have been pushed into enlargement by "rhetorical entrapment,"[55] having itself always pushed the idea during the Cold War when it was entirely impossible, it rebounded quickly by making sure that enlargement would take place on its own terms. Dragging the process out over a decade and a half of training programs, association agreements, and precise instructions to the various parliaments about the legislation they needed to pass, the old members managed to reduce not only eastern expectations but its economic benefits as well (in comparison to previous poorer entrants Spain, Portugal, and Greece) and to make accession into an arrangement that should benefit the old members quite well.[56] Bargaining was tough. Stephen Holmes mentions a host of ways in which the West has used its advantage in order to maintain and even to expand that advantage in the "united" Europe, such as withholding the structural adjustment funds awarded previous entrants, maintaining barriers on eastern imports while eliminating them on western exports, cutting agricultural subsidies for new entrants, dampening the new member states' contact with their eastern neighbors (because of immigration issues), continuing the ban on free access of the eastern workforce to the EU labor market, and creating new EU governing processes that allow the West to monitor the East even after the latter are full members.[57]

The terms of the accession, the style of the negotiations (which Wade Jacoby likens to a "dialogue" between "the priest and the penitent"),[58] the enforcement of uniformity—all this makes East European governments less likely, because less able, to protect the interests of their domestic actors. In many cases, the plethora of EU norms (or as Bruszt and Stark call it, "*norm*alization")[59] are likely to destroy thriving eastern industries unable to afford the costs of modern regulation. The conundrum, then, to quote Bruszt and Stark again, is that as Eastern Europe becomes more embedded in the EU economy, "the greater will be the pressure on their governments to use regulation more as a means of *adjustment* to the short-term requirements of increasing global competitiveness and less as a means to create newly enlarged, more inclusive, alliances coordinating diverse local considerations."[60] In other words, as integration proceeds, look for domestic ties to be further sundered and local actors to be passed over in favor of international ones. Needless to say, such domestic exclusion is the soil on which illiberalism grows.

Of course, previous EU entrants also faced new superregulatory regimes, yet they often managed to preserve and even strengthen their economic institutions, such as tripartite social dialogue. But this gets us back to the content of this book. Previous entrants were able to preserve domestic inclusivity to the extent that EU integration had *not* been preceded by an assault on trade unions and the attempt to dismantle domestic networks. With unions, business associations, and former economic coordination mechanisms marginalized by years of neoliberal policies, East European societies find themselves in a weaker position vis-à-vis the EU than previous entrants did.

So what are the implications for politics? One essay in the *EEPS* collection makes an argument similar to mine, about the tendency of an overreliance on economic liberalism to lead to political illiberalism. Governments, say Grzymala-Busse and Innes, have had no choice but to pursue the prescribed neoliberal politics. People have been free to choose which parties win, but not which policies win; there is "electoral accountability but not policy accountability."[61] (As Holmes puts it, "voting starts to resemble a pointless act of protest when policy remains unchanged even after incumbents are tossed out by a disappointed electorate.")[62] In this context, they say, irresponsible populist and nationalist parties have an edge, for the outlandish things they propose make it *look* as if they offer some alternative.[63]

We are, it seems, back to the book's starting point—the exasperated outburst by the eminent Berkeley professor who said "Labor *must* lose. No one can do anything about it." As I've argued throughout, to say this and nothing more is tantamount to an acceptance of an un-inclusive form of democracy and an illiberal polity. It is the assumption of "no alternative" that is the problem. For when political liberals assume there's no choice in economic policy, and when the "only acceptable" policy is one that benefits them while excluding and angering so many others, they willy-nilly drive voters into the arms of illiberals.

If the aim is to promote the possibility of broad political democracy, the assumption of "no alternative" must be replaced by one of ongoing negotiations and concessions over economic issues. And such negotiations are always possible, whatever the overarching budget constraints, when they are understood as concerning concessions, not capitulation. In this sense, there are always alternatives. Both sides need to recognize this. Non-elites do so when they organize along economic cleavages, and elites need to encourage such cleavages and allow room for concessions. That was the path to successful democratization in Western Europe. By contrast, we can recall that when Solidarity unionists demanded concessions in 1993, the liberal government insisted on capitulation instead, resulting in its ouster and in the illiberal turn of Solidarity.

The claim that there is "no alternative" is of course the mantra of globalization. As countless critics have pointed out, however, it is itself an ideological claim, not a neutral statement of reality. Bienefeld, for example, shows how the claim delights the greedy by making greed less morally objection-able. Greider shows how it legitimates corporate negligence of workplace safety, on the grounds that such negligence is necessary for global competi-tiveness.[64] The assumption, in other words, is a *pre-eminently* political claim. Repeating the assumption reinforces the politics behind it.

And so it seems to me that Ken Jowitt, concluding the *EEPS* special issue, has it right when he says we need *more* ideology—more bold ideas that go counter to what's allegedly "impossible," more heroism, and more activism. Democracy in the West came about in large part due to the persuasiveness of a powerful liberal ideology, and the passion that ideology instilled in people originally excluded by it. Shunning ideology now in favor of pragmatic eco-nomics, as most advisers recommend, will only "disarm Western liberal capi-talist democracy by abandoning the terrain of ideology to proto-ideological movements of resentment." It is "the EU's obsession with economic costs," Jowitt notes, that *produces* such "anti-Western movements of rage," but the ob-session can only be overcome by a "partisan and passionate" ideology advo-cating a different vision.[65] So the question (to use somewhat different words) becomes, which kind of anger is going to prevail? The kind that challenges economic "rationality" by reactionary, illiberal appeals to nation, race, civi-lization, and religion, or the kind that recalls how pro-Enlightenment west-ern thought has challenged the "no alternative" fallacy in the past and comes up with an inclusive program equivalent to the postwar economic settlement?

This is not the place to discuss the many viable programs and proposals (such as the Tobin Tax, or social clauses on trade treaties) developed by dem-ocratic critics of neoliberal globalization. It is, however, worth noting that while liberals still tend to treat such proposals as idealistic, unrealistic, and thus not worthy of political attention[66]—despite recent successes such al-ternative policies have had in Argentina[67]—the political right, as this book should make clear, has not ignored the issue at all. On the contrary, they rail at the demise of economic inclusion and come up with all sorts of danger-ously concrete programs to fight it. So have they done in Western Europe and the United States, where for years the right has been deftly milking pop-ular anxiety about the end of the postwar economic boom. As solutions, they propose programs aimed against minorities and civil liberties, promising physical safety in lieu of economic security. If and when the enlarged EU fails to deliver the goods that many are still hoping for, we may reach a time when an extreme right in both East and West will finally have its chance at power. Unless they're no longer the only ones to seriously contemplate alternatives.

Jowitt says that the needed response is "a revitalized and recast liberal ide-ology," and he calls for a revisionist European capitalism to challenge the neoliberal American orthodoxy.[68] I have argued for a new engagement with class. Again: a *new* engagement, not the old one. As Jowitt argues that abandoning ideology only means conceding the terrain to others, so I have shown how Polish liberals (and the left) gave up on class language and concerns, allowing the right to mobilize labor instead. To say class is no longer relevant because it no longer explains social dynamics or because we live in a postmodern world where such narratives no longer make sense[69]—this is to concede the terrain of class organization to others, which the Le Pens and Leppers of the world are more than happy to do. That the old liberal, social democratic concept of class no longer "unites" as it once did only means it's necessary to find a new language, for as is all too clear from the example of postcommunist society, the realities class evokes still produce pain and anger. Parties still have to organize people shaped by those experiences. Class certainly needs to be rethought to take into account the diverse experiences of today. This is the only way it can become appealing once again. And we toss it out only at a steep price to democracy.

Notes

Introduction

1. Marian Krzaklewski, "16 rocznica Sierpnia," in *Tygodnik Solidarnosc*, September 13, 1996.
2. Philadelphia: Temple University Press, 1990.
3. See, for example, Christopher Beem, *The Necessity of Politics* (Chicago: University of Chicago Press, 1999); and Lani Guinier and Gerald Torres, *The Miner's Canary: Enlisting Race, Resisting Power, Transforming Democracy* (Cambridge: Harvard University Press, 2003), ch. 4.
4. Ost, *Solidarity and the Politics of Anti-Politics*, 203.
5. Ken Jowitt, "The Leninist Extinction," in his *New World Disorder* (Berkeley: University of California Press, 1992).
6. Ibid., 262.
7. By Christianity he means Catholicism. The rise of Protestantism was a sign of the collapse of Christian civilization, just as Khrushchev's and Brezhnev's innovations signaled the beginning of the end of Leninism. Ibid., 255–57.
8. Ibid., 270.
9. Ibid.
10. Ibid., 275.
11. Ibid., 278.
12. See Valerie Bunce, *Subversive Institutions: The Design and the Destruction of Socialism and the State* (Cambridge: Cambridge University Press, 1999).
13. Susan Woodward, *The Balkan Tragedy* (Washington, D.C.: Brookings Institute, 1995).
14. Albert O. Hirschman, *The Passions and the Interests* (Princeton: Princeton University Press, 1977); Christopher Lasch, *The True and Only Heaven: Progress and Its Critics* (New York: Norton, 1991).
15. David Reiff tells of how Serb paramilitary soldiers turned ordinary Bosnian Serbs into killers by first making them kill their neighbors under threat that they would be killed if they refused. Everyone in the village soon understood that ethnicity now mattered. *Slaughterhouse: Bosnia and the Failure of the West* (New York: Simon and Schuster, 1996).
16. Bruce Parrott, "Perspectives on Post-Communist Democratization," in *The Consolidation of Democracy in East-Central Europe*, ed. Karen Dawisha and Bruce Parrott (Cambridge: Cambridge University Press, 1997), 4, 5–6.

205

17. Gil Eyal, Ivan Szelenyi, and Eleanor Townsley, *Making Capitalism without Capitalists: Class Formation and Elite Struggles in Post-Communist Central Europe* (London: Verso, 1998), 3.

Chapter 1. Democracy and the Organization of Anger

1. Michael Burawoy, *The Politics of Production* (London: Verso, 1985), 15.
2. "What Happened in Eastern Europe in 1989?" in *The Crisis of Leninism and the Decline of the Left*, ed. Daniel Chirot (Seattle: University of Washington Press, 1991), 5.
3. *Rocznik Statystyczny 1991* (Warsaw: GUS, 1991), 500.
4. Ibid., xxv.
5. Alexander Matejko, *Social Change and Stratification in Eastern Europe* (New York: Praeger, 1974), 74.
6. Thanks to Jeff Strohl for calculating figures from data set collected for "Social Stratification in Eastern Europe After 1989," research project organized by Ivan Szelenyi and Donald Treiman. Data collected 1993–94. Available at http://archiv.soc.cas.cz/SSEE/SSEE.data.html.
7. Jan Pakulski and Malcolm Waters, "The Reshaping and Dissolution of Social Class in Advanced Society," in *Theory and Society* 25:5 (October 1996), 667–91.
8. Grzegorz Ekiert and Jan Kubik, "Contentious Politics in New Democracies: East Germany, Hungary, Poland, and Slovakia, 1989–1993," in *World Politics* 50:4 (July 1998), 547–81; Ion Bogdan Vasi, "The Fist of the Working Class: The Social Movements of Jiu Valley Miners in Post-Socialist Romania," in *East European Politics and Societies* 18:1 (Winter 2004), 132–57.
9. Barbara Gaciarz, "Dynamika zbiorowych stosunkow pracy," in *Rozpad Bastionu?: Zwiazki Zawodowe w gospodarce prywatyzowanej*, ed. Juliusz Gardawski, Barbara Gaciarz, Andrzej Mokrzyszewski, and Wlodzimierz Pankow (Warsaw: Institute of Public Affairs, 1999), 214.
10. Adam Przeworski, "Some Problems in the Study of the Transition to Democracy," in *Transitions from Authoritarian Rule: Comparative Perspectives*, ed. Guillermo O'Donnell, Philippe Schmitter and Laurence Whitehead (Baltimore: Johns Hopkins University Press, 1986), 63.
11. Leszek Balcerowicz, *Socialism, Capitalism, Transformation* (Budapest: Central European University Press, 1995).
12. Maria Jarosz, "Krajobraz po prywatyzacji," in *Globalizacja, Gospodarka, Praca, Kultura*, ed. Juliusz Gardawski and Jolanta Polakowska-Kujawa (Warsaw: Szkola Glowna Handlowa, 2003), 216. See also her "Suicides as an Indicator of Disintegration of Polish Society," in *Polish Sociological Review* 3 (1999).
13. Bela Greskovits, *The Political Economy of Protest and Patience: Eastern European and Latin American Transformations Compared* (Budapest: Central European University Press, 1998). The main reasons for the lack of protest, he says, is that some old social welfare mechanisms are still in place and that dissatisfaction is more likely to be expressed by voting for opposition parties than by organizing collectively.
14. Grzegorz Ekiert and Jan Kubik, *Rebellious Civil Society: Popular Protest and Democratic Consolidation in Poland* (Ann Arbor: University of Michigan Press, 1999).
15. Greskovits does talk about the need for governments to offer "compensation" to workers in order to get them to accept the costs of transition. But in this very focus on what elites must do to consolidate democracy, he maintains the assumption that labor "counts" only as a potential threat. Greskovits, *The Political Economy*, ch. 7. One of the few exceptions to this tendency is David Stark and Laszlo Bruszt's *Postsocialist Pathways* (Cambridge: Cambridge University Press, 1998). Unlike Greskovits and Ekiert and Kubik, they do not write much about labor, but they do devote a section to the beneficial results of "institutionalized deliberations" (186) between the political authorities and labor representatives, thus stressing the active and positive role labor can play in postcommunist transformation.
16. Most would-be class analysts either had to posit the discovery of a "new class" or argue, contrary to common sense and the absence of private ownership of the means of production, that Eastern Europe was indeed a form of capitalism, namely "state capitalism."

17. Gil Eyal, Ivan Szelenyi, and Eleanor Townsley, *Making Capitalism Without Capitalists: Class Formation and Elite Struggles in Post-Communist Central Europe* (London: Verso, 1998). See also George Konrad and Ivan Szelenyi, *The Intellectuals on the Road to Class Power* (New York: Harcourt Brace Jovanovich, 1979); and Ivan Szelenyi, *Socialist Entrepreneurs* (Madison: University of Wisconsin Press, 1988).

18. Eyal, Szelenyi, and Townsley, *Making Capitalism*, 33.

19. See *Workers after Workers' States: Labor and Politics in Eastern Europe after Communism*, ed. Stephen Crowley and David Ost (Boulder: Rowman & Littlefield Press, 2001); Paul Kubicek, "Organized Labor in Postcommunist States: Will the Sun Set over It, Too?," in *Comparative Politics* 32:1 (October 1999); and Stephen Crowley, "Explaining Labor Weakness in Post-Communist Europe: Historical Legacies and Comparative Perspective," in *East European Politics and Societies* 18:3, Summer 2004, 394–429.

20. Eyal, Szelenyi, and Townsley, *Making Capitalism*, 9.

21. Arlie Russell Hochschild, *The Managed Heart: Commercialization of Human Feeling* (Berkeley: University of California Press, 1983), 56, 75.

22. For more on this and on other themes developed here, see David Ost, "Politics As the Mobilization of Anger: Emotions in Movements and in Power," in *European Journal of Social Theory* 7:2 (2004), 229–44. Istvan Meszaros, "Political Power and Dissent in Post-Revolutionary Societies," in *New Left Review* I/108 (March-April 1978), 3–21 discusses the political implications of transparent versus opaque power.

23. Valerie Bunce, *Subversive Institutions: The Design and the Destruction of Socialism and the State* (Cambridge: Cambridge University Press, 1999), 31.

24. Antonin Liehm, "Intellectuals on the New Social Contract," in *Telos* 23 (1975).

25. It is different, of course, in capitalist *dictatorships*. There, power is also transparent, which explains why such regimes also manage over time to unify society against the authorities, as happened in Latin America or southern Europe in the 1970s.

26. Karl Marx, *Capital: Volume One*, ch. 1.

27. It is worth quoting Hirschman here in full: "As economic growth in the nineteenth and twentieth centuries uprooted millions of people, impoverished numerous groups while enriching some, caused large-scale unemployment during cyclical depressions, and produced modern mass society, it became clear to a number of observers that those caught in these violent transformations would on occasion become passionate—passionately angry, fearful, resentful. . . . Social scientists . . . recorded these developments and analyzed them under the terms of alienation, *anomie, ressentiment, Vermassung*, class struggle, and many others." Albert O. Hirschman, *The Passions and the Interests* (Princeton: Princeton University Press, 1977), 126.

28. The term "market society" comes from Karl Polanyi, who also shows how it necessarily arouses widespread, if imprecise, resistance. *The Great Transformation* (1944; repr., Boston: Beacon Press, 2001).James Scott makes use of Polanyi's ideas, as well as Polanyi's other concept of "moral economy," to document antimarket resistance in southeast Asia in his *Moral Economy of the Peasant* (New Haven: Yale University Press, 1976).

29. Debra Javeline, "The Role of Blame in Collective Action: Evidence from Russia," in *American Political Science Review* 97:1 (February 2003), 119.

30. Donatella Della Porta and Mario Diani, *Social Movements: An Introduction* (Oxford: Blackwell, 1999), 70.

31. Carl Schmitt, *The Concept of the Political* (1927; repr., Chicago: University of Chicago Press, 1996), 28.

32. Ibid., 29.

33. The seminal text here is Seymour M. Lipset and Stein Rokkan, "Cleavage Structures, Party Systems, and Voter Alignments," in their *Party Systems and Voter Alignments* (New York: Free Press, 1967).

34. For a fuller discussion of interests, see David Ost, "The Politics of Interest in Post-Communist East Europe," in *Theory and Society* 22 (August 1993).

35. Frances Fox Piven and Richard A. Cloward, *Poor People's Movements* (New York: Vintage Books, 1977), 15; and Greskovits, *The Political Economy*.

36. Social movement theory discusses these issues in terms of "frames." Movements, it is said, succeed not only by organizing effective actions but by getting people to accept and inhabit the cultural, symbolic, and ideological universe that movement theorists propose. Before a movement can succeed in redressing grievances, it must get people to accept its definition ("frame") of what the grievance is and its claim about how it can be redressed. This is what is meant by movements "constructing" social problems. The "construction" involves two elements: identifying something as a problem and identifying the "enemy" that must be targeted in order to correct the problem. See Della Porta and Diani, *Social Movements*, 68–74; William Gamson, *Talking Politics* (Cambridge: Cambridge University Press, 1992); and David Ost, "Politics as the Mobilization of Anger," in *European Journal of Social Theory* 7:2 (2004), 229–44.

37. Richard Hofstadter, *The Paranoid Style in American Politics* (New York: Knopf, 1965); Seymour Martin Lipset, *Political Man* (New York: Doubleday, 1960).

38. John D. McCarthy and Meyer Zald, "Resource Mobilization in Social Movements: A Partial Theory," in *American Journal of Sociology* 82 (May 1977), 1212–34.

39. Robert Dahl is commonly cited as the inspiration behind the consensus against "substantive democracy"; surely his wonderfully imagined dialogues between "Jean-Jacques" and "James" in *Democracy and its Critics* make the case very well (New Haven: Yale University Press, 1989; esp. ch. 16). But behind Dahl, and even more important, lies Isaiah Berlin's *Four Concepts of Liberty*, with its demonstration that not all good things are commensurable, along with the claim that the attempt to make them so usually leads to something even worse.

40. The early transition theorists were not unsympathetic to the problem. They said they defined democracy procedurally because this definition was consistent with different material outcomes, with more or less redistribution. They themselves seemed to favor more redistribution. Przeworski, Schmitter, and O'Donnell called themselves social democrats. Yet the thrust of their approach necessarily led in a neoliberal direction. While democracy may be compatible with high levels of redistribution, their procedural definition continually leads them to advise against it, since any moves toward redistribution might upset the propertied classes and thus the democratic consensus. In the end, the proceduralist definition amounts to blackmail with a human face: we would like to do good for you but we can't, because if we try to we may end up doing even worse for you. Albert Hirschman identifies this as the "futility thesis," a staple of what he calls *The Rhetoric of Reaction* (Cambridge: Harvard University Press, 1991).

41. See James Scott's description of pre-market Indochina, where consistent elite intervention to avert the ever-present danger of starvation kept society coherent and kept peasants from demanding "democracy." European feudalism or Chinese Confucianism maintained similar reciprocal ties that, *when functioning*, kept people from demanding "democracy." *Moral Economy of the Peasant* (New Haven: Yale University Press, 1976).

42. See ibid. Scott explains the revolutionary turmoil in southeast Asia as the result of a market economy upsetting the rules of the traditional moral economy. This, of course, is also Polanyi's key point in *The Great Transformation*.

43. On the crucial role of the nation-state in embedding capitalism, see Immanuel Wallerstein, "The Agonies of Liberalism" and "Liberalism and the Crisis of Nation-States," in *After Liberalism* (New York: New Press, 1995). For more theoretical reflections on inclusion, see Iris Marion Young, *Inclusion and Democracy* (Oxford: Oxford University Press, 2000).

44. Dietrich Rueschemeyer, Evelyne Huber Stephens, and John D. Stephens, *Capitalist Development and Democracy* (Chicago: University of Chicago Press, 1992), 8. In nineteenth-century France, bourgeois liberals repeatedly solicited workers' support for the struggle against the old feudal elites, only to abandon them once the monarchists were ready to deal with the liberals. While such deals may have furthered the specific interests of the bourgeoisie, they did little as far as achieving democracy was concerned. See Ronald Aminzade, *Class, Politics, and Early Industrial Capitalism: A Study of Mid-Nineteenth Century France* (Albany: State University of New York Press, 1981). Of course, workers have themselves often played the same duplicitous role

vis-à-vis others, achieving rights for themselves but not for women, ethnic minorities, or racial others. Nevertheless, labor inclusion remains the key democratic turning point because it obliterates the exclusionary "rational" criteria of liberalism, according to which only elite-certified rational human beings have political rights. The great liberal John Stuart Mill could justify his calls for the exclusion of colonized peoples or for multiple votes for the educated on the grounds that Africans were not rational beings—and workers not fully so. The racial exclusions favored by workers, however, most notably in the United States and South Africa, were based on prejudice and interest alone, without any theoretical principle to back it up. It was the destruction of any *theoretical* obstacle to full inclusion that makes labor's struggle for inclusion the moment at which the democratic ideal becomes universal.

45. Alexander Hicks, Joya Misra, and Tang Nah Ng, "The Programmatic Emergence of the Social Security State," in *American Sociological Review* 60 (June 1995), 329–49.

46. Gregory Luebbert, *Liberalism, Fascism, or Social Democracy: Social Classes and the Political Origins of Regimes in Interwar Europe* (New York: Oxford University Press, 1991).

47. Ibid., 258.

48. Ruth Berins Collier and David Collier argue that systemic political outcomes in Latin America are the product of the particular way in which labor is incorporated there. *Shaping the Political Arena* (Princeton: Princeton University Press, 1991).

49. As Adam Przeworski and John Sprague write, "Class position structures daily experience, generates a certain kind of knowledge, and may even evoke . . . a feeling of solidarity. But this experience need not become collectivized as one of class." *Paper Stones: A History of Electoral Socialism* (Chicago: University of Chicago Press, 1986), 8.

50. The literature on the interconnection between class and ethnicity is quite large, most of it focusing on particular cases rather than the broad theoretical problem. See, for example, Albert Lindemann on French anti-capitalism becoming anti-Semitism, Charters Wynn on the same phenomenon in tsarist Russia, Allister Sparks on Afrikaner anti-capitalism turning into racism, Ronald Takaki on American class anger becoming anti-Chinese anger, and David Roediger on American labor's resistance to the move from artisanal to industrial capitalism as the foundation for its racist concept of "whiteness." Lindemann, *The Jew Accused* (Cambridge: Cambridge University Press, 1991); Wynn, *Workers, Strikes, and Pogroms* (Princeton: Princeton University Press, 1992); Sparks, *The Mind of South Africa* (New York: Ballantine, 1990); Takaki, *Iron Cages* (Oxford: Oxford University Press, 1990); Roediger, *Wages of Whiteness* (London: Verso, 1991).

51. Wynn, *Workers, Strikes, and Pogroms.*

52. *The End of the American Era* (New York: Random House, 2002), 37.

53. As Hirschman puts it, in the voice of the eighteenth-century theorists, "The passions that most need bridling belong to the powerful, who are in a position to do harm on a huge scale and were believed to be particularly well endowed with passions in comparison to the lesser orders." The latter were seen as concerned only "with subsistence and material improvement, generally as ends in themselves," and thus as beings without passions. *The Passions and the Interests*, 69–70, 112.

54. Raymond Williams, *Keywords: A Vocabulary of Culture and Society* (New York: Oxford University Press, 1976), 52.

55. There is a long history of the political right trying to organize workers along non-class lines, such as the *Zubatovshchizna* (the tsarist Russian government's attempt to keep workers away from radicals), or the Catholic trade unionism so prominent in southern Europe. For when socialist movements became increasingly prominent in the twentieth century, conservatives counterattacked. As Michael Mann puts it, "they appealed to workers, but not *as* workers." Mann, "Sources of Variation in Working-Class Movements in Twentieth-Century Europe," in *New Left Review* 212 (July-August 1995), 36.

56. Vladimir Tismaneanu, *Fantasies of Salvation: Democracy, Nationalism, and Myth in Post-Communist Europe* (Princeton: Princeton University Press, 1998), 9, 6. See also Sabrina Ramet, ed., *The Radical Right in Eastern Europe* (State College: Pennsylvania State University Press, 1999).

Chapter 2. Solidarity Against Itself

1. Peter Hall, ed., *The Political Power of Economic Ideas: Keynesianism Across Nations* (Princeton: Princeton University Press, 1989), 369.

2. Ryszard Kapuscinski, "Notatki z wybrzeza," in *Kultura* (Warsaw), September 14, 1980; reprinted in Grazyna Pomian, *Polska Solidarnosci* (Paris: Instytut Literacki, 1982).

3. "Hopelessness" was a common theme of the intelligentsia in the early 1970s. The term was introduced by Leszek Kolakowski in an article on all the reasons why the communist system could not be reformed. "Hope and Hopelessness," English translation in *Survey* 17:3 (Summer 1971).

4. The gender implications of this turn are also quite significant, heralding a postcommunist tendency to idealize the home-bound woman who protects the private sphere from state intrusion.

5. Conversation with Kijowski in New York City, November 23, 1983.

6. Wajda made a similar turn from subtlety to agitprop. In 1979, right between *Man of Marble* and *Man of Iron*, Wajda made one of his best films, *Without Anesthesia*, a subtle dissection of the compromises intellectuals make to hold onto their privileges. In 1982, during martial law, when Wajda staged *Antigone* in Krakow, he made his point by having the choir hold up banners saying, "Solidarity with Antigone!"

7. Quoted in *Citizens*, Richard Adams's superb 1984 documentary film of the Solidarity period.

8. Friedrich Schiller, *Naive and Sentimental Poetry* (1795; repr., New York: Ungar Publishers, 1966).

9. From Adams's film *Citizens*.

10. David Ost, *Solidarity and the Politics of Anti-Politics* (Philadelphia: Temple University Press, 1990), chs. 1–2. Conservative intellectuals also embraced Solidarity, but between 1980 and 1990 they were far less influential in the organization than the liberals and ex-socialists who came out of the KOR (Workers Defense Committee) movement of the 1970s. Conservatives saw workers not as future democratic "citizens" but as good moral representatives of the Catholic nation that communism had been unable to defeat.

11. All citations from Adam Michnik, *Takie Czasy* (Warsaw: Nowa, 1986), 26–31.

12. Ost, *Solidarity and the Politics of Anti-Politics*, 165–69.

13. Interview with Geremek, Warsaw, July 1984.

14. The 1981 slogan of "no economic reform without political reform," meant to highlight the constitutive role of an active citizenry, turned into "no political reform without economic reform" by the middle of the decade.

15. Eyal, Szelenyi, and Townsley, *Making Capitalism* (London: Verso, 1998), 11, 85.

16. Jan Kubik, *The Power of Symbols against the Symbols of Power: The Rise of Solidarity and the Fall of State Socialism in Poland* (University Park: Pennsylvania State University Press, 1994), 238.

17. Transcript of conversation between Kaczynski and Andrzej Paczkowski, recorded and transcribed as part of *Negotiating Revolution in Poland: Conversion and Opportunity in 1989*, a research project coordinated by Michael Kennedy, Brian Porter, and Andrzej Paczkowski, sponsored by the National Council for Eurasian and Eastern European Research and the University of Michigan. A few dozen participants were interviewed for the project. Referred to below as "[Interviewee] Transcript."

18. Litynski Transcript; interviewer: Padraic Kenney.

19. Rakowski Transcript; interviewer: David Ost.

20. The main exception was Silesian miner Alojzy Pietrzyk, who rose, however, not just because of his own contribution but because he belonged, albeit temporarily, to Litynski's network. Litynski introduced him to Michnik and wrote his first speech at the Round Table meetings. See Litynski Transcript.

21. The one substantive issue concerned cost-of-living adjustments for rapid inflation, an issue on which Solidarity took a more moderate stance than OPZZ.

22. Litynski Transcript.

23. Zyta Oryszyn, "Ludzie sa zmeczeni," in *Tygodnik Solidarnosc*, August 18, 1989, 2. Solidarity's reluctance to support the strikes is laid bare in its Executive Committee's feeble statement of August 9, saying that in light of hyperinflation and the recent absurd personnel changes, the union would ask the regions to "consider" organized protest action on behalf of reform. See Ludwika Wujec, "Prezydium KKW: Co robic?" in *Tygodnik Solidarnosc*, August 18, 1989, 2.

24. Personal interview with Kaczynski, April 1999.

25. *Tygodnik Solidarnosc*, August 25, 1989, 15 (emphasis mine). The reference here to "working people" was quite untypical of union statements at the time. Solidarity activists at all levels usually attacked the government for driving the "country" or "nation" to ruin, not "workers."

26. *Tygodnik Solidarnosc*, August 25, 1989, 15.

27. These and other quotations here from "Czym jest, czym ma byc NSZZ Solidarnosc?," in *Tygodnik Solidarnosc*, June 9, 1989, 8–9.

28. This and other quotations here from Wojciech Arkuszewski, "Od gory do dolu," in *Tygodnik Solidarnosc*, September 22, 1989, 1–2.

29. Quoted in "Ile Wytrzymacie?" in *Tygodnik Solidarnosc*, September 29, 1989, 2. This is a report from the September 19 meeting of the KKW, written by Pawel Lawinski.

30. Interview with *Gazeta Wyborcza*, cited in *Tygodnik Solidarnosc*, October 20, 1989, 23.

31. Zbigniew Bujak, "Chcialbym zachowac niezalezna pozycje," in *Gazeta Wyborcza* 2, May 9, 1989, 5.

32. Quoted in "Ile Wytrzymacie?"

33. Cited in ibid.

34. *Tygodnik Solidarnosc*, November 17, 1989, 23.

35. Aleksandra Zawlocka and Pawel Bujalski, "W regionach," in *Tygodnik Solidarnosc*, January 5, 1990, 19.

36. A[leksandra] Z[awlocka], "Bez niespodzianek," in *Tygodnik Solidarnosc*, February 23, 1990, 19.

37. "It is clear that since 1981, membership has dropped five-fold." Aleksandra Zawlocka and Pawel Bujalski, "W regionach," in *Tygodnik Solidarnosc*, January 5, 1990, 19.

38. A[leksandra] Z[awlocka], "Bez niespodzianek," in *Tygodnik Solidarnosc*, February 23, 1990, 19.

39. Quoted in "Ile Wytrzymacie?"

40. The first estimate comes from Anna Bikont's interview with Wladyslaw Frasyniuk, "Zwyciezylo i cos peklo," in *Gazeta Wyborcza*, January 29, 1990, 4–5. The second figure, calculated for the union's national congress in March 1990, is from "Maly wielki zwiazek," *Gazeta Wyborcza*, March 5, 1990, 1. This figure made Wroclaw (Lower Silesia) the second-largest Solidarity in the country, behind Katowice's (Silesia-Dabrowski) 272,000, and ahead of third-place Warsaw's (Mazowsze) 210,000. Nationwide, the National Commission estimated 2.5 million members in 13,764 union cells.

41. Aleksandra Zawlocka and Pawel Bujalski, "W regionach," in *Tygodnik Solidarnosc*, January 5, 1990, 19.

42. Ibid.

43. Aleksandra Zawlocka, "Sztab bez armii," in *Tygodnik Solidarnosc*, December 1, 1989, 22.

44. State-owned firms in 1989 were formally governed by employee-elected councils, a result of the 1981 law on enterprise self-management that had been suspended during martial law and revived after the Round Table talks. These councils had final say on all key managerial decisions, including investment and wage policy.

45. Initial evidence, on the contrary, suggested that they were not. See Janusz Dabrowski, Michal Federowicz, and Anthony Levitas, "Polish State Enterprises and the Property of Performance: Stabilization, Marketization, Privatization," in *Politics and Society* 19:4 (December 1991), 403–38.

46. Maurice Glasman, "The Great Transformation: Polanyi, Poland, and the Terrors of

Planned Spontaneity," in *The New Great Transformation*, ed. Chris Bryant and Edmund Mokrzycki (London: Routledge, 1994).

47. Krzysztof Czabanski, "Pytanie do rzadu," in *Tygodnik Solidarnosc*, December 8, 1989, 1.

48. Andrzej Zarebski, "Obrady KKW," in *Tygodnik Solidarnosc*, November 24, 1989, 23.

49. "Demokracja albo autorytaryzm," an interview with Zbigniew Romaszewski by Jerzy Sczcesny, in *Tygodnik Solidarnosc*, October 19, 1990, 10.

50. Marcin Przybylowicz, interviewed by Aleksandra Zawlocka, in "Nie ma nas," *Tygodnik Solidarnosc*, January 12, 1990, 19. The exception here was Grazyna Staniszewska, a parliamentarian from Bielsko-Biala who regularly interrogated legislation from the perspective of a regular union member. According to Przybylowicz, she spoke so often on such matters–and others so little—that other Solidarity deputies began to find her voice quite tiresome.

51. The quotation and the calculation are from Anna Bikont, "Zwyciezylo i cos peklo," in *Gazeta Wyborcza*, January 29, 1990, 5.

52. See, for example, Alex Callinicos, *The Revenge of History: Marxism and the East European Revolutions* (College Park: Pennsylvania State University Press, 1991). A more sophisticated presentation of this argument, tracing the emergence of the elite dissidents' new class interests to developments in the communist era, can be found in Giovanni Arrighi, Terence K. Hopkins, and Immanuel Wallerstein, "1989: The Continuation of 1968," in *After the Fall: 1989 and the Future of Freedom*, ed. George Katsiaficas (New York: Routledge, 2001.)

Chapter 3. Market Populism and the Turn to the Right

1. Nearly 10 percent said they had not heard of the plan. "Doswiadczani Balcerowiczem," in *Gazeta Wyborcza*, January 30, 1990, 2.

2. *Gazeta Wyborcza*, January 27–28, 1990, 1.

3. On economic developments in this period, see Kazimierz Poznanski, *Poland's Protracted Transition* (Cambridge: Cambridge University Press, 1996), esp. ch. 7. Ben Slay notes problems of statistics-gathering that may overestimate the crisis, such as limited data about the private sphere, despite which he confirms the claim of a large decline in wages and economic activity during this period. *The Polish Economy* (Princeton: Princeton University Press, 1994), esp. ch. 3. For more on problems in statistical calculations of economic decline, see Tomasz Mickiewicz and Janice Bell, *Unemployment in Transition: Restructuring and Labour Markets in Central Europe* (Amsterdam: Harwood, 2000).

4. See Jacek Kuron and Jacek Zakowski, *Siedmiolatka, czyli Kto Ukradl Polske?* (Wroclaw: Dolnoslaskie, 1997), 28–29.

5. Marek Czyzewski, Kinga Dunin, and Andrzej Piotrowski, introduction to their edited collection *Cudze Problemy* (Warsaw: Osrodek Badan Spolecznych, 1991), 6.

6. Quoted in Anna Bikont, "Zwyciezylo i cos peklo," in *Gazeta Wyborcza*, January 29, 1990, 4–5.

7. Izabella Greczanik-Filipp et al., "Po co komu Solidarnosc?" in *Tygodnik Gdanski*, April 22, 1990, 9.

8. Jagienka Wilczak, "Parasol z powylamywanymi drutami," in *Polityka*, May 5, 1990, 6.

9. This account of the origins and genesis of the railway strike borrows extensively from Kazimierz Kloc, "Przyczyny i Przebieg Strajku na PKP w maju 1990," in *Studia nad Ruchami Spolecznymi*, vol. 5 (Warsaw: Institute of Sociology, Warsaw University, 1990), 159–201. All quotations in this section are taken from this article.

10. The industry was indeed top-heavy with administrators. At the beginning of 1990, the railways employed some 23,000 administrators (of 430,000 total employees) and had over eighty "key directorial positions." But this stemmed from the overall nature of the industry. The fare structure had been constructed so as to make the transport of raw materials, particularly coal, very cheap. Deficits were thus built into the industry, forcing it to rely on heavy subsidies from the state, which in turn allowed politicians to continually intervene, leading to bad bureaucratic

management. Solidarity was thus right to point to the need for restructuring, but wrong to see the problem as due to bad management alone. On the other hand, it was right to point to the financial limits of the industry. The previous year had been particularly painful for the rail industry. The sharp drop in passenger and commodity transport due to the economic crisis combined with a drop in subsidies due to the Balcerowicz Plan—these two factors left the industry in a hole that was not likely to change soon. Altering the September tax base was easy, but a 110 percent guarantee was not.

11. E. Isakiewicz, "Kto zwodzil Slupsk?" in *Tygodnik Solidarnosc*, June 1, 1990.

12. Quoted in Wlodzimierz Slowinski, "Koleje strajku," in *Gazeta Wyborcza*, May 28, 1990, 5.

13. Because Labor Minister Kuron steadfastly refused to meet with anyone outside of an official union and national Solidarity refused to serve as the strikers' representative, the strikers finally authorized OPZZ leader Alfred Miodowicz to meet with Kuron. But Miodowicz was authorized only to urge Kuron to come to Slupsk himself. When Kuron refused, there was nothing left for Miodowicz to discuss, and he walked out.

14. "Lech Kaczynski w Slupsku," in *Gazeta Wyborcza*, May 22, 1990, 1.

15. Maciej Zalewski, "Nie zdazymy," in *Tygodnik Solidarnosc*, April 6, 1990.

16. Kurt Weyland, "Neoliberal Populism in Latin America and Eastern Europe," in *Comparative Politics* 31:4 (July 1999), 379–401. An indication of the strength of this pro-capitalist sensibility is that even Walesa's political rivals agreed with him on this point. Andrzej Gwiazda, Solidarity's 1980–81 vice president who later became one of Walesa's chief populist opponents, denouncing his commitment to negotiations with the Party and rebuking him for betraying Polish workers, charges for which Walesa excluded him from all Solidarity leadership roles in the late 1980s—even Gwiazda agreed with this naïve conception of capitalism. When I asked him in early 1990 what he thought of Poland's new capitalism, he looked at me as if I were the innocent babe: "Capitalism is where workers can *afford* the goods that are produced," he cried. "Look around today! This is not capitalism." Interview with Gwiazda in Gdansk, April 1990.

17. Quoted in Konstanty Gebert, "Rola antysemityzmu," in Miroslawa Grabowska and Ireneusz Krzeminski, *Bitwa o Belweder* (Warsaw: Mysl, 1991), 242–67.

18. Quoted in Tomek Grabowski, "The Party That Never Was: The Rise and Fall of the Solidarity Citizens' Committees in Poland," in *East European Politics and Societies* 10:2 (Spring 1996). As Grabowski puts it, for Kaczynski "social discontent had to be expressed [and] organized . . . rather than hushed up amidst appeals for national solidarity."

19. See Peter Gowan, "Neo-liberal Theory and Practice for Eastern Europe," in *New Left Review* 213 (September-October 1995), 3–60.

20. Kazimierz Kloc, "Polish Labor in Transition, 1990–1992," in *Telos* 92 (Summer 1992).

21. Even after he was president—and thus complicit—Walesa still tried to maintain his old line. Thus, he regularly told labor protesters that he supported their struggle and that if he were in their shoes he'd probably be doing the same thing. But since he was president, he would add, he *had* to be on the other side. "But I support you still!" he would conclude. Rapidly declining poll numbers showed that few accepted this attempt to be everything to everybody.

22. Several well-publicized scandals in 1991 buttressed Olszewski's view of Polish capitalism as bandit capitalism. The most notorious was known as "Art-B," the name of a highly touted new entrepreneurial firm supposedly in the entertainment business but actually focusing on bilking the banking system by transferring huge sums of money faster than the system could process it, thereby earning simultaneous interest. Tipped off by someone inside the government, the owners fled the country just before they were arrested, taking several hundred million dollars with them. Coming at a time when average wages were about 200 dollars a month—wages that many firms were unable to pay anyway—Art-B served for Olszewski as the poster boy of bad capitalism.

23. See Seymour Martin Lipset's famous thesis of "working-class authoritarianism," according to which workers seek simplistic, and thus dangerous, political solutions because of their "lower-class way of life." *Political Man* (New York: Doubleday, 1960), 98.

24. Louisa Vinton, "Polish Government Faces New Strike Challenge," in *RFE/RL Research Report*, May 21, 1993.

25. The IMF insisted on budget cuts and a small deficit in return for a recommendation to western creditors to cancel some of Poland's burdensome foreign debts.

26. From September 1991 to September 1992, real wages declined 2% for urban workers, 4% for peasant-workers, and 8% for retirees. Food consumption declined about 3%, 9%, and 15%, respectively. People spent more for housing, less for food, and 20–25% less for entertainment, travel, and vacations. There was a steep decline in housing construction. "W kraju," in *Polityka*, December 19, 1992.

27. Slogans included "We want deputies, not donkeys" [*poslow a nie oslow*] and "Embezzlers to prison." See Janina Paradowska, "Konwersacja Wielopietrowa," in *Polityka*, May 2, 1992, 1.

28. Jagienka Wilczak, "Pozegnanie z mitem," in *Polityka*, June 20, 1992, 5.

29. For more on Tychy Fiat, see Guglielmo Meardi, "Trade Union Consciousness, East and West: A Comparison of Fiat Factories in Poland and Italy," in *European Journal of Industrial Relations* 2:3 (1996), 275–302; and Meardi's *Trade Union Activists, East and West* (London: Ashgate, 2000).

30. Jan Dziadul, "Granice rozsadku," in *Polityka*, September 12, 1992, 1.

31. Waldemar Kuczynski, "Strajkowanie przeciwko przyszlosci?" in *Zycie Gospodarcze*, August 23, 1992.

32. "W kraju," in *Polityka*, October 10, 1992, 2.

33. Wojciech Blasiak, "Gorniczy Strajk Generalny na Slasku," in *Gornicy Gornoslascy—ludzie zbedni, ludzie luzni?* ed. Marek Szczepanski (Krakow: amp, 1994), 19.

34. For more on the 1993 protest actions, see Grzegorz Ekiert and Jan Kubik, *Rebellious Civil Society: Popular Protest and Democratic Consolidation in Poland* (Ann Arbor: University of Michigan Press, 1999), ch. 6.

35. The Non-Party Bloc had been created by President Walesa only a few months earlier as a feeble attempt to build his own political party. The awkward name was chosen for its initials—BBWR—the same as the party founded by Marshal Pilsudski in the 1930s for his own presidential dictatorship. The Union of Labor, the only explicitly left-wing party to emerge from Solidarity, gained a surprising 7.3 percent of the vote, more than triple its 1991 total, in part through a strong campaign against gender discrimination that attracted liberal and professional women. The Confederation of Polish Independence was an explicitly right-wing party, formed illegally in the late 1970s, that appealed to youth fighting for "radical" change.

36. Many of the policy enactments discussed here as accomplishments of the DLA were in fact first proposed as part of the Pact on State Enterprises that Suchocka's Labor Minister Jacek Kuron negotiated with trade unions in 1992–93. The creation of a Tripartite Commission, the replacement of the wage tax by negotiated increases, requirements for all firms to establish "social funds," debt relief for firms, free shares for employees of privatized firms—all this was part of the Pact on State Enterprises that the Suchocka government signed with trade unions in February 1993. I associate them with the DLA government, however, for two reasons. First, all of these measures were implemented by that government. Second, it is far from clear that Suchocka could have pushed these bills through parliament even if her government had survived. When Kuron first announced the measures, the chief opposition came from within the government's own ranks, specifically from former Solidarity liberals and conservatives who thought these bills gave the unions too much power. Saying the pact would create a "unionocracy," some pro-Suchocka parliamentarians proposed a contrary bill *taking away* some rights of trade unions. In other words, even during the Suchocka government, these measures could have won parliamentary approval only with DLA support, and even then it was not clear that sufficient numbers of "pro-Solidarity" parliamentarians would have supported it. When the DLA came to power, it tried to push the pact forward quickly, and indeed it did so with the provisions on the wage tax and the Tripartite Commission, before meeting strong opposition from its coalition partner concerning the pact's other measures—as well as from Solidarity, which now adopted an intransigently anti-government stance. So I present these measures as accomplishments of the

DLA government, despite their origins in the turn away from neoliberalism first proposed by Labor Minister Kuron.

37. The wage tax died when its replacement, which had been pushed through by DLA liberals, was vetoed by President Walesa. Some months later, a softer version of wage controls was reinstated by parliament, but it died of desuetude as the Tripartite Commission began functioning and enterprise collective wage bargaining reappeared.

38. On matters as crucial as wage rules, prior Solidarity governments had left on the books language such as this: "The Council of Ministers, in order to realize the centralized wage and benefit policies of the national socio-economic plan, and after consultation with the national union organization . . ."—despite the fact that there was no longer a "centralized wage and benefit policy," no "national plan," and no all-embracing "national union organization." Labor Code, sec. 11, ch. 1, art. 240, par. 2 of *Kodeks Pracy*, 1993.

39. It would be wrong to see such measures simply as irresponsible populist gestures, an easy—if expensive—way to get votes. In early postcommunism, citizens viewed pensions as the tribute paid by the generation able to profit from the new economy to the generation who built that economy but was never able to profit from it.

40. This was a widespread practice, and not only in small firms where paying the standard 45-percent benefits package could be a severe burden. A young marketing expert I knew was employed by Coca-Cola in Warsaw the same way: a recurring one-month contract for nearly two years.

41. Ludwik Dorn, "Po burzy: proba bilansu," in *Rzeczpospolita*, February 21, 1995.

42. For example, at the same time that the Suchocka government had steadfastly refused to raise public sector allocations in 1993 on the grounds that there was just no money available, it had privately promised a small farmers' party additional agricultural subsidies in order to lure it into its coalition.

43. Personal conversation, Warsaw, September 1993.

44. OPZZ representatives accounted for more than a third of the DLA's parliamentary contingent, 66 of 171, 32 of which came from the Union of Polish Teachers. The UPT president headed the parliamentary commission on education, while another official became deputy minister of education.

45. This and other quotations in the paragraph from interview with Adam Glapinski in *Tygodnik Solidarnosc*, April 29, 1994.

46. See the series of articles on the topic in *Eastern European Constitutional Review* 6:2/3 (Spring/Summer 1997).

47. The country had been muddling through since 1989 under the old constitution, changing it as necessary to allow here a presidency, there a parliamentary right to veto, and wherever else to match the new institutions created on the fly. In late 1992, a "little constitution" was adopted to regulate relations between the president and prime minister.

48. Quoted in Pawel Spiewak, "The Battle for a Constitution," in *Eastern European Constitutional Review* 6:2/3 (Spring/Summer 1997). Available at http://www.law.nyu.edu/eecr.

49. *Tygodnik Solidarnosc*, August 30, 1996, 14.

50. According to Gregor Koso, an American union adviser working with Solidarity on this project. Conversation with Koso, Warsaw, July 1999.

51. See Ekiert and Kubik, *Rebellious Civil Society*.

52. Interview with Olinowicz (a pseudonym), Mielec, May 1993.

53. Ekiert and Kubik, *Rebellious Civil Society*, 180. Emphasis in original.

54. Ibid., 187–88.

55. Ibid., 187.

56. Ibid., 149.

57. Ibid.

58. Bohdan Cywinski, in "Plus-Minus" section of *Rzeczpospolita*, April 2–4, 1994.

59. Richard Sennett and Jonathan Cobb, *The Hidden Injuries of Class* (1977; repr., New York: Norton, 1993).

60. More on this in chapter 6. See also David Ost, "The Weakness of Strong Social Movements," in *European Journal of Industrial Relations* 8:1 (March 2002), 33–51; and David Ost, "Labor and Union Identity in Poland, 1989–2000," in *Workers After Workers' States*, ed. David Ost and Stephen Crowley (Boulder, CO: Rowman & Littlefield, 2001).

61. E. P. Thompson, *The Making of the English Working Class* (New York: Vintage, 1966), 212.

62. Elizabeth Dunn, *Privatizing Poland: Baby Food, Big Business, and the Remaking of the Polish Working Class* (Ithaca, NY: Cornell University Press, 2004), 92

63. Ibid., 93.

64. Ibid., 85.

65. Maryjane Osa, "Creating Solidarity: The Religious Foundations of the Poland Social Movement," in *East European Politics and Societies* 11:2 (Spring 1997), 339–65.

66. Some Silesian scholars tend toward even more critical views about Solidarity's role in the strike, noting that by starting the strike at the exact moment that export contracts were being negotiated, Solidarity prevented mines from locking in long-term exporting contracts that would have significantly improved their financial picture. They also point out that unlike other strikes at the time, the liberal press seemed to sympathize with the demands. Their point is that the strike only looked like a defense of miners but was meant all along to facilitate their demise. See Wojciech Blasiak, "Gorniczy Strajk Generalny na Slasku," note 33.

67. Guglielmo Meardi, "The Trojan Horse for the Americanization of Europe? Polish Industrial Relations Toward the EU," in *European Journal of Industrial Relations* 8:1 (March 2002), 77–99.

68. Maryjane Osa, "Contention and Democracy: Labor Protest in Poland, 1989–1993," in *Communist and Postcommunist Studies* 31:1 (1998), 29–42; Jonathan A. Terra, "Influence, Assets and Democracy: Who Got What After the Fall of Communism in East Central Europe?" Ph.D. dissertation, Stanford University, 2003.

Chapter 4. How Liberals Lost Labor

1. For a discussion of the diverse and fluid meanings of liberalism in Eastern Europe, see Jerzy Szacki, *Liberalism after Communism* (Budapest: Central European Press, 1995).

2. See Andrzej Walicki, "Mysli o sytuacji politycznej i moralno-psychologicznej w Polsce," in *Aneks* (London) 35 (1984).

3. Witold Gombrowicz, *Diary: Volume One*, translated by Lillian Vallee (Evanston: Northwestern University Press, 1988), 27.

4. Maryjane Osa makes good points in her work on the Christian roots of Solidarity. But insofar as she stresses the mass reception of the movement rather than its intellectual leadership, her work does not challenge my emphasis on Solidarity's left-liberal master-frame. "Creating Solidarity: The Religious Foundations of the Polish Social Movement," in *Eastern European Politics and Societies* 11:2 (Spring 1997), 339–65. Any close study of Solidarity's politics in the 1980s, and particularly in 1980–81, will show that Solidarity always felt closer to the Church than the Church felt to Solidarity.

5. Listen to how one conservative writer at the time assessed Solidarity's 1989 election list:

Behind the vast all-embracing screen of the union hides the left-wing post-KOR opposition, taking up almost its entire space. Solidarity, the main social and political force in Poland today, has become the playing field for only one ideological option. . . . We can of course understand why they're doing this. Imagine if they started to seek votes on their own political account—not as "the left," of course, and certainly not as the "secular left," but as a modern social democratic formation. . . . How many votes would they have gotten then? . . . I don't mean to take away from these people all they have shown and given through their talent, determination, and courageous resistance. I respect their views, though I do not share many of them. I also respect the fact that they stood for Solidarity from the very beginning, that they maintained in it an unshakable faith even at times when so many others were wavering. They worked for the union in its most difficult conditions, went to jail on its behalf, and did a great deal, maybe more than anyone else, for its revival. They have every right, even a moral right, to speak in its name. I deny them only one thing: their claim to exclusivity. Solidarity is not their property, regardless of the enormous contribution they gave to it. (Tomasz Wolek, "Czy opozycja jeszcze istnieje?" in *Polityka Polska* 14 (1989), 8–9.)

The quotation is useful not just for its critique of the liberal left's behavior—the right, after all, was simply jealous—but for its expression of the extent of the left's domination of the union in the eyes of other political activists. We might also note that Wolek here calls them what many of them ideally wished to be—social democrats—ignoring the fact that in 1989 they behaved simply like free-market liberals. But this only points to a broader problem for Polish socialists in the twentieth century: because of the weakness of liberal capitalism, they were always unable to be simple social democrats (that is, democratic critics of a market economy) but usually had to choose instead between liberalism and communism. They sided with the former at the time of independence in 1918 and with the latter right after World War II. In 1989, they came to see themselves as the group that would have to build a liberal capitalist society themselves—even if only so that later, as some liked to say, they could protest against it. It was only during the 1980–81 Solidarity period that they were able to appear as a fully independent force, since the Party made sure that both social democratic "enemies," capitalism and clericalism, were kept under wraps. In that context, they appeared as participatory democrats and adherents of "anti-politics." In 1989, they appeared as liberals. Wolek is right that it is the "same" group, but their role changed dramatically depending on the context. On the leftism of Solidarity in 1980, see my *Solidarity and the Politics of Anti-Politics* (Philadelphia: Temple University Press, 1990), ch. 1. On the links between that leftism and liberalism, see my introduction to the English version of Adam Michnik's *The Church and the Left* (Chicago: University of Chicago Press, 1993).

6. Jacek Kuron from a 1991 TV show, quoted in Grzegorz Ekiert and Jan Kubik, *Rebellious Civil Society* (Ann Arbor: University of Michigan Press, 2001), 170.

7. On the erosion of civil society thought in the East, see Marc Morje Howard, *The Weakness of Civil Society in Postcommunist Europe* (Cambridge: Cambridge University Press, 2003) and David Ost, "The Politics of Interest in Post-Communist East Europe," in *Theory and Society* 22 (August 1993).

8. Szacki, *Liberalism After Communism*, 202.

9. John Campbell and Leon Lindberg, "Property Rights and the Organization of Economic Activity by the State," in *American Sociological Review* (October 1990).

10. On the liberal substitution of progress for passion, see Christopher Lasch, *The True and Only Heaven: Progress and its Critics* (New York: Norton, 1991).

11. Bronislaw Geremek, *Rok 1989* (Warsaw: Plejada, 1990), 366.

12. Ibid., 380. Robespierre was frequently invoked by liberals as the quintessential symbol of what happens when passion is embraced by non-elites. See, for example, Maciej Kozlowski, "Noworoczne wrozby," in *Tygodnik Powszechny*, January 8, 1989.

13. Grzegorz Gorny, "Strajk gornikow," in *Gazeta Wyborcza*, January 22, 1990. The discussion and quotations are taken from this article.

14. From *The Unbearable Lightness of Being* (New York: Harper and Row, 1984), part 6.

15. For example, the reaction to the jingoist and anti-Semitic remarks of Szczecin Solidarity leader Marian Jurczyk in October 1981 focused largely on the rumor that an agent provocateur speechwriter had written them. The urge to explain away domestic irrationality extended to history as well. With previously taboo topics newly subject to open inquiry, oppositionists relished in exposing Soviet crimes but took refuge in the notion of "provocation" when discussing subjects like anti-Jewish pogroms in postwar Poland. (The operative narrative became that of the communist police urging ordinary Poles to do bad things so that the communists could show the world that Poles ought not to be trusted with democracy.) Crimes against Poles were told in

an active voice, crimes by Poles in a passive voice. When the historian and democratic socialist Jan Jozef Lipski broke these rules in 1981 by publishing a pamphlet naming and denouncing Polish crimes—and was widely criticized for doing so—liberal intellectuals acknowledged his courage but largely declined to join his effort. It should be noted that Adam Michnik's critical comments on Solidarity in 1985, quoted in chapter 2, were printed only in one of his more obscure underground publications; he never wrote such things for general public consumption.

16. Wlodzimierz Pankow, "Funkcje zwiazkow zawodowych w zakladach pracy," in *Rozpad Bastionu?: Zwiazki Zawodowe w gospodarce prywatyzowanej*, ed. Juliusz Gardawski, Barbara Gaciarz, Andrzej Mokrzyszewski, and Wlodziemierz Pankow (Warsaw: Institute of Public Affairs, 1999), 166.

17. Wieslawa Kozek, "Destruktorzy: Tendencyjny obraz zwiazkow zawodowych w tygodnikach politycznych w Polsce," in *Instytucjonalizacja stosunkow pracy w Polsce*, ed. Kozek (Warsaw: Scholar, 2003).

18. Arlie Russell Hochschild, *The Managed Heart: Commercialization of Human Feeling* (Berkeley: University of California Press, 1983), 172.

19. Ibid., 173.

20. Quoted in Tomek Grabowski, "The Party That Never Was," in *East European Politics and Societies* 10:2 (Spring 1996), 242. For an account of the role, significance, and fate of the Center Alliance, see Janina Paradowska, "Ruch dwoch," in *Polityka*, July 21, 2001.

21. Letter to editor, *Tygodnik Solidarnosc*, July 27, 1990, 5.

22. On how market transition changes stratification, see Victor Nee, "A Theory of Market Transition: From Redistribution to Markets in State Socialism," in *American Sociological Review* 54 (1989), 663–81; and Yang Cao and Victor Nee, "Comment: Controversies and Evidence in the Market Transition Debate," in *American Journal of Sociology* 105:4 (January 2000), 1175–89. On the role of dissidents in the postcommunist elite, see Gil Eyal, Ivan Szelenyi, and Eleanor Townsley, *Making Capitalism Without Capitalists* (London: Verso, 1998).

23. Frances Fox Piven and Richard A. Cloward, *Poor People's Movements* (New York: Vintage Books, 1977), 17, 18.

24. Miroslawa Grabowska, "Socjologia nie skonsumowana," in Miroslawa Grabowska and Ireneusz Krzeminski, *Bitwa o Belweder* (Warsaw: Mysl, 1991), 87–106.

25. See, for example, Piotr Pacewicz, "Stan 'drugiej Polski,'" in *Gazeta Wyborcza*, November 26, 1990.

26. See, for example, R. Markowski and T. Zukowski, "Wrozba dla Polski," in *Polityka*, December 8, 1990. Also K. B. Kruszewski, in *Gazeta Wyborcza*, December 1–2, 1990.

27. See Father Jozef Tischner's comments in *Tygodnik Powszechny* on January 6, 1991, and in *Gazeta Wyborcza* on January 12–13, 1991.

28. Grabowska, "Socjologia nie skonsumowana," 101. With the interpretation most sociologists were giving, she said, "the overwhelming majority of the population would be part of Poland 'B.' . . . If politics is unclear or incomprehensible to them, this bodes ill not for them but for the politicians."

29. Mitchell Orenstein, *Out of the Red: Building Capitalism and Democracy in Post-Communist Europe* (Ann Arbor: University of Michigan Press, 2000).

30. Eyal et al., *Making Capitalism Without Capitalists*; Janine Wedel, *Collision and Collusion: The Strange Case of Western Aid to Eastern Europe 1989–1998* (New York: St. Martin's, 1998).

31. See David Stark and Laszlo Bruszt, *Postsocialist Pathways: Transforming Politics and Property in East Central Europe* (Cambridge: Cambridge University Press, 1998), esp. ch. 1.

32. Gregory Luebbert, *Liberalism, Fascism, or Social Democracy* (New York: Oxford University Press, 1991).

33. The Democratic Union's internal newsletter, *Biuletyn Informacyjny*, ran articles at the time urging local activists to stress the party's pro-business stance and to try to bring intellectuals back in while maintaining silence about labor issues. It is probably not accidental that the one DU region that did *not* ignore labor, in Wroclaw, got the party's highest 1993 vote, over 20 percent, nearly double the national average. In Rzeszow, the DU polled only 6.6 percent, just

over half the national average. In 2001, after the Freedom Union was voted out of office, it chose Wroclaw leader and veteran Solidarity activist Wladyslaw Frasyniuk to be its new leader.

34. Jan Litynski, "Unia ma goraczke," in *Gazeta Wyborcza*, December 3, 1998.

35. Some of its support passed to a new neoliberal party that did enter parliament: the "Civic Platform," headed by former LDC-ers.

36. In March 2004, 53 percent of a national sample said they trusted Lepper, second only to President Kwasniewski. See internet daily *Donosy*, March 30, 2004.

37. In addition to Hochschild, there is a long tradition of both left and right political thought connecting rationality to class privilege, from Horkheimer and Adorno's *Dialectic of Enlightenment* to Friedrich von Hayek's *Road to Serfdom.*

38. In part, what is going on here is the kind of clash between working-class and middle-class social movements that frequently goes on in capitalist democracies, but not in state socialist systems or even capitalist dictatorships when the two kinds of movements in the struggle for democracy are united. Fred Rose writes about this in *Coalitions Across the Class Divide*, his wonderful book on social movement conflict in the United States. Offering a structural and cultural interpretation of differences between the two types of movements, Rose argues that because of their different relationships to the labor process, working class movements "tend to frame their approaches to politics and social change in the language and logic of interests. Middle-class organizations, on the contrary, tend to conceive of their organizing in the language and framework of values and education." The two groups will clash when the leader of each group does not recognize the differing styles and motives of the other. The example Rose offers—of middle-class environmentalists in the Pacific Northwest failing to understand the timber unions, thereby driving them into the arms of the timber industrialists—is similar to my account of Polish liberals driving labor into the arms of the political right. The conclusion would be that liberals must also adopt the language and address the matter of interests, or else they will drive labor into the arms of those who do. *Coalitions Across the Class Divide* (Ithaca, NY: Cornell University Press, 2000), 17.

39. Jodi Dean, following Foucault, describes something similar in the very different world of "ufology," or the widespread belief in UFOs, arguing that people who maintain such "irrational" beliefs are precisely those who are deprived of the officially sanctioned tools for truth-seeking (i.e., scientific knowledge) but want to participate in scientific discussion anyway. *Aliens in America: Conspiracy Cultures from Outerspace to Cyberspace* (Ithaca, NY: Cornell University Press, 1998).

40. For discussion of those attitudes, see David Ost and Marc Weinstein, "Unionists Against Unions: Towards Hierarchical Management in Post-Communist Poland," in *East European Politics and Societies* 13:1 (Winter 1999).

41. This may be the reason why Ekiert and Kubik believe that radicals caused labor discontent, rather than the other way around. Radicals were able to get the publicity that more moderate rank-and-file critics were unable to attract, precisely because of their break with consensus. Wrzodak, for example, burst onto the national scene only after he organized street demonstrations and provoked a physical confrontation with the police—the first use of force against labor since 1989. See the accounts in *Polityka*, June 3 and 10, 1995.

42. Other important factors explaining Czech labor's better position were that Czech unions were centralized while Polish ones were fragmented, and the Czech economy was in better shape—particularly after shedding Slovakia in 1993—with far less indebtedness to the West. Still, a look at the record shows an assertiveness already in 1990 on the part of Czech unions that was lacking in Poland. Insofar as this challenges cultural stereotypes about Czech passivity versus Polish insurrectionism, it lends support to the claim about the importance of organizational autonomy. See Martin Myant, "Czech and Slovak Trade Unions," in *Parties, Trade Unions, and Society in East-Central Europe*, ed. Michael Waller and Martin Myant (Essex: Frank Cass, 1994); and Orenstein, *Out of the Red.* For a development of this analysis on Czech-Polish union differences, see David Ost, "Can Unions Survive Communism?" in *Dissent* (Winter 1997). In Slovakia, things turned out differently. With its higher unemployment, weaker unions, and

stronger Catholic political traditions, many workers there did become mobilized along illiberal lines, though in this case chiefly by ex-communist nationalists. See Jonathan Stein, "Neocorporatism in Slovakia: Formalizing Labor Weakness in a (Re)democratizing State," in *Workers After Workers' States: Labor and Politics in Eastern Europe After Communism*, ed. Stephen Crowley and David Ost (Boulder, CO: Rowman & Littlefield Press, 2001). For a fuller account of changes in the Czech workplace, see Anna Pollert, *Transformation At Work* (London: Sage, 1999).

Chapter 5. Communist and Postcommunist Experiences of Class

1. Victoria Hattam, *Labor Visions and State Power: The Origins of Business Unionism in the United States* (Princeton: Princeton University Press, 1993).

2. On the erosion of labor's control over the work process, see David Montgomery, *The Fall of the House of Labor: The Workplace, the State, and American Labor Activism* (Cambridge: Cambridge University Press, 1986). On the political dislocations this caused, see Christopher Lasch, *The True and Only Heaven: Progress and Its Critics* (New York: Norton, 1991), 203–25; and Sean Wilentz, *Chants Democratic: New York City and the Rise of the American Working Class* (New York: Oxford University Press, 1984. David Roediger links labor dissatisfaction over the loss of its autonomy to the rise of working-class racism, where "whiteness" comes to provide the dignity and higher income (race as rent) that controlling the labor process once did. *The Wages of Whiteness: Race and the Making of the American Working Class* (London: Verso, 1991).

3. This is how Hattam characterizes Gompers' views. *Labor Visions*, 138.

4. Michael Burawoy and Janos Lukacs, *The Radiant Past: Ideology and Reality in Hungary's Road to Capitalism* (Chicago: University of Chicago Press, 1992).

5. Padraic Kenney notes that even during the early Stalinist period, workers were permitted to express their grievances directly in open workplace meetings while other groups already had to toe the official line. See his *Rebuilding Poland: Workers and Communists, 1945–1950* (Ithaca, NY: Cornell University Press, 1997).

6. See Michael Burawoy, *Manufacturing Consent: Changes in the Labor Process under Monopoly Capitalism* (Chicago: University of Chicago Press, 1979).

7. Marx's claim of the proletariat as the universal class was a philosophical rather than an empirical observation, its universality stemming from its being forced to sell as a commodity the labor-power that Marx identified as the human essence. Politically, though, it is capital that, in a capitalist system, can always more easily lay claim to universality, since it is the one that provides jobs. As Adam Przeworski and John Sprague put it, "A classless vision of society is in the class interests of capitalists." *Paper Stones: A History of Electoral Socialism* (Chicago: University of Chicago Press, 1986), 47.

8. The numerous private farmers in Poland after 1956 were still deprived of control over the products of their labor due to the state purchasing monopoly, and faced severe limitations on controlling their own labor process due to restrictions on land hiring and land purchasing. They do not, therefore, constitute a significant exception. That they also saw themselves as workers was made clear by their eagerness to join with Solidarity in 1980.

9. *Breaking the Barrier: The Rise of Solidarity in Poland* (New York: Oxford University Press, 1991), 61.

10. The best account of the 1956 events in English is Lawrence Goodwyn, *Breaking the Barrier*, ch. 2. His account is based heavily on Jaroslaw Maciejewski and Zofia Trojanowicz, *Poznanski Czerwiec* (Wydawnictwo Poznanskie: Poznan, 1981).

11. See Goodwyn, *Breaking the Barrier*; Roman Laba, *The Roots of Solidarity* (Princeton: Princeton University Press, 1991); Jan Kubik, "Who Done It: Workers, Intellectuals, or Someone Else?" in *Theory and Society* 23 (1994), 441–66; and Andrzej Tymowski, "Workers vs. Intellectuals in Solidarnosc," in *Telos* 90 (Winter 1991–92); 157–75.

12. Solidarity called its first national strike, in October 1980, to protest the government's

failure to fulfill an agreement for wage increases. It never again called a national strike over a wage dispute. In its entire sixteen months of legality, Solidarity regularly put economic issues on hold in order to concentrate on social and political ones, such as access to mass media, regular consultations, and an end to harassment. Indeed, traditional "bread and butter" issues became so habitually marginalized that in September 1981, Solidarity miners threatened to strike against a government plan to *increase* wages. The miners did not want to be seen as profiting during a time of collective suffering, and they objected to the government adopting the plan unilaterally instead of after negotiations with the union.

13. Because of this group's creative aspirations, Jacek Kurczewski calls them a "new middle class." *The Resurrection of Rights in Poland* (Oxford: Oxford University Press, 1993).

14. The concept of the public sphere comes from Jurgen Habermas, *The Structural Transformation of the Public Sphere* (Cambridge: MIT Press, 1991). For its use in the context of Poland and Solidarity, see David Ost, *Solidarity and the Politics of Anti-Politics*, ch. 2.

15. For a brilliant account of how prewar communists became postwar Stalinists without really wanting to, see Isaac Deutscher, "The Tragic Life of a Polrugarian Minister," in his *Heretics and Renegades* (1957; repr., Indianapolis: Bobbs-Merrill, 1969).

16. See Paul W. Drake, *Labor Movements and Dictatorships* (Baltimore: Johns Hopkins University Press, 1996), esp. ch. 3.

17. See Charles Sabel and David Stark, "Planning, Politics and Shopfloor Power: Hidden Forms of Bargaining in Soviet Imposed State Socialist Societies," in *Politics and Society* 11 (1982), 439–75; and David Stark, "The Micropolitics of the Firm and the Macropolitics of Reform," in *States versus Markets in the World-System*, ed. Peter Evans et al. (Los Angeles: Sage, 1985).

18. For discussion of communist-era factory life under piece-rate systems, see Miklos Haraszti, *Worker in a Worker's State* (New York: St. Martin's, 1978); and Burawoy and Lucacs, *The Radiant Past*.

19. As David Stark and Laszlo Bruszt put it, local authorities were "responsive responsibles," needing to represent local interests, not just enforce national policies. *Postsocialist Pathways* (Cambridge: Cambridge University Press, 1998), 113.

20. In contrast to Goodwyn and Laba, then, who see workers and intellectuals as belonging to different classes with diverse interests during the communist era, I would argue that it was the two of them together that constituted the communist-era working class. Under communism, intellectuals and professionals had a legitimate basis to consider themselves workers, such as their status as employees, subjection to Party (*nomenklatura*) domination, and the ideology of the system that required alternative views to be presented as pro-labor views. And that claim was accepted by workers themselves, who regularly voted for them as leaders. Intellectuals dominated the labor movement (that is, dominated labor when it became a movement) legitimately in the communist era, even while it was this very domination that would leave labor so lost afterwards. So while I agree, for example, with Robert Biezenski's view that the Polish self-management movement favored technocrats over workers, I disagree with his implication that this constituted a betrayal of its alliance with labor. For my point is that the technocratic domination of the labor movement was overdetermined by the communist system itself. When labor appeared publicly as a class, it naturally fought for universal interests—and was represented by intellectuals. This domination was a profound problem for the working class in the postcommunist period, as we have seen in previous chapters. In the communist period, however, this alliance was simply how class was naturally expressed. See Biezenski, "Workers' Self-Management and the Technical Intelligentsia in People's Poland," in *Politics and Society* 22:1 (March 1994).

21. See my introduction to the English translation of Adam Michnik's *The Church and the Left* (Chicago: University of Chicago Press, 1993).

22. On the effect of changing democratic discourses on working-class politics, see Ronald Aminzade, "Class Analysis, Politics, and French Labor History," in *Rethinking Labor History*, ed. Lenard Berlanstein (Urbana: University of Illinois, 1993), esp. the section on "republican discourses of representation," 105–8.

23. Of course, trade unions have often incorporated such non-class discourses themselves,

as in North American or South African "white" unions, but these imposed racial frames onto class paradigms, rather than using them as a substitute for the latter. This sunders democracy, to be sure, although the prevalence of the underlying class paradigm holds out the possibility, as eventually happened in the American case, of jettisoning the racism and preserving the unionism. It is the belief in the salience of class that is central to trade unionism.

24. One prominent exception is Henryk Domanski. See, for example, his *On the Verge of Convergence: Social Stratification in Eastern Europe* (Budapest: Central European University Press, 2000). Ivan Szelenyi has of course spent much of his career writing on class theory and class stratification in Eastern Europe, though mostly focusing on dominant rather than subordinate classes. For his analysis of postcommunism, see Gil Eyal, Ivan Szelenyi, and Eleanor Townsley, *Making Capitalism without Capitalists* (London: Verso, 1998).

25. Jerzy Szacki, *Liberalism after Communism* (Budapest: Central European University Press, 1995).

26. Guglielmo Meardi, "Trade Union Consciousness, East and West: A Comparison of Fiat Factories in Poland and Italy," in *European Journal of Industrial Relations* 2:3 (1996), 275–302, quotation 285.

27. Ibid., 283.

28. Ibid., 289, 288.

29. Ibid., 288. Emphasis in original.

30. "Od gory do dolu," in *Tygodnik Solidarnosc*, September 22, 1989, 1.

31. Meardi, "Trade Union Consciousness," 285. Emphasis in original. Carola Frege found a similar situation prevailing in postcommunist Hungary, with workers believing they have the same interests as management. As a result, she says, "Workplace relations were shaped by management" and "marked by marginalization of the unions." See her "The Illusion of Union-Management Cooperation in Postcommunist Central Eastern Europe," in *East European Politics and Societies* 14:3 (Fall 2000), 640.

32. Meardi, "Trade Union Consciousness," 285.

33. Solidarity vice president at the WSK aircraft manufacturing plant in Mielec, June 1994.

34. Meardi, "Trade Union Consciousness," 293.

35. For a full discussion of the survey's findings, see David Ost and Marc Weinstein, "Unionists Against Unions: Towards Hierarchical Management in Post-Communist Poland," in *East European Politics and Societies* 13:1 (Winter 1999). I am heavily indebted to Marc Weinstein for the discussion in the following paragraphs.

36. We administered surveys, in spring 1994, to leaders of the firm's two largest trade unions (almost always Solidarity and OPZZ) in 95 firms drawn from a variety of different ownership structures, in towns and cities throughout Poland.

37. On these, as on most questions, there was not a great deal of difference between Solidarity and other trade unionists. Indeed, we found that despite the very tense relations among national union activists, on the shopfloor level representatives of Solidarity and of OPZZ, the former communist trade union federation, get on rather well. Less than 30 percent of our respondents stated that there existed many points of conflict between the unions; well over half claimed that union relations at their particular plant were friendly.

38. "Non-private" refers to both state-owned firms and "corporatized" ones, a kind of intermediary position when the state is actively preparing for the company to be sold. Our survey showed that nearly two-thirds of non-private firms had regular meetings between union and management at least once a month as opposed to less than one-third of private firms, and that only in non-private firms were strategic enterprise matters put on the agenda.

39. It should also be noted that when Solidarity originally spoke of privatization, it did not have employee stock ownership in mind. When a proposal advocating such a solution was soundly defeated at the union's second national congress in April 1990, union vice president Lech Kaczynski "considered this a great success: another utopia had fallen." (Jagienka Wilczak, "Parasol z powylamywanymi drutami," in *Polityka*, May 5, 1990, 6.)

40. Juliusz Gardawski, *Robotnicy 1991* (Warsaw: Friedrich Ebert Foundation, 1992), 28.

41. Ibid.

42. Workplace surveys conducted by Artur Czynczyk and Andrzej Chelminski, summarized by Marc Weinstein in personal communication, November 1992.

43. The chief exception was military-related work in nuclear and rocket technology, carried out in the Soviet Union in distant "closed cities." See Victor Zaslavsky, "Closed Cities and the Organized Consensus," in *The Neo-Stalinist State* (Armonk, NY: M.E. Sharpe, 1982). The claim that skilled workers and employees could no longer do their jobs professionally and with dignity was one of the key points stressed by Leszek Kolakowski in his influential 1970 essay that helped precipitate the modern Polish democratic opposition. See his "Hope and Hopelessness," in *Survey* (London) 17:3 (Summer 1971).

44. The formal name of the plant is *Wytwornia Sprzet Komunikacyjnych, Polskie Zaklady Lotnicze* (Transport Equipment Manufacturing, Polish Aviation Company), commonly shortened to WSK PZL "Mielec." WSK had branches in several cities, of which Mielec was the largest.

45. Figures from Zbigniew Ziolo, "Przemiany spoleczno-ekonomiczne," in *Mielec: Studia i Materialy z dziejow miasta i regionu*, Vol. 2, ed. Feliks Kiryk (Rzeszow: Krajowa Agencja Wydawnicza, 1988).

46. In this section, people are identified by pseudonyms.

47. Surveys from 1990–94 and a study in 1998 show that engineers and others with higher education who belonged to Solidarity in 1980–81 and who stayed out of OPZZ in the mid-1980s did *not* return to Solidarity after 1989. Juliusz Gardawski, "Czlonkowie i zakladowi liderzy zwiazkow zawodowych," in *Rozpad Bastionu?*, ed. Gardawski et al. (Warsaw: Institute of Public Affairs, 1999), 116. On engineers in early Solidarity, see Michael D. Kennedy, *Professionals, Power and Solidarity in Poland* (Cambridge: Cambridge University Press, 1991).

48. I. Yellowitz, quoted in V.V. Zagladin et al., *The International Working-Class Movement*, Volume 2 (Moscow: Progress Publishers, 1976), 80.

49. Conversation with Wojciech Grzeszek, May 11, 1994.

50. Interview with Lugosz (a pseudonym), September 1993.

51. Interestingly, gender probably explains why union leaders in the textile city of Lodz seem to have been more militant than those in heavy industrial areas. The key factor is not the women who worked in the plants but the frustrated men who did, and who usually headed the unions there. Men seem to have gotten more involved with the union because they saw it as a way to improve their status (i.e., assert their manhood). Male workers in the core industries did not need the union for this, as their labor itself was their badge of manhood. Lodz textile plants, however, did not belong to the pantheon of the socialist economy, and the industry itself seemed to be without much future. In fact, this was not necessarily true: with its experienced, low-wage workers, Polish light industry had, and has, a comparative advantage over its western neighbors. But Polish workers imagined only heavy, male, industrial production as the source of wealth. Men working outside of this sector lacked the sense of dignity and worth that came naturally to the Braneks and Olinowiczes, which probably explains their greater militance.

52. See discussion in David Ost, "Labor, Class, and Democracy: Shaping Political Antagonisms in Post-Communist Society," in *Markets, States, and Democracy: The Political Economy of Post-Communist Transformation*, ed. Beverley Crawford (Boulder, CO: Westview Press, 1995).

53. In state-owned firms, this was due to the direct election of management by the enterprise councils. In the reformed, "corporatized" firms, where management was appointed by government, this was due to the government being in the hands of former oppositionists. That began to change soon after the former communists returned to power in 1993.

54. Jacques Ranciere, *The Nights of Labor* (Philadelphia: Temple University Press, 1989), 20.

Chapter 6. Unions in the Workplace

1. Kazimierz Kloc, "Polish Labor in Transition, 1990–1992," in *Telos* 92 (Summer 1992); Halina Szostkiewicz, "Trade Unions in Employee-Owned Companies," in *Management Em-*

ployee Buy-Outs in Poland, ed. Maria Jarosz (Warsaw: Institution of Political Studies of Polish Academy of Sciences, 1995).

2. Conversation with Litynski, Warsaw, October 1998.

3. Conversation with Grosz (a pseudonym), Mielec, May 1994.

4. Conversation with Branek, Mielec, May 1994.

5. Eric Hanley, "Cadre Capitalism in Hungary and Poland: Property Accumulation among Communist-Era Elites," in *East European Politics and Societies* 14:1 (Winter 2000), 143–78; and David Stark and Laszlo Bruszt, *Postsocialist Pathways* (Cambridge: Cambridge University Press, 1998).

6. Hanley, "Cadre Capitalism," 152.

7. Simon Clarke and Veronika Kabalina, "Privatisation and the Struggle for Control of the Enterprise," in *Russia in Transition: Politics, Privatisation and Inequality,* ed. David Lane (London: Longman, 1995), 145. Lynn Nelson and Irina Kuzes confirm this assessment with additional information in their "Privatisation and the New Business Class," in the same volume.

8. The government needed this legislation because of a unique characteristic of the country's ownership structure. Although state firms were formally "owned" by the particular ministry that created them, the self-management law, passed in 1981 but implemented only in 1989, gave control over the disposition of those assets to the enterprise councils. Calling them "state-owned" firms was thus something of a misnomer, as the state, ironically, did not control the firms that it formally owned. In 1990, it asked to regain that control.

9. Juliusz Gardawski, "Trends in the Ownership and Authority Structure of Employee-Owned Companies," in *Management Employee Buy-Outs in Poland,* ed. Maria Jarosz, 63.

10. In state treasury firms, also called "corporatized" or "commercialized" firms because of the new legal code they come under, employee councils are replaced by a board of directors, two-thirds of whose members are appointed by the state, with the other third elected by employees. Final decisions on the sale of the firm's assets go to the state, but unions retain consultation rights. The 1994 enterprise survey conducted by Weinstein and me showed that unions took those rights seriously and remained active in such firms until the state succeeded in selling them off. See Ost and Weinstein, "Unionists Against Unions," in *East European Politics and Societies* 13:1 (Winter 1999).

11. It is worth pondering this paradox for a moment, as it illustrates the degree to which "privatization" and "market reform" are often just so much ideology. In the official parlance, then, as well as the official statistics, firms whose assets were controlled by workforce-elected employee councils were considered "state-owned" firms, while firms whose assets were controlled directly by the state were considered "private." In this way, the proliferation of state treasury firms, with their typically high revenues and asset valuations (because they were usually large manufacturing firms), was treated as proof that Poland had undergone a privatization revolution. Such stories began appearing in the western press, helping make Poland in the mid-1990s the new darling of economic reform, replacing the Czech Republic, whose star waned when the extent of the corruption in the privatization process became clear. In fact, Poland experienced a privatization "revolution" *only because* of this strange accounting practice listing state treasury firms as private firms. In the end, "private ownership" did not necessarily mean private ownership. It only meant that an employee council would no longer intervene. Even an employee council acting according to strict market principles would not be considered as "pro-reform" as the most lethargic state-appointed board of directors. It is here that we see the extent of the victory of Solidarity neoliberals. The very concept of "market reform" had come to be as much about ending participatory forms of management as about promoting profit-seeking behavior—and sometimes even more. "Civil society" had become subjugated to "bourgeois society" in the very terms themselves.

12. Andrzej Mokrzyszewski, "Charakterystyka badanych zakladow pracy i ich pracownikow," in Juliusz Gardawski, Barbara Gaciarz, Andrzej Mokrzyszewski, and Wlodzimierz Pankow, *Rozpad Bastionu?* (Warsaw: Institute of Public Affairs, 1999), 46.

13. Witold Pawlowski, "Uscisk typu podwojny nelson," in *Polityka,* February 18, 1995, 7.

14. Quoted in Cezary Lazarewicz, "Bylo ich siedemnascioro," in *Gazeta Wyborcza*, August 29, 2000.

15. Michnik explained to me his resistance to unions as the result of his fear, in 1990, that Walesa would use unions to carry out his vendetta against the paper. Later on, the publishers of *Gazeta* explicitly promoted employee stock ownership as an alternative to unionism. Conversation with Michnik, July 2002.

16. Gardawski, "Trends in the Ownership," 59.

17. See Marek Belka, "Trzeba sie na cos zdecydowac," in *Rzeczpospolita*, August 30, 1994, 9.

18. Danuta Zagrodzka, "Bez bolu sie nie obejdzie," in *Gazeta Wyborcza*, April 11, 1994.

19. Quoted in Ost and Weinstein, "Unionists Against Unions," 23.

20. Quoted in ibid., 21.

21. Gardawski, Gaciarz, Mokrzyszewski, and Pankow, "Zwiazki Zawodowe w Polsce," in *Rozpad Bastionu?* 15.

22. Conversation with Solidarity activist from Bytom, at a Solidarity demonstration in Warsaw, May 27, 1994.

23. The quotation is inexact, based on a conversation with a human resource manager for a Fortune 500 company, at a convention of human resource managers at the School of Industrial and Labor Relations, Cornell University, May 1991.

24. The Polish word is the same: *strajk.* The Polish Statistical Yearbook counts only work stoppages in its listing of strikes. Newspaper accounts are different: what reporters and the unionists they write about call "strikes" may refer to little more than the "flagging" mentioned by our informant. In this vein, it is interesting to note that the 1998 study of over 200 Polish enterprises found that while 78 percent of union activists said there had been "strikes" in their firms, only 34 percent of the directors of these same firms said so. Barbara Gaciarz, "Dynamika zbiorowych stosunkow pracy," in *Rozpad Bastionu?* 228. For a fuller account of industrial conflicts in the early 1990s, carried out by industrial sociologists working as conflict arbiters, see Kazimierz Kloc and Wladyslaw Rychlowski, *Spory zbiorowe i strajki w przemysle* (mimeo printed by Szkola Glowna Handlowa, Warsaw, 1994).

25. "Krzaklewski: chodzi o ustroj," in *Rzeczpospolita*, May 7–8, 1994, 1.

26. "Piatek 'S,'" in *Gazeta Wyborcza*, May 7–8, 1994, 3.

27. Quoted in Mariusz Janicki, "Panstwo zwiazkowe," in *Polityka*, July 6, 1996, 17.

28. The speech is in *Tygodnik Solidarnosc*, September 13, 1996, with the title "16 rocznica Sierpnia."

29. Conversation with Gregor Koso, Warsaw, July 1999.

30. Janice Bell, "Unemployment Matters: Voting Patterns During the Economic Transition in Poland, 1990–1995," in *Europe-Asia Studies* 49:7 (1997), 1263–91.

31. Krzysztof Jasiewicz, "Portfel czy rozaniec?: Ekonomiczne i aksjologiczne determinanty zachowan wyborczych," in *Wybory Parlamentarne 1997*, ed. Radoslaw Markowski (Warsaw: Institute of Political Studies, 1999).

32. Unlike Walesa, Krzaklewski maintained a parliamentary seat too, but he stayed out of its limelight, preferring to exercise his control out of the public eye.

33. Tomaszewska quotation from personal conversation, Warsaw, May 1999. Other quotation and comment from Barbara Gaciarz and Wlodzimierz Pankow, *Dialog Spoleczny po polsku: fikcja czy szansa* (Warsaw: Friedrich Ebert Foundation, 2001), 42, 45.

34. Juliusz Gardawski et al., *Rozpad Bastionu?* The researchers studied five manufacturing sectors (automotive, chemical, lumber and paper, food processing, and construction) and also health and education. The first five were chosen because their high growth rates, high degree of privatization, success in job creation, small and medium size (except for automotive), and geographical diversity made them good representatives of the emerging sectors of the economy. Their informants included 202 directors or board members, 148 union leaders, and 1225 employees, both unionists and non-members. For one of the best accounts of union erosion in the mid-1990s and of similar union lack of interest in building up their organizations, see Jane Hardy and Al Rainnie, *Restructuring Krakow: Desperately Seeking Capitalism* (London: Mansell, 1996).

35. Gardawski et al., "Zwiazki Zawodowe w Polsce," in *Rozpad Bastionu?* 19. Many unionists said that they saw no evidence of union activity in their workplaces. Among workers overall, only 7.1 percent said that unions "are effective and that the workforce has much to thank them for."

36. Barbara Gaciarz, "Dynamika zbiorowych stosunkow pracy," in *Rozpad Bastionu?*

37. They were not even upset that they had been misled about the new plant providing opportunities for local miners about to lose their jobs. The SEA government had cited this as the reason why it was giving large tax breaks to GM, but only 5 percent of the plant's employees had previously worked in the mines.

38. Wieslawa Kozek, ed., *Instytucjonalizacja stosunkow pracy w Polsce* (Warsaw: Scholar, 2003); Tadeusz Kowalik, ed., *Nierowni i rowniejsi* (Warsaw: Innowacja, 2002); Henryk Domanksi, Antonina Ostrowska, and Andrzej Rychard, eds., *Jak Zyja Polacy* (Warsaw: IfiS PAN, 2000).

39. Much of this discussion is based on Jacek Mojkowski, "Marsz na Akcje," in *Polityka*, March 22, 1997.

40. The bill finally became law in April 1997.

41. *Tygodnik Solidarnosc*, May 31, 1996, 1. The evidence presented here, as well as in liberal newspapers, suggests that many old *nomenklatura* individuals had kept dominant positions not in factories, where Solidarity had been active, but in banks, trading, and insurance companies. This makes sense, since success in these fields relied more on elite contacts and less on maintaining good industrial relations. Such enterprises did not have to worry much about meddlesome unions and employee councils seeking to "protect the national wealth," since, in classic industrial age style, labor in 1989 generally understood only machinery as the wealth they did not want plundered. The *nomenklatura*, a step ahead, knew differently. As it turns out, the *nomenklatura* did not hang onto this property. By 2001, most Polish banks were foreign-owned.

42. Mariusz Janicki, "Krzak: ile jeszcze tak?" in *Polityka*, November 3, 2001, 16. This constituted a 50 percent decline from 1989.

43. Quoted in Juliusz Gardawski, *Zwiazki Zawodowe na Rozdrozu* (Warsaw: Instytut Spraw Publicznych, 2001), 251.

44. By 2001, Gardawski found that both Solidarity and OPZZ activists universally rejected the idea of union participation in politics. In ibid., 250.

45. Ibid., 247. The unionist telling this story, showing his new awareness of comparative industrial relations, remarked that the managers' policy seemed "as if taken from an American manual on how to destroy a union in three days." For other union-busting techniques employed by the hypermarkets, see 245–50.

46. Mariusz Janicki, "Nowa walka klas," in *Polityka* 47, 2000.

47. Gardawski, *Zwiazki Zawodowe na Rozdrozu*, 213–19.

48. Quoted in ibid., 201–2.

49. Ibid., 76–79.

50. Ibid., 229.

51. Ryszard Socha, "Masz pan byc podmiotem," in *Polityka*, November 3, 2001, 64.

52. Gardawski, *Zwiazki Zawodowe na Rozdrozu*, 236–38.

53. Quoted in ibid., 268.

54. For more on these models, see Kate Bronfenbrenner et al., eds. *Organizing to Win: New Research on Union Strategies* (Ithaca, NY: ILR Press, 1998).

55. See David Ost, "The Weakness of Strong Social Movements: Models of Unionism in the East European Context," in *European Journal of Industrial Relations* 8:1 (March 2002).

56. This and other quotations from conversation with Stanislaw Ciepiera, in Gliwice, July 30, 2002.

57. Membership figures from Mark Carley, "Trade Union Membership 1993-2003," report posted May 21, 2004, on European Industrial Relations Observatory On-Line: http://www.eiro. eurofound.eu.int/2004/03/update/tno403105u.html; 2001 density figure from Juliusz Gardawski, "Declining Trade Union Density Examined," report posted August 21, 2002, on Euro-

pean Industrial Relations Observatory On-Line: http://www.eiro.eurofound.eu.int/2002/08/feature/pl0208105f.html.

58. Typical of Nowa Huta Solidarity attitudes were the following comments from 1998: "It was very hard to change the mentality of the people," lamented one union official, recalling the early postcommunist years. But "there was a new Poland and we had to tell the workers that they're not needed on the job and that they'd have to go." The plant's Solidarity president, meanwhile, who was also a parliamentary deputy from 1997 to 2001, boasted that Solidarity was the one restraining workers' pay demands. See Miroslaw Banasiak, "Solidarni z Huta," in *Gazeta Wyborcza*, November 30, 1998. In the 2001 elections for employee representatives to the firm's Supervisory Board, Solidarity lost to both OPZZ and Solidarity '80. Jerzy Palosz, "Chwieje sie Twierdza 'Sendzimir,'" in *Gazeta Krakowska*, June 1, 2001.

59. Gay Seidman, *Manufacturing Militance: Workers' Movements in Brazil and South Africa, 1970–1985* (Berkeley: University of California Press, 1994), 2.

60. Sam Gindin of the Canadian Auto Workers, quoted in Kim Moody, "Towards an International Social-Movement Unionism," in *New Left Review* 225 (September/October 1997).

61. Interview with Marian Kokoszka, WSK Solidarity vice president, Mielec, May 2001.

62. On the class basis of business unionism, see Victoria Hattam, *Labor Visions and State Power: The Origins of Business Unionism in the United States* (Princeton: Princeton University Press, 1993). "Rather than looking to government as their saviors," she writes, the business union approach "argued that workers would be better off if they directed their energy and resources to trade union organizing and protest on the shop floor" (157). Howard Kimeldorf makes a similar point when he speaks of the militance of craft workers in mid–twentieth century America in *Battling for American Labor: Wobblies, Craft Workers, and the Making of the Union Movement* (Berkeley: University of California Press, 1999).

63. For a fuller presentation of this argument, including a discussion of its relevance elsewhere in Eastern Europe as wall as in the West, see Ost, "The Weakness of Strong Social Movements."

Chapter 7. Class, Civil Society, and the Future of Postcommunist Democracy

1. Wieslawa Kozek, "Destruktorzy: Tendencyjny obraz zwiazkow zawodowych w tygodnikach politycznych w Polsce," in *Instytucjonalizacja stosunkow pracy w Polsce*, ed. Kozek (Warsaw: Scholar, 2003).

2. The official rate hit 20% at the end of 2003, and by April 2004 stood at 20.5%. Government statistics as reported in internet news bulletin *Donosy*, February 23 and April 22, 2004.

3. Jonathan Stein, "Neocorporatism in Slovakia: Formalizing Labor Weakness in a (Re)democratizing State," in *Workers After Workers' States: Labor and Politics in Eastern Europe After Communism*, ed. Stephen Crowley and David Ost (Boulder, CO: Rowman and Littlefield Press, 2001), 59–60.

4. Czech unions owed their relative strength, paradoxically, to their tardiness in undergoing reform—not in the early 1980s, as in Poland, but only in 1990, when market reformers were already in power. So whereas in Poland independent unions mobilized against a communist enemy, making them gravitate to capitalism as the putative other, in the Czech Republic postcommunist unions started out with marketizers as the relevant other, forcing them to show some early militance simply in order to define themselves. It was this relative union strength, together with the government's focus on privatizing firms rather than restructuring them, that gave Czechs the lower unemployment rates and higher living standards that continued until the market bubble burst in 1997. For a comparison of Czech and Polish unions, see David Ost, "Can Unions Survive Communism?" in *Dissent*, Winter 1997. On Czech economic policies, see Mitchell Orenstein, *Out of the Red: Building Capitalism and Democracy in Post-Communist Europe* (Ann Arbor: University of Michigan Press, 2000). As for unemployment, the Czech Republic's

3.5% unemployment rate of 1993, the first year after the break-up of the country, was one-third that of the country with the next-lowest unemployment rate, Romania, with 10.5%.

5. See Anna Pollert, "Labor and Trade Unions in the Czech Republic, 1989–2000," in *Workers After Workers' States*, ed. Crowley and Ost.

6. See David Ost, "Illusory Corporatism in Eastern Europe: Neoliberal Tripartism and Postcommunist Class Identities," in *Politics and Society* 28:4 (December 2000), 503–30.

7. Laszlo Bruszt, "Reforming Alliances: Labour, Management, and State Bureaucracy in Hungary's Economic Transition," in *Acta Oeconomica* 46:3–4 (1994), 317. Such market opportunities helped make Hungarian workers more quiescent than in Poland, where the lack of individualistic strategies for advancement pushed the more energetic workers more into public activity. For more on this comparison, see Michael Burawoy, *The Politics of Production* (London: Verso, 1985), 199–200.

8. This account comes largely from the writings of, and my several conversations with, two Hungarian labor researchers, Maria Lado and Laszlo Neumann. See also Andras Toth, "The Failure of Social-Democratic Unionism in Hungary," in *Workers After Workers' States*, ed. Crowley and Ost; and Carola M. Frege, "The Illusion of Union—Management Relation in Postcommunist Central Eastern Europe," in *East European Politics and Societies* 14:3 (Fall 2000).

9. Tina Rosenberg, "From Dissidents to MTV Democrats," in *Harper's*, September 1992, 46–52.

10. Susan Woodward, *The Balkan Tragedy* (Washington, D.C.: Brookings Institute, 1995), esp. ch. 2.

11. On the role of formalized ethnic institutional arrangements in the disintegration of East European communism, see Valerie Bunce, *Subversive Institutions: The Design and the Destruction of Socialism and the State* (Cambridge: Cambridge University Press, 1999); and Rogers Brubaker, *Nationalism Reframed: Nationhood and the National Question in the New Europe* (Cambridge: Cambridge University Press, 1996).

12. V.P. Gagnon Jr., "Ethnic Nationalism and International Conflict: The Case of Serbia," in *International Security* 19:3 (Winter 1994–95), 130–66. See also his book *The Myth of Ethnic War* (Ithaca, NY: Cornell University Press, 2004). Though Gagnon talks here mostly about Serbia, it is important to note that this pattern prevailed throughout the country. A parallel reading of Woodward's book makes this clear. For although Woodward puts more blame on Slovenia and Croatia, and Gagnon on Serbia, both agree that republican elites threatened by federal reforms explicitly sought to capture popular anger at current or impending economic problems and direct it at national others instead, with devastating effects for the country. The most tragic channeling of anger took place, of course, in Bosnia, as Serb nationalist paramilitaries used terror and propaganda to take the enmities of poor Bosnian Serb peasants against the more wealthy residents of Sarajevo and convert it into rage against Muslims instead.

13. Victoria Hattam, *Labor Visions and State Power* (Princeton: Princeton University Press, 1993).

14. To the extent that people organize against an ethnic other as a stand-in for a class other, that is not organizing along class lines. For when the class other is identified as a national other instead, against what Amy Chua calls a "market-dominant minority," the ensuing fight almost always becomes an ethnic fight instead. Riots against Jews in tsarist Russia or against Chinese in post-Suharto Indonesia had a class element, but were not class conflicts insofar as only one nationality was targeted. See Amy Chua, *World on Fire: How Exporting Free Market Democracy Breeds Ethnic Hatred and Global Instability* (New York: Doubleday, 2002).

15. For a discussion of the differences between the two notions, see Erik Olin Wright, "The Continuing Relevance of Class Analysis," in *Theory and Society* 25:5 (October 1996), 693–717.

16. Adam Seligman, *The Idea of Civil Society* (New York: Free Press, 1992), 166–67.

17. Adam Przeworski and John Sprague, *Paper Stones: A History of Electoral Socialism* (Chicago: University of Chicago Press, 1986), 10.

18. James C. Scott, *Weapons of the Weak: Everyday Forms of Peasant Resistance* (New Haven: Yale University Press, 1985), 43.

19. Running on such a platform, Kaczynski decisively won the first ever Warsaw mayoral election in 2002. These three parties won nearly 28% of the vote in the 2001 parliamentary elections and combined for just under 40% of the vote in the 2004 European Parliament elections.

20. The right's fixation on an all-powerful "communism" despite the collapse of the communist system, or on the domination of secular liberals despite the great privileges enjoyed by the Catholic church, dovetails well with Douglas Hofstadter's definition of the "paranoid style," according to which "history is a conspiracy, set in motion by demonic forces of almost transcendent power." Douglas Hofstadter, *The Paranoid Style in American Politics* (New York: Vintage, 1967, 29.

21. Bela Greskovits characterizes my argument about economic liberalism endangering political liberalism as a claim that democratization is impossible. My point was not that postcommunist democracy was "impossible" and would necessarily "break down" but only that dogmatic neoliberalism would produce a democracy less inclusive and less politically liberal than most observers at the time were claiming would arise. See his *The Political Economy of Protest and Patience* (Budapest: Central European University Press, 1998), 7, as well as his more developed critique in "The Path-Dependence of Transitology," in *Postcommunist Transformation and the Social Sciences*, ed. Frank Bonker et al. (Lanham, MD: Rowman and Littlefield, 2002), 219–46.

22. David Ost, "Is Latin America the Future of Eastern Europe?" in *Problems of Communism* 41:3 (May-June 1992).

23. Thus, Thomas Friedman's notion of the "golden straitjacket," in his *The Lexus and the Olive Tree* (New York: Anchor, 2000).

24. See Guy van Gyes et al., *Can Class Still Unite? The Differentiated Workforce, Class Solidarity and Trade Unions* (Aldershot, UK: Ashgate, 2001).

25. See Kate Bronfenbrenner et al., *Organizing to Win: New Research on Union Strategies* (Ithaca, NY: ILR Press, 1998). For a new theoretical imagination of class that connects it with lived reality in contemporary America, see Robin D.G. Kelley, *Yo Mama's Disfunktional: Fighting the Culture Wars in Urban America* (Boston: Beacon, 1997).

26. For a critique of this tendency, see Christopher Lasch, *The Revolt of the Elites* (New York: Norton, 1996).

27. A concept made popular by Seymour Martin Lipset in *Political Man* (New York: Doubleday, 1960).

28. Proceedings of conference on "Intellectuals and Social Change in Central and Eastern Europe," published in special issue of *Partisan Review* LIX:4 (1992). See also Vladimir Tismaneanu, *Fantasies of Salvation: Democracy, Nationalism, and Myth in Post-Communist Europe* (Princeton: Princeton University Press, 1998).

29. I could not address Laba's and Goodwyn's claims about worker domination of Solidarity in my 1990 book since it was published before theirs, but a reading of all three books will show, I think, just what I state here: that workers built the union organizationally, but the politics the union pursued followed that of KOR intellectuals. Insofar as their books focus on Solidarity's origins and not its 1980–81 policies, they cannot be read as challenges to my claim about Solidarity's policies.

30. The two are alternate translations of the same German term that is their source: *bürgerliche Gesellschaft.*

31. On the original East European model of civil society, see chapter 2 of my *Solidarity and the Politics of Anti-Politics* (Philadelphia: Temple University Press, 1990); and Andrew Arato, "Civil Society vs. the State: Poland 1980–81," in *Telos* 47 (Spring 1981).

32. For a superb account of how both state and market constrain freedom, an account produced by the milieu of this democratic East European opposition, see Jeffrey Goldfarb, *On Cultural Freedom: An Exploration of Public Life in Poland and America* (Chicago: University of Chicago Press, 1982).

33. Most people writing about democracy and civil society today are quite aware of the debt they owe the East Europeans. See, for example, Adam Seligman, *The Idea of Civil Society* (New

York: Free Press, 1992), and Christopher Beem, *The Necessity of Politics* (Chicago: University of Chicago Press, 1999).

34. The term is now generally used without the radical democratic connotations of the past, and no doubt the East European elites' repudiation of their old notion has contributed to this. As Margaret Somers writes, the "civil society" that emerged from Eastern Europe in the 1980s, with its emancipatory claims of "a place where citizens can participate in the practices of citizenship free of both coercion and competition" (i.e., free of both state and market), had by the late 1990s turned into a concept denoting chiefly "the private, . . . market side" of the dichotomy. It is increasingly used to denote little other than the volunteer sector, with the "empowerment of civil society" coming to mean allowing the state to cut back its obligations to citizens. See Somers, "The Privatization of Citizenship," in *Beyond the Cultural Turn*, ed. Victoria Bonnell and Lynn Hunt (Berkeley: University of California Press, 1999), 122–23.

35. As Wlodzimierz Pankow puts it, "Polish political thought and transformative practice believed that there was a clear contradiction between . . . the 'general good' and . . . particular interests. But this maxim did not apply to the so-called 'middle class,' which was seen as the carrier of the 'good' and the 'better tomorrow' of all of society. This meant that in the name of the future national interest, personified today by the middle class, it was necessary to sacrifice, or at least drastically limit, the immediate interests of all other social groups." "Niezamierzone Efekty Neoliberalnej Rewolucji," in *Kontynuacja czy Przelom?* ed. Witold Jakobik (Warsaw: Institute for Political Studies, 1994), 144. Bill Lomax, meanwhile, shows how liberal Hungarian intellectuals turned from democrats into meritocrats, redefining the concept of "civil society" to justify their own power and privileges. "The Inegalitarian Nature of Hungary's Intellectual Political Culture," in *Intellectuals and Politics in Central Europe*, ed. Andras Bozoki (Budapest: Central European University Press, 1999).

36. Quoted in "Quiet Voices from the Balkans," *The New Yorker*, March 15, 1993, 6.

37. For more on the crisis of interests in postcommunist society, see David Ost, "The Politics of Interest in Post-Communist East Europe," in *Theory and Society* 22 (August 1993).

38. Thanks to Marc Weinstein for help on this section. For a work that does take ideas seriously, see Peter Hall, ed., *The Political Power of Economic Ideas* (Princeton: Princeton University Press, 1989). In another account, Marc Howard Ross subsumes the study of ideas in politics into a more general cultural framework, but this seems only to legitimate the study of ideas while depriving it of any specificity. See his "Culture and Identity in Comparative Political Analysis," in *Comparative Politics: Rationality, Culture, and Structure*, ed. Mark Lichbach and Alan Zuckerman (Cambridge: Cambridge University Press, 1999).

39. Adam Przeworski, *Democracy and the Market* (Cambridge: Cambridge University Press, 1991); Stephen Haggard and Robert Kaufman, *The Political Economy of Democratic Transformation* (Boulder, CO: Westview, 1995).

40. Crowley and Ost, eds., *Workers After Workers' States*.

41. Quoted in David Mandel, *Rabotyagi: Perestroika and After Viewed from Below* (New York: Monthly Review, 1994), 184.

42. As Margaret Levi points out, rational choice theory "is methodologically individualist, yet its focus is not on individual choice but on the aggregation of individual choices." See "A Model, a Method, and a Map: Rational Choice in Comparative and Historical Analysis," in *Comparative Politics*, ed. Lichbach and Zuckerman.

43. This is an argument about uncertainty, not "false consciousness." I am not saying I know their interests, only that they did not, due to lack of experience of a market economy. On the uncertainty of interests, see my "Politics of Interest in Post-Communist East Europe," and also Valerie Bunce and Maria Csanadi, "Uncertainty in the Transition: Post-Communism in Hungary," in *East European Politics and Society* (hereafter *EEPS*) 7:2 (Spring 1993), 240–75.

44. David Stark and Laszlo Bruszt, *Postsocialist Pathways: Transforming Politics and Property in East Central Europe* (Cambridge: Cambridge University Press, 1998); and Kathleen Thelen and Sven Steinmo, "Historical Institutionalism in Comparative Politics," in *Structuring Politics*, ed. Steinmo, Thelen, and Frank Longstreth (Cambridge: Cambridge University Press, 1992).

45. Conversation with Kowalik, July 2002, about his article, "Moj rok osiemdziesiaty dziewiaty," in *Gazeta Wyborcza*, March 23–24, 2002.

46. Kuron died in June 2004 at the age of 70. For an essay representative of his new ideas, see "Jak upadl realny socjalizm," in *Gazeta Wyborcza*, July 1, 2000. On his connections with young activists, see Jacek Zakowski, "Kuszenia Jacka Kuronia," in *Polityka*, June 26, 2004.

47. Artur Domoslawski, *Swiat nie na sprzedaz: rozmowy o globalizacji i kontestacji* (Warsaw: Sic!, 2002).

48. See David Ost, "Letter from Poland," in *The Nation*, November 25, 2002.

49. Janine Wedel, *Collision and Collusion: The Strange Case of Western Aid to Eastern Europe, 1989–1998* (New York: St. Martin's, 1998).

50. Marek Pliszkiewicz, "Trojstronnosc w krajach Europy Srodkowej i Wschodniej," in *Syndykalizm Wspolczesny i jego Przyszlosc* (Lodz: Wyd. Uniwersytetu Lodzkiego, 1996), 259.

51. Much of the credit for this is due to the energetic head of the Warsaw office, Frank Hantke, formerly an official with the German trade union confederation DGB, responsible for coordinating EU policy. Hantke estimates that the Warsaw office has published over a hundred books and sponsored many dozens of workshops, seminars, and conferences. Personal communication with Hantke, March 3, 2003.

52. This program is different from that of industrial sociology, which has been a major field in Poland for a long time, including throughout the communist period, when Poland was the one Soviet-bloc country where sociology flourished as a discipline. So far, Kozek says, students tend to get jobs with businesses, not with unions. Personal communication, March 3, 2003.

53. See Dorothee Bohle and Bela Greskovits, "Capital, Labor, and the Prospects of the European Social Model in the East," *Working Paper 58* in Program on Central and East European Working Paper Series, Harvard University, 2004. The strong unionism typical of postwar Western Europe is due to "the dominance of capital and skill-intensive . . . industries in the production profile of the West European economy," they argue, while in Eastern Europe it is the "labor-intensive export industries [that] have become the leading sectors."

54. *EEPS* 17:1 (Winter 2003).

55. Frank Schimmelfennig, "The Community Trap: Liberal Norms, Rhetorical Action, and the Eastern Enlargement of the European Union," in *International Organization* 55 (Winter 2001), 47–80.

56. Andrew Moravcsik and Milada Anna Vachudova show how the existing states have structured an enlargement process that benefits them first of all. See "National Interest, State Power, and EU Enlargement," in *EEPS* 17:1.

57. Stephen Holmes, "A European *Doppelstaat*?" in *EEPS* 17:1.

58. Wade Jacoby, "Priest and Penitent: The European Union as a Force in the Domestic Politics of Eastern Europe," in *East European Constitutional Review* 8:1–2 (Winter-Spring 1999).

59. Laszlo Bruszt and David Stark, "Who Counts?: Supranational Norms and Societal Needs," in *EEPS* 17:1, 74.

60. Bruszt and Stark, "Who Counts?" 77. Emphasis in original.

61. Anna Grzymala-Busse and Abby Innes, "Great Expectations: The EU and Domestic Political Competition in East Central Europe," in *EEPS* 17:1, 66.

62. Holmes, "A European *Doppelstaat*?" 114.

63. Grzymala-Busse and Innes, "Great Expectations," 67. Technocratic parties, they point out, also gain a competitive edge here, and this, as Grzymala-Busse argues in her own book, is what has given ex-communist parties their electoral support in Hungary and Poland. See her *Redeeming the Communist Past: The Regeneration of Communist Parties in East-Central Europe* (Cambridge: Cambridge University Press, 2002).

64. Manfred Bienefeld, "Capitalism and the Nation State in the Dog Days of the 20th Century," in *Socialist Register 1994*, ed. Ralph Miliband and Leo Panitch (London: Merlin Books, 1994), 94–129; William Greider, *One World, Ready or Not* (New York: Simon & Schuster, 1997).

65. Ken Jowitt, "May the Boundaries Fall . . . ," in *EEPS* 17:1, 123.

66. For an excellent exception, however, arguing how the struggle for economic inclusivity

is central precisely to realist politics, see David Goldfischer, "Prospects for a New World Order," in *Globalization, Security, and the Nation State: Paradigms in Transition*, ed. Ersel Aydinli and James N. Rosenau (Albany: SUNY Press 2005).

67. Larry Rohter, "Argentina's Economic Rally Defies Forecasts," in *New York Times*, December 26, 2004.

68. Jowitt, "May the Boundaries," 122, 124.

69. For examples of the first critique, see Jan Pakulski and Malcolm Waters, "The Reshaping and Dissolution of Social Class in Advanced Society," in *Theory and Society* 25:5 (October 1996), 667–91; Terry Nichols Clark and Seymour Martin Lipset, "Are Social Classes Dying?," in *The Breakdown of Class Politics*, ed. Clark and Lipset (Washington, D.C.: Woodrow Wilson Center Press, 2001); and Paul W. Kingston, *The Classless Society* (Stanford: Stanford University Press, 2000). For examples of the second critique, see Ulrich Beck, *World Risk Society* (Cambridge, UK: Polity, 2000). However, for evidence that voters do still vote much along class lines, see Jeffrey Stonecash, *Class and Party in American Politics* (Boulder, CO: Westview, 2000).

Index

abortion, 62, 85
AFL-CIO, 86, 122–23, 160, 168, 190, 198
agricultural subsidies, 81
American Council of Learned Societies, 199
anesthesiologists, 161
anger: "anger regimes," 21–24, 196; and
   capitalism, 22–23; "economic anger," 9,
   23, 186–87; in immediate postcommunist
   period, 6–9, 61–65; liberal attitude to,
   96–97, 100–106, 116–17; and politics, 1,
   5–9, 17–26
anti-communism, 131–33
anti-Semitism: in general, 25, 31, 74,
   209n50, 228n14; in Poland: 67, 86, 98,
   116, 217n15
Arkuszewski, Wojciech, 52, 134

Baczkowski, Andrzej, 80
Balcerowicz, Leszek: elected head of Free-
   dom Union, 114; as Finance Minister, 55,
   68, 71, 161; in mid-1980s, 42
Balcerowicz Plan: criticized, 61, 66, 69, 72;
   liberals on, 98; Solidarity's support for,
   55–57; and wages, 63, 154
banks, 153, 170, 226n41
Baranczak, Stanislaw, 40
Belchatow, 82
Bielecki, Krzysztof, 68, 79
Bienenfeld, Manfred, 202
Biezenski, Robert, 221n20
Blumsztajn, Seweryn, 100

Boeing, 143
bonuses, 129, 131, 146
Borusewicz, Bogdan, 54
Bosnia, 205n15, 228n12
Bourdieu, Pierre, 19, 91
Brecht, Bertolt, 109
Brezhnev era, 129, 138, 205n7
Bruszt, Laszlo, 182, 201, 206n15
Bugaj, Ryszard, 57
Bujak, Zbigniew, 53
Bulgaria, 129
Bunce, Valerie, 22
Burawoy, Michael, 13
business unionism, 177–78, 227n62
Bydgoszcz, 54
Bytom, 88

Cambodia, 31
Catholic Church, 2–3, 66, 84–85, 160–61,
   216n4
Center Alliance, 71, 107, 116
Central Industrial Region, 11, 140
China, 31
Chua, Amy, 228n12
Ciepiera, Stanislaw, 174–75, 197
Civic Committee, 34
Civic Platform, 219n35
civil society: changing meaning of, 98, 112,
   190–94, 224n11, 230n34; original mean-
   ing of, 3, 40–41, 132; weakness of, 15,
   150

233

CPSIA information can be obtained
at www.ICGtesting.com
Printed in the USA
LVHW030837020822
724972LV00003B/180